Laughing with the Animals

I

Laughing with the Animals

Judith Chase

B
P

BRAMBLEWOOD PRESS, LLC
SANTA BARBARA

ISBN-13: 978-1-932762-76-1
ISBN-10: 1932762760

Cover design by Greg Wadsworth

Illustrations by Kristina Devries, Aimee and Leslie Pepper, and Sharon Williams

This book was written, printed and bound in the United States of America.

Bramblewood Press, LLC
729 De La Vina Street
Santa Barbara, CA 93101

editor@bramblewoodpress.com
http://www.bramblewoodpress.com

Table of Contents

For Dan, our children, and our many animals

Chapter 1
A Real Ranch

After two days of squishing through sticky clay mud in the middle of a wild and late winter storm, my family finally finished moving all of our animals, baled hay, and belongings from our old eight-acre farm in San Luis Obispo, California, to a large new ranch several miles down in the Los Osos Valley.

With only a station wagon and a single-wide horse trailer as our moving equipment, everything we owned, including our bedding and clothing, arrived soggy wet. While transporting mountains of our past, I couldn't help but wonder whether this new parcel of land would finally be our permanent home, or merely another way-station before more faint and winding trails.

The Los Osos Valley had sprung to life in the recent rains, and now all the lower hills were green with volunteer oats and weeds; the ranch was a beautiful, rain-soaked, washed-fresh world. Prefumo Canyon Creek, which most of the year existed as little more than a bed of dry rocks, curved through the southern side of our property. The day we arrived the creek was a rushing torrent of muddy water, tumbling and bubbling just beyond the ranch lane. The creek's music rang in our ears like a joyful orchestra and made a fine introduction to this big change in our lives. Hearing it reminded me of truly how far we had traveled from our long ago dry and hot years in Arizona.

As we unloaded the last boxes safely into the house, the rain ceased its pattering and the wonderful fragrance of damp eucalyptus permeated the atmosphere. Just a few dark clouds lingered behind the trees, and soon the afternoon sun broke through and turned the leaves a clean, silvery green. I knew that I would always remember this marvelous first sight.

The window in our new kitchen perfectly framed the trees to the west. As I gazed out at the fresh splendor, I announced to Dan, "Look–on top of this lovely hill, sunsets are going to come later than in the valley, and sunrises will come earlier."

"Sure," he countered, "now you can get up at four o'clock instead of five!"

We had moved our daughter Nancy's horse, Blue One, to the ranch the day before, and despite our short time away, it was a joyful reunion. Blue raced up and down in her field beside the lane, tossing her head and whinnying long and loud to welcome us. She had obviously felt lonely and frightened in our absence—this young mare loved friendship and conversation, and she had repeated her welcoming act every time we came ferrying another load of our belongings.

Our Jersey cow, April, mooed impatiently in her large wooden corral at the top of the lane. She had also missed us and needed reassurance, alfalfa, and Dan to come milk her.

Treve, our bright shepherd dog, was the last to reach the farm. He was ecstatic with relief when he finally realized he hadn't been left behind. This herder and family caretaker would immediately see infinite possibilities for hunting and exploring on our expansive new acreage, with large barns and a garage that could always provide him with shelter.

Treve's steadfast love for the family kept him busy taking care of the children, and he now had far more land to patrol for strange noises and intruders. He quickly began to go far above and beyond his necessary guard duties by hurtling down the lane, roaring and trying to chew the tires off of every car that left the ranch except ours. I never managed to break him from the habit of herding cars, but luckily this was his only obnoxious habit. Treve had no need for a doorbell—as soon as anyone even contemplated a drive or walk up our lane, Treve's loud bark sounded out the question, "Are you friend or foe?"

Treve was a wonderful dog, and proved to be more loyal, trustworthy, and reliable than even some people. "Please," I thought, "let there be more time on Oak Hills for this intelligent and human-like dog and me to converse!" I believed he viewed all of us as members of his pack—with the children as junior members and, Dan, I, and Treve as co-leaders. His kindness, loyalty, and love were unconditional, although he sometimes clearly wondered why we made so many dumb decisions; why did I often leave him home when I went in the car with the kids? Why did Dan leave us so many mornings each week and not bring back dinner for his pack?

Shandy, our independent orange cat, also took on the role of home guardian. He, however, defended against smaller intruders—by trying to banish the armies of rodents and ground squirrels from the open fields and higher hills, as well as doing away with every mouse and rat in the sheds and barns. He was such a keen and relentless hunter, and incredible tracker, we kept him in the house for the first two weeks we were there, because otherwise he would probably find his way back to our former home.

My Oak Hills Actors' Guild did not only contain animals—we had a full house of people as well. With our four energetic children, life would be rural but hardly serene. The very first day we arrived, the children and Treve began to explore the ranch, but as night fell, all four were too weary to do more than drink some hot canned soup, eat a few crackers and cheese, and try to get some warm sleep in their new bedrooms.

Nancy, at fourteen, was the oldest of the children and would spend a lot of time riding Blue and attending school. Danny was twelve and a lover of music, machines, hunting, school, and Boy Scouts. He often joined Nancy as she explored the land (though he rode a bicycle instead of a horse). Douglas, age five would soon begin first grade, and he and Jeffrey, age two, also liked to hunt, but mainly with Mason jars and a kitchen strainer, capturing frogs, lizards, and various bugs.

In a suit and tie, my husband, Dr. Dan, taught at the university (and was developing a new Agricultural Management Department there). He still managed to fit in the tasks of nighttime teacher, father, husband, dairyman, and confidence-builder.

I was the dowdy farm-wife and mother. I had an undying love for the land and the down-home atmosphere of country living, but I always felt like a bumbling novice in everything I tackled. Still, I already felt different, almost reborn, in this wonderful new ranch setting.

Geraniums and bougainvilleas girded the foundations of the wood-sided ranch house nestled on the southeastern edge of the flat-topped knoll. The gray slate roof of the house had grown a bit of gray-green moss after this very wet year. The house also had a rugged lawn of Bermuda grass that would turn brown at the first hint of a chill and rest in the winter. This grass surely needed this time to rest in order to survive the traffic now of six human beings and a host of animals. It's definitely a hard job to survive being a ranch lawn.

Glory be! At long last, our kingdom had become a ranch house on a hill, with rolling hills and lush fields. If I had known how to do cartwheels, I'd have cartwheeled all around this farm that first day.

The Los Osos Valley and Laguna Lake rested just below the ranch on the far side of Los Osos Road, and stretching beyond was San Luis Mountain, a beautiful peak that separated us from the town of San Luis Obispo. This mountain was one of nine peaks of volcanic origin that stretched out like a necklace from south of San Luis Obispo up north to Morro Bay. A host of other scenic mountains loomed farther away to the southeast and north. When we arrived in that idyllic valley, it was still mostly open country, with only two ranch houses visible to the south.

Down at the lower end of the ranch lane, Prefumo Canyon Road led us to Los Osos Road if we turned left, but a right turn passed our large red mailbox and then followed the creek in a steep and tortuous route up the canyon walls to the top and then became See Canyon Road as it dropped down the other side to Avila Beach.

The locals called these hills and mountains on the eastern sides of the Los Osos Valley the "Irish Hills" because each spring they remained green longer than the valley floor and the hills across the valley toward town. The Irish Hills were breathtaking that time of the year and often kept our swimming cove at Avila Beach warmer than some others.

Our move to this new home was only made possible because our longtime family friends, the Smiths, who had two ranches in the north county, wanted another ranch close to San Luis Obispo. They invited us to locate one and to manage it for them, so during the previous autumn I had diligently begun searching. When I finally found Oak Hills Ranch for sale, all the fields were golden with dry oats, and a warm breeze stole my heart as it rustled the leaves. We and the Smiths were sold.

The previous owner of Oak Hills Ranch had tried to raise turkeys. The farmer had slaved for a number of years trying to make good profits, yet various things had kept going wrong. One year, on an extra-hot day, a great many of his adult birds got spooked by the heat and fled for the shade of those eucalyptus trees lining the far edge of the parking area. Most of them wound up dying as they frantically piled on top of each other. The dejected farmer let out a sigh and lamented, "I would have been significantly better off if I had never even brought a single turkey on the place and just stayed in the house and watched TV." With that he gave up turkey farming and set out to sell the ranch, which now had hundreds of acres of new green oats growing on its rolling hills. This grazing and hay land largely stretched out on the long side of the property to the west beside Los Osos Road, but also wrapped its friendly arms around the house and barns.

The first of the outbuildings on this property was a long, low, unpainted shed with a corrugated tin roof; the shed ended at the barnyard, which was a large flat parking area of red rock. This building had been used for the failed turkey project, and it had a number of small windows to let in air and light. The far side of the shed opened to three fenced fields.

The next building on that side of the property was a whitewashed concrete barn with a wooden fenced corral adjacent. The barn was relatively new and had probably been used for hay storage or dairy cows we unearthed several large milk cans that were stored in a far corner.

A third shed was an open one along the back of our wide parking area to the west and it contained a large amount of firewood stacked in it! This was a great relief given the fact that our house lacked any adequate source of central heating, and the generally temperate coastal climate could still become very chilly in the winter.

The last building was the garage, next to the house. This was another welcome sight—for the first time our car would have shelter from sun and rain!

I also discovered a special treasure down the hill and out of sight from the house. There sat another large barn—this one ancient, brown, and sagging from lack of repairs. It must have been there for well over a century. It had a beauty of line in the steeply pitched shake roof and the lower, side roofs, even though many of the roof's wooden shingles were lost, and a few of the long siding boards were also missing or rotting nearby in the matted grass. The barn's big, heavy doors had probably once opened to bring in hay, animals, or, perhaps, a wagon or carriage. Small windows marked the places where stalls had once held animals.

The hinges on the barn's heavy doors were now frozen with rust, and the earth around the doors had gradually filled in and become higher as countless years of weeds and soil had washed down the hill. Because the big doors had been left open, the barn could still give shelter and some protection from rain and wind to horses, a resident barn owl, and many swallows and other birds. The owl, sitting alone on a high rafter, appeared fat and fairly tame. Not until I walked almost under him did he hastily flap outside to the eucalyptus trees. The barn must have provided him a banquet of mice, gophers, and birds. With such shelter and food available, I always wondered why he seemed to have no mate.

As those first weeks went by, I made occasional excuses to steal away for a short spell, to wander down the hill, perch on an old partition, and think and relax in the quiet dimness of Old Barn. With the house up the hill full of animals, kids, and some their school friends, who came visiting to see this new home, the barn offered solitude and a place to renew strength. It had a special silence and a poignancy, plus a feeling of continuity and survival. If only the barn could have talked and given some clues to its history! Surely, generations of early settlers had used it for their horses, cattle, hay storage, and wagons. Now it appeared vulnerable and abandoned. Unless we could someday buy this part of the ranch, the next owners would surely tear it down—probably to make a development of subdivisions.

Slightly up the hill from this barn were the remains of a couple of old wagons. Had these wagons lumbered over faint trails from eastern states, carrying pioneering families and their belongings to this verdant valley full of wildlife, trees, and grasses? On one wagon, there remained only one wheel and some of the floor and sideboards. A second wagon had two wheels and most of one side and the bed intact. The third wagon was actually some sort of carriage, with larger wheels that were almost whole, plus a few parts rusting or rotting a short distance away, deep in the grass and partly buried in the rock-hard soil.

Going in to San Luis Obispo once a week, or maybe once a month, must have been a main social event in those earlier times, as well as a means of obtaining sugar, flour, yardage, nails, sacks of grain, and other staples. Like the turkey farmer, we were always too busy to dig the deeply buried wagons and carriage out of the weeds, rock, and hardpan; hence, they remained there, constant reminders of those early settlers who had the courage to set out on new trails.

Chapter 2
Never-Never Land

I've got a million things to do!" Whoever first spoke that tired lament may well have been a farm wife. The next morning, long before the sun rose to a cold and damp dawn, I lay awake in my new room doing a lot of thinking. Dan and I had trouble following the "take it one day at a time" philosophy. Our philosophy was more like "grab every minute and fill it to overflowing." Right away it became evident that Oak Hills Ranch would become another never-never land—no matter how I sliced it, work would never be finished. There would never be enough time in any hour, day, month, or year, and there would never be enough money. Nevertheless, though we were in mid-career and mid-life, we were also at a new beginning. We finally had some of the big things like food and shelter, but both tiny and large jobs needed my constant attention.

Time had always felt like a gale-sized wind pushing me back and keeping me from making progress. In college it had been lack of time to prepare for tests, write term papers, read books, and get to all my classes on time. Then came marriage, which brought abject poverty and a drive to reach goals—goals of raising a family and large numbers of animals, improving little farms that operated well below a subsistence level, and constantly seeking more income.

I had always wondered what "getting there" meant. Where was "there," and how would either Dan or I know when we had arrived? This ranch was certainly special, and we hoped to be here for many years; yet, if getting there involved only a place to live, this ranch wasn't it, for we didn't own the ranch. Maybe being "there" would mean being in a place where we were not only happily surrounded by a family of children and animals, but also living on our own land in another landscape of hills and valleys.

On this ranch the stage was set: for the first time ever, we lived on a ranch with a bonanza of authentic sheds, barns, a roomy house with four bedrooms, and even a garage. It was certainly a wonderful place compared to the measly blank slate that had been our first farm in Arizona, a two-room shack on two acres without even a single tree.

My troupe was on hand, and they all desired leading parts. They'd get parts, certainly, but often not the ones they wanted; instead, their parts would involve lots of hard work, and on this stage there were few exits, with town too far away for easy walking and no neighbors nearby.

As before, I'd get more time in the spotlight than I wanted. In our plotting and planning sessions, usually lasting late into the night, Dan and I made the decision that again, instead of my getting a teaching job, I would continue to stay home with the kids, critters, and farm work. He took on the role of "bringing home the bacon," which would probably involve adding extra jobs onto his teaching and administrative role at California State Polytechnic College (some years later changed to "University") in San Luis Obispo.

There remained two big enemies: time and money. Our life was constantly assaulted and restricted by both. I was a firm believer in adapting to what couldn't be changed, yet time wasted might likely affect our later years. "Time is of the essence," I reminded Dan. "Let's choose income over full time home and hearth occupations for a while. Maybe I can serve brunch on Saturdays and Sundays, and thus omit the work of two meals?"

Dan answered, "Well, a lot will depend on how much time you and I save and how much work we can add. We're both perpetual starters, not stoppers—we'll figure things out. Losing, or giving up, aren't options."

Years ago I'd heard an elderly friend of my mother say to her, "As you get older, time will go by like a freight train on a downhill track. Stay young, at least in heart, my dear!" Time was flying by just as she said, but I hoped there were still lots of trails ahead. I believed fully in the Puritan work ethic—never look to others for help, do as much as possible for as long as possible, and believe that working hard can be fruitful and bring happiness.

We never took to heart Ben Franklin's old adage, as our schedules and jobs on that new large ranch immediately made us both "Late to bed and early to rise." I never came drowsily out of bed, but instead jumped up totally awake and ready for action. With seldom even a cup of coffee, I continued to feel full of caffeine during the countless long days that followed.

"Just how much can we change schedules and how can we become 'un-poor'? There seems to be something urgent every second. I won't turn into a pumpkin at midnight...or was it into a maid? I'm already the maid and a farm hand. However, I have a problem with deadlines—as soon as I meet one successfully, new ones pop up all over the place."

One reason deadlines were hard to meet was that I continued to lose things. A larger house should have helped me organize and put everything in its special place, but the extra rooms and closets just provided more room for stuff to hide. I'd honed my skills by managing to lose things in a series of homes with few rooms, closets, and drawers, and had squandered hours searching for such things as my purse, a pen, or someone's library book. Of course, it wasn't my fault if I'd found only one glass to set on the table for dinner the first night on Oak Hills. It was a sure bet that there were already a couple of glasses in each bedroom and a few in the living room, plus several others out in the hay barn.

With more brainstorming in the dark hours of the following night, I came up with the idea that we could probably save "thirty years of our lives" by continuing to be different from other people—not all people, but lots of them. Half-whispering, I added, "Our inner clocks are going to run out. I don't want to be old and poor—not in money, memories, achievements, or needing help from the children. Do you really think I should stay home and continue raising this crop of kids and just try to match your hours of work?"

Dan mumbled, "Sounds good to me, but what are your thoughts with all these years piling up and you still home every day?"

"I've no choice until all the children leave home...really no choice at all."

Dan then came fully awake to discuss a blizzard of ideas that must have been scurrying around in his head. "Yeah, it's fine for me to be a college prof, but it'd be nice to have that American dream of getting ahead and making more money.

"For starters, we've both decided to board horses. Tomorrow I'll put up a few notices at school. Since kids majoring in Animal Husbandry now and then bring one or two of their own cows to the dairy unit, I bet more members of the rodeo team and other aggies would bring their horses to college if there were a cheap and safe place nearby to board them.

"I'll continue to teach summers, and we can continue to do the yearly Farm Broker conferences. I've also been wondering about teaching some real estate classes for the Adult Evening School at the high school and for the junior college. We made enough mistakes in buying that Santa Margarita place to provide a whole bunch of lecture notes. And there was that near calamity when we got the five rental units. I could take students on field trips to see how and how not to do things. They'd love to see some of the mistakes their prof has made."

Dan turned on a lamp and grabbed a pencil. "Look here, if we save even two hours a day of unnecessary stuff, that's 14 hours per week, 56 a month, 672 a year, and 6,720 hours every 10 years. Imagine what can be done with that many hours, and they come free!" The die was cast: our shifts of work would change and become longer. Since I could hardly harness the children for much work when school and activities other than farm labor were taking more and more of their time as they grew up, it would be up to me.

It was almost morning before we figured out how to save time in order to toil longer with more jobs. "Of course," I continued to ponder at breakfast that morning, "Even if we save thirty years, it's still gone, so I guess we mean it's looking at things from an offbeat angle and doing what we want."

"Sure," Dan answered, "you don't want to play bridge. Since you've never played, you won't miss it. We'll play Fish or Rummy with the smaller kids when they're old enough. A good game of tennis takes an hour, instead of four hours for golf or an evening of bridge. It's the priorities, kiddo."

The house suddenly became quiet after everyone left for school, and I started mulling over these decisions. Many friends would say, "You're crazy! Think of all the fun you're missing by staying home way out here in the country and doing so much work." They had a point. And yet, I'd heard so many relatives and friends procrastinate and say things like:

"It's just too late for us to tackle."

"I never go out to shop until the rain stops."

"I'll get a job when we have enough money for a second car."

"We'll wait until the kids are grown."

"I'll never be able to afford to buy a house."

"I'd love to be a nurse, but it's six miles out there to take classes."

"We'll finally see Jack's relatives in England once we retire and have more time and money."

Much of what those people achieved in the meantime seemed like prologues with few main events. No, this was it for me, this day and henceforth; if it's true that busy people have the most time, I was on the right track. Even if I stumbled often, maybe just forging ahead would mean fewer falls.

From past experience, I knew some of the choices to make about saving time. For one thing, I would avoid having barbecues unless family or friends came and helped with the work. Hadn't the human race gotten rid of burned chunks of meat eons ago after moving from caves to houses? Now not even the fire is often from wood—it's from an uneven pile of charcoal briquettes that need a blowtorch to light them. By the time the charred chicken or steak is brought to the picnic table, often yellow jackets are already feasting on salad, beans, and butter-soaked and under-toasted French bread. Our dogs and cats will miss the leftovers, but, sure, I can manage to do without time-consuming barbeques.

We never had taken any real vacations, and now we wouldn't for a long time. So far, none of the kids had even been left alone with a sitter, not even for one evening. Could we wait till after we retired to see the world? I'll gamble a "Yes" on that scenario.

Housecleaning could be a snap, since I would have no trouble going forward without perfection—I'd always felt too much tidiness was depressing, so, as in the past, the house wouldn't have to get very clean or tidy until the day before company arrived. One day of frenzied cleaning by the family could achieve most of it, and by getting up about 3 A.M. on the day the company was to arrive, I could finish the job in time to do the cooking. Before long, even the dogs and cats tried to hide before company came, sensing that I planned to quickly drag them into the tub to get shiny clean and smell less like manure and more like doggy tar shampoo.

All this last-minute work would surely beat such things as daily spraying and polishing the piano, cleaning the floor of the shower, or the kitchen windows above the sink. It helped that I almost never saw any TV commercials showing constantly smiling, pretty women in attractive dresses, new hairdos, and painted nails, spending their days making floors glow with all kinds of solvents, cleaners, and waxes. These women seemed to enjoy taking the "wax buildup" off and then re-waxing all over again. Except on the day when company arrives, no one will risk breaking a leg on any slippery-clean floors in this house.

And I had my own daytime soap operas. Dealing with the children and the critters, I felt no need to watch any news programs; there were enough real life jobs to handle on this hilltop without hearing about the latest on the day's murders, fires, wars, or car crashes.

I also decided to be better about phone calls from strangers who wanted to take surveys, sell tickets to a ball for deep-sea divers, or inform me I have to vote for Joe Blow or the country will go to the dogs. I'll just say, "Sorry, I never talk to strangers who invade my home with ringing bells."

This morning, from my early morning command post in the kitchen, I now began revving up more of the usual "Didjas"—"Didja feed the dog? Didja put your sheets in the wash? Didja wash your hands?" Thank heavens that when they were old enough the younger two kids could wear their regular clothes for gym classes at their two-room school, just a few blocks down Los Osos Valley Road. Doug was already enrolled there for the fall and Jeff would begin first grade before too long. The boys would come home with their clothes filthy and sometimes torn, but at least Doug and Jeff wouldn't have to take a second outfit of gym clothing or athletic gear for a number of years, as Nancy and Danny's often did. All gym outfits seemed to hate to accompany the older children to school. Instead, they hid out in the washing machine, on the bedroom floors, under the car seat, or were still in their locker at school.

"You want them when? Those gym clothes just went in the washer this morning a few minutes ago. They aren't even spinning yet! Come on, child! Don't sweat the small stuff! Others must miss gym clothes now and then."

"Mom!" the boy then screamed while trying to paw through the wet wash still in the machine, "It's not small stuff! I'll die! The team will kill me!" Actually, if I could find the wayward items and had the car to drive that day, I would taxi the clothes to school in time for a gym class, a tennis match, or a water polo game. However, even with my best efforts, the older kids "died" a lot—their clothes sometimes arrived late, or not at all. Fortunately for me, each of our blessed animals had only one fur or feather outfit to wear: they knew how to keep life simple.

I also didn't need to take time learning about wines or serving them. Milk glasses were enough to wash. After all, Dan and I were born during the early years of Prohibition. Besides, with my obsession about ranch living, the kids, the animals, and food, I hardly needed another addiction. Perhaps some of my ancestors had been in the Anti-Saloon League. At any rate, Dan and I had made our own prohibition vow: never serve or drink any alcoholic beverages until the last of the children leave home. Of course, with the number of soft drinks the kids consumed, they were probably rotting their teeth instead of their livers.

Still, for about fifteen years, every summer some dear friends of ours in the State Farm Broker group brought us a case of "fine valley wines." Cases and cases of wine gradually piled up beneath and around Nancy's saddle in her tack closet, but we didn't like the taste and were never able to tell good wine from bad.

Because of Treve's intense barking frenzies whenever a car turned up the lane, few salespeople tried to even get to the door to make inroads on my time. Our interests were also beginning to focus on purchasing rental houses, not insurance, so I never did learn about such things as whole life, term life, or comprehensive liability coverage.

There was also no need for a gym or an exercise program for me. The only iron I pumped was the iron I used to remove the wrinkles from school clothing. There was also no taking my pulse or time for 'tired blood.' With all the time I saved by not going to a gym, I might even revert to being a child again.

There was, of course, no end to the ways I could save little pieces of time: I could talk with my mouth full, talk on the phone while stirring the cereal cooking on the stove, and even put the cat's food in my ice cream dish after dinner, thereby avoiding the need to wash the dish twice.

Stalling began to work very well. Suddenly I might leave the kitchen, saying, "I think Jeff is calling me." Doug might then decide he had to make his own sack lunch for school.

I also gave much thought to saying "No" more successfully and more often. I needed a polite way that wouldn't become a "Yes" for invitations to dinner, club memberships, working on committees, or baking cakes and cookies. I'd continue with the school stuff, but the kids could often sell a purchased cake to take to school just as well as one made from scratch. While I tried to keep volunteering for such groups as the League of Women Voters, the Scouts, and the Camp Fire Girls, the rest of the time I'd just say, "I'm really too busy to add another thing for at least the next five years." It took a while to learn not to say, "I'm busy tomorrow," or, "I'm fully booked this week," because many of those callers might switch from current needs and come up with year-long agendas and projects needing staff for the next twenty years.

The bottom line was that time is lost forever once it goes, and every moment had to count. Time might become a tyrant, but it would hopefully have good consequences. The omens seemed right—the large rain storm was past, and spring would soon arrive. An almost tangible peace and stillness came to the room after the older two kids departed for school, leaving Jeff and Douglas in their room, bundled up in heavy jackets and finding new-old treasures in some rain-soaked boxes of toys. Treve and the cat, Shandy, lay quietly nearby on the kitchen floor.

I began to implement my plans after breakfast. This ranch would be my turf, and happiness found in immediately cleaning the barn,and mucking out the long turkey shed to remove its deep layer of turkey droppings before any potential horse-boarding students arrived to check out this shed as shelter for their horses when they didn't want the horses out in a field.

Chapter 3
We-Haul and You-Haul

After thinking more about how to save time, I came to Dan with an impassioned plea. "Help! It's a necessity! It's life or death! I desperately need wheels! Somehow, we have to buy a second car! Since we're a little farther from your job, if I need the car for the day I have to spend a great deal of time taking you all the way to campus and picking you up there again in the late afternoon. With four kids, growing numbers of animals, and a new full schedule, I need to save time and have the freedom to move."

Fortunately, Dan agreed. "I know, you've needed a car since last year. How about you use the wagon, and maybe I can start looking for another vehicle."

We had a penchant for big, utilitarian vehicles, and I started growing excited at the prospects. At that time in the '60s, station wagons were extremely popular, and I loved ours. The kids did not appreciate the fact that it took such a large car to accommodate the family whenever we all went places together, and scathingly dubbed the wagon as the Tank or the Whale. Unglamorous, utilitarian, and inexpensive pick-up trucks were next in our sights, and really seemed the best choice for a second vehicle. Dan could use it as for work and hauling large objects, and I could use the station wagon to run a taxi service for the kids.

"Hon," I concluded, "nothing can stop me if I just have wheels."

All this dreaming, and suddenly, hallelujah! A new blue Ford pick-up, economy model was parked out beyond the gate. I was far more excited about this truck than I would have been about any fancy sports car. Whenever I sat behind the wheel it reminded me that I belonged in the country. A real cowgirl! I reveled in the high seats that allotted us a beautiful view over our valley.

While most of the pick-up's disadvantages were minor, the main one was that occasionally we had to squeeze four of us into the only seat—which didn't adjust. It was by no means a plush automobile—the windows had to be hand-cranked, the engine was so noisy we had to shout to be heard, the radio was nearly useless, and the seat bounced us around wildly with any hint of pavement imperfections. The extra-stiff springs on that truck did not always make it pleasant to drive on the ever deteriorating roads and byways of central California. Still, it was a wonderful auto, and I constantly extolled its usefulness.

I found that some of the most wonderful properties of cars don't even involve taxiing people around. My car became a dandy place to let my thoughts catch up with me, to rest my aching back against the seat and gaze out upon open fields—land where nothing had to be fed, cleaned, or nurtured by me. I felt like my car was a mini day spa, where I occasionally found a moment to relax and renew my body and soul—all without guilt or wasted time. Running errands or waiting for the kids gave me such an escape! On the other hand, these vacations did not come free—both the big station wagon and the pickup drank gasoline as if it were water.

After moving to Oak Hills, I started making lists and lists to hold tightly in my fist, lists that became necessary when I drove to town. Tying a string around my finger was no longer a sufficient memory aid. I may have been too busy, dumb, or absentminded to remember all the errands and things to buy or do on each trip, but with my lists I would have no trouble recalling all the stops to be made.

Unfortunately, the lists began to look like large treasure-hunt maps. At first I drove to the north end of town for one thing, then over to the west side for something else, then over to the east side, and back to the south side. To avoid half a day of crisscrossing back and forth, I soon began numbering my list, and plotted the sequence of my errands on a grid that represented the different areas of town. To top it off, four kids who were all into sports, had almost daily needs for new gym shorts, tennis rackets to be re-strung, caps for water polo, and rides to and from games or practice. And yet their activities didn't even end at sports… scout activities quickly proved to be quite time consuming. Each child needed constant lifts to Boy Scout or Camp Fire Girls meetings and activities. It took countless trips to get stuff for projects so that the kids could win the badges and patches that I then had to sew onto their uniforms. Moms and dads should be made "Eagle Go-For Scouts" and "Torch Light-Bearers" when the kids won their scouting honors, for by the time the three boys became Eagle Scouts and Nancy a Torchbearer, I had become a barely flickering house wren.

Over a twenty-year period, I sat and waited in a dark car while each child took piano lessons. Most of the time I transported Danny and Nancy together, and then Doug and Jeff together, but the wait was still for four separate lessons every week. I didn't complain though—it was the most rest I got all day.

Only a mom who has gone through it would also realize how many years' worth of trips it takes to get teeth straightened. In addition to braces, each of our four children needed to have his or her wisdom and cuspid teeth removed. It's a wonder I didn't become frozen into the con-figuration of the letter E—head forward, scanning the road, arms for-ward clenching the wheel, and feet forward pressing the pedals.

And, if only there had been a supermarket that would have sold to me wholesale! Since I usually filled six human tummies about six times each day, supplies of food quickly disappeared. Even with home-produced vegetables, milk, and meat, I needed to take the pick-up to hold all the food needed for a week—especially since the children brought an extra child or two home from school now and then. Dan and I were really hauling—every year we put between 30,000 and 45,000 miles on each vehicle. Dan was driving to and from school, and then going back into town almost every evening after dinner to moonlight at the junior college, the high school, or the various locations of our Lumbleau Real Estate

School. We also bought property in Santa Maria and Grover City (now Grover Beach), and Dan taught real estate classes in those towns every week for what seemed like a thousand years.

I don't know whether it was worse or better when the two older children began to drive and I no longer hauled them everywhere. Especially at night, the clock and I ticked off the minutes together, while I mentally drove with them from the moment they left until the time I saw the headlights of their cars shining on the lane and through our bedroom window as they returned safely.

After all the business of hauling around kids, our wonderful animals were a cinch to care for. The barn only had to be filled chuck-full of oat and alfalfa hay once a year. Since I forced the kids to do most of the feeding and watering of the large animals, I mostly fed small critters and did clean-up duty. Of course there were the occasional rushed trips to the feed or farm supply stores when we ran out of grain, pellets, mash, or other critter food, but these were nothing compared to trips for the kids.

Chapter 4
Home Is the Kitchen

With our emphasis on heavy schedules and saving time, we barely had time to dream—even though I had always wished for a ranch home with a long veranda and steps leading up to it. Sitting on the steps on warm summer evenings there would be a guitar player wearing jeans, boots, and a plaid shirt, playing his guitar and singing tunes like "Don't Fence Me In," "Tumbling Tumbleweeds," "Wagon Wheels," and "Twilight on the Trail." There on the porch, family and friends would gather and share in talk, laughter, and songs. A couple of dogs would lie nearby, and there would always be a pitcher of lemonade and a freshly baked cake.

The other dream I nursed when I was completely exhausted was of me alone on that long porch, sitting in a cushiony rocking chair, resting my back while sipping a glass of tea and watching sleek, graceful horses grazing in nearby green pastures.

Oak Hills Ranch house had a porch all right, but the porch and big front door were on the wrong side of the house, without even a good walkway around the house from the parking area to the door. Everyone living on the ranch had obviously always gone through the back door to the screened-in porch and then through a second door into the kitchen—a most unceremonious entrance. Yet that made sense to me since the back yard had the garage, a large parking area, the barns and sheds nearby, the only gate into the yard, and a cement walkway to the back door. Because of this arrangement, not much time was spent on the porch, and very soon much time was spent in the kitchen.

With its no-nonsense linoleum floor, the kitchen was ready for heavy use, including muddy kids' shoes and animal paws coming and going all day long, Dan, carrying full-to-the-brim pails of warm frothy milk or bags of groceries, Nancy carrying her saddle, ropes, and bridle back and forth, and my constant food preparation.

The living room immediately changed its role and become both a bedroom and a playroom for Doug and Jeff. There was room enough for their train tracks, building blocks, and half-finished puzzles. The one downside with the space was there were no closets—their clothing multiplied all over the floor and furniture. I gave them a large dresser to share, but pulling dresser drawers open seemed to be too much work for them; they would just as soon store their laundry in piles around the room.

Back then, people didn't go in for a lot of plumbing—a large percentage of the old houses still had just one bathroom, and this house was no exception. In the bathroom there was a wonderful bathtub but no shower. The tub, resting on large cast-iron paws that looked like lions' feet, was long enough for me to stretch out in and sink blissfully into hot water. The tub quickly became my respite for weary muscles or a throbbing head—a sink-in-and-forget pool, as well as a soap-and-cleanup tub, especially necessary after a day spent mucking out horse sheds or cow corrals.

One of our friends wondered, "Don't you all have to take numbers, sign up on a waiting list, or tear your hair and scream to get to the john?"

"No," I answered, "just a small groan or yell now and then."

One bathroom worked out all right, but we surely needed more than one little fireplace. This was the coldest house we had ever encountered.

Inadequate heating was hardly a strong enough statement to convey the extent of the problem. Since Dan and the older children would be away much of the time in school, I complained, "You'll find me somewhere inside two ski caps, three jackets, and two pairs of pants. Even with a roaring fire, the temperature in this high-ceilinged house is barely higher than outside, and the large stack of wood will be gobbled up in no time. I can't keep feeding the fire's endless appetite all day long! And who's going to cut more wood? A crackling fire is lovely, but it doesn't even begin to do the job of that floor furnace in our last house."

Dan just laughed, "Guess you'll just have to warm up by working harder and faster." Damn.

Throughout the house, my daily refrain quickly became, "Close the door, will ya? That means the refrigerator door, too!" The kids had younger and warmer fuel coursing through their veins. The words "close the door" must come with middle age!

With no insulation in the walls, ceilings, or floors, the cold seeped in and frigid drafts found their way through every crack. To top it off, we had no carpeting—not even area rugs; in the mornings I swear I could have ice skated into the kitchen. The only source of warmth other than the fireplace was a small wall-mounted heater in the hall near the bedrooms, but this heater burned expensive propane, so I only turned it on for a few minutes while the family was dressing on the coldest of mornings.

Because the kitchen was the only warm place, soon all activity centered there. Every day at about 5:30 A.M., I would turn on the oven and leave the door open, letting it serve as a heater (a very dangerous practice). Soon the room would burst with voices, action, and warmth. Steaming hot oatmeal, the smell of bacon and eggs frying, and the sound of coffee perking made the room seem even warmer, and it echoed with the spirited chorus of everyone needing to eat, make lunches, find homework, and figure out the day's schedules.

In the kitchen, our lovely maple table and its matching chairs, burnished and satiny brown, stacked high day and night with books, school work, clothes to be sorted and folded, toys, and, for the first few years, jars of frogs, tadpoles, beetles, or moths brought in by the younger two boys. At mealtime all such clutter had to be moved to the lonely table in the dining room, but the minute the dishes were removed the kitchen table filled with projects again.

Whenever the kitchen counter was full, the table also doubled as the place to fix food for the dog and cat, make sack lunches, pay bills, and spread out homework. Jeff and Doug even listened to their bedtime stories as we sat around that table.

Birthdays for the younger children were usually celebrated at the kitchen table, which could accommodate up to ten squirming, excited participants. My cakes had a reputation for messy, thick frostings covering lop-sided layers. They were certainly "kitchen-table cakes," and I tried to keep them hidden from any parents who dropped off their children—I was afraid that they would be appalled by my deplorable baking efforts.

Needless to say, the kitchen chairs never made it to old age. They were used as rockers by the kids, who tilted them back and forth as they ate and talked. Since the kitchen was closer at hand than any closets, the chairs also often held sweaters, wet jackets, slickers, and coats. I borrowed the chairs to stand on to reach high shelves or when painting ceilings. Dan used them as barber's chairs when he cut the boys' hair. When we needed to change light bulbs in high-ceilinged fixtures, we carried these chairs to all rooms in the house. I also sat on one chair and put my feet up on another each time I fixed string beans or tackled other sit-down chores.

The only time these chairs received any loving care was when large groups or special guests came to dine. Then I tried to scrape the rungs clean of food and mud, scrub the backs and sides, and give them a coat of polish over the dents, scratches, and any bare wood. I glued and re-glued the rungs, legs, and backs, and eventually even repaired some of them with screws.

Other than the table, another popular focal point in the kitchen was our only telephone. Firmly attached to the kitchen wall, it was in the perfect location to prevent any long, chatty calls, since we had to stand up to use it and few secrets were possible with so many people in and out of the room. The older children usually cast furtive glances around to see who was listening. There was also a lot of giggling and whisper-ing, "I can't talk now," or, "You ask me, and I'll answer 'Yes' or 'No.'"

A cork bulletin board hung on the wall next to the phone and held a large calendar, frequently overflowing with messages of mostly outdated appointments and reminders. Any leftover space on the board often held the school artwork of the younger boys. Some of this artwork overflowed to the door of the laundry room. Nothing could be tacked or taped to the door frame, however, because that was reserved to mark the birthday heights of each child for each year that we lived on the ranch. This became quite a record, even though we left the ranch before the last of the gang stopped growing. Their growth was impressive—they grew to be six, six-four, six-five, and six-eight feet tall.

Whether on the phone or in person, each morning I tried to catch any red-flag words, such as, "My history report is due Friday," or, "Camp Fire Girls (meeting) has to be here tomorrow because Jane's mom is sick," and, "Sure we can bring some cookies tomorrow." There were also plenty of desperate crises, like, "Mom, will you make Danny feed the horses? I've got a math test tomorrow, and I don't know any of the stuff!" All this talk carried over and expanded at mealtime, which involved my almost absolute law for this jungle clan: everyone had to eat both breakfast and dinner sitting down together at the table unless the excuse was extremely important. Often I'd tell them, "You're mistaken if you think you can skip dinner or eat later. Sit down this minute!"

That law made for so much chatter in the kitchen that a speech therapist at school later discovered that our youngest child, Jeff, was leaving out syllables when speaking some words and decided it was "probably due to the older children and parents talking too much and too fast." Jeff couldn't get his words in edgewise or fast enough to speak properly. I then spent a summer taking him to see a speech-doctor to improve his oral communication. The therapist gave me the homework assignment of making a picture scrapbook from magazines and newspapers with the names of the objects in the photos containing the letters and sounds that Jeff dropped or misplaced—I then pointed to the pictures while Jeff practiced saying the words correctly.

Other than Jeff's speech correction, I had quickly decided to ignore much of what was going on. If the kids hid broccoli or turnips under the table, fed bits of dinner to Treve, or read by flashlight at night, I usually feigned ignorance. Not insisting on perfect behavior can be the salvation for both mother and child as long as the kids' transgressions consist of "small stuff."

Next to the kitchen was the laundry room. We had no clothes dryer except the sun, so five long lines of wash, clipped in place with wooden clothespins, flapped in the backyard breeze six days a week, unless it rained. When it rained, or looked like it might, there were enough wet clothes and sheets hanging everywhere inside to make a humidity meter predict rain inside the house. If the house had been properly heated, I'd have lived in a steam bath on most cloudy or rainy days.

The laundry room eventually also became the best place for temporarily housing new small pets—sometimes in the laundry tub, sometimes on the floor. The new momma rabbit lived there until a hutch could be built; an injured dove stayed there, and so did a hamster whose cage had been taken over by a large snake for couple of days earlier. If a dog got a bath on a rainy day, the laundry room became his drying room. When certain company came, wearing silk stockings and nice dresses, or with an overwhelming fear of animals, the laundry room became an immediate kennel for any dogs and cats who might try to sit on the wrong lap.

We had a long Formica counter built across one end of the laundry room where Doug could sit on a barstool to do his chemistry set experiments. However, after I saw one or two of those experiments, I hurried back to the store and bought a second barstool for the use of a Cal Poly chemistry student that we hired to teach and observe Doug so that he wouldn't blind himself or blow up the house.

Thus, life in the house, yard, barns, and gardens quickly became my rut, a daily program of work with few options and little variety (aside from my many adventures as a taxi driver)—mow the lawn, pay the bills, spend less than our bank balance each month, wash and dry loads of laundry, and wash the car, dogs, and Jeffrey (until he began screaming, "Let me take my own bath!"). Ruts can be comfortable places, giving a strange sense of serenity as well as providing a daily, endless routine with few intermissions. Best of all, my ruts only required a daily costume of old jeans, faded flannel shirts, torn jackets, tennis shoes too ancient to grace any tennis court, and my perpetually straight stringy hair. Acquiring a pair of new rubber boots to use when I cleaned the horse sheds or when it rained became a rare and exciting purchase.

Chapter 5
Love on the Hoof

Nancy's addiction to horses never lessened as she got older. It had been a long hard trail, taking us many years before Nancy could own her own lovely horse. Nancy had taken a few lessons from Monty Roberts, who, with his uncanny insight into horse behavior and soundness, had found Nancy her horse, Blue. Nancy started to enter horse shows, and won ribbons of many colors in the local arenas around the county. The large bulletin board on the wall behind her bed gradually became a collage of blue, purple, green, red, yellow, white, and pink ribbons.

The brainstorm idea to board horses belonging to university students became an immediate success. Blue soon had more horse friends than she wanted, and I was in the horse-boarding business.

All the horses we boarded that first year belonged to female college students. These horses had an emotional side that included a need for a caring home with people, plus a chance to run, be brushed, and be ridden. All had a great need to feel safe and were quick to sense danger or trouble, whether it be the sound of thunder, a gun going off farther up the canyon road, or just a truck rattling by on Los Osos Road.

The three or four horses in each large field quickly became friends and loved to race around as a herd, especially while they were waiting impatiently for their hay every morning and early evening. The thundering hooves of these horses were not the sounds of wild mustangs, but of docile, well-mannered, and beloved mounts of young college students.

With the students' first horse-boarding checks, I ordered enough oat and alfalfa hay to get by until there were new cuttings the following year. "Easy-keeper" Blue could continue to grow overly plump, just as she had done on our small O'Connor Way farm.

I always loved the fragrance of newly baled alfalfa hay that filled the air when I tossed flakes to the horses. I also loved seeing the orderly stacks of baled hay in the barn and knowing that the supply would last until new crops were harvested and the barn could be filled to the ceiling again.

With the introduction of the new horses, Nancy's normally docile and gentle mare Blue became a different horse. This land had quickly become her assumed personal spread, and had furnished her with solo dinners and breakfasts. Now she had to share the pasture and she thought she was being made to share her food. Stamping her hoof and squealing, she bared her teeth and tried to bite and kick as she charged toward a new horse. Blue's ears went back in an effort to eat the lion's share of every flake of hay.

We reduced this problem by tossing the flakes of hay farther apart over the fence along the lane leading down the hill and by putting out one more flake of hay than there were horses. With that the horses played a version of musical chairs, as, with mouths full of hay, they went rushing, circling, and swerving to different flakes. After a while, the jockeying for position pretty much stopped, and they adjusted to one another. Then another new horse would arrive, and would get kicked and nipped by the others for several days before feeling accepted. Sometimes we placed flakes of hay halfway down the hill to keep the peace.

When it rained, the horses willingly trotted into the adjacent long turkey shed to be fed. Fortunately, the shed had been made with a series of small windows, and whoever was feeding the horses could load the new pick-up truck or the wheelbarrow and still feed the horses by throwing separate flakes through the numerous open windows.

Even in the coastal areas of Central California, where temperatures seldom go below 30 degrees, the horses grew long, shaggy, winter coats. Then, in the spring, as the days grew longer and warmer, the horses began to shed. That was when the whole hilltop began to look as if it were molting, since the students often brought their horses up to the barn to currycomb, brush, and feed them. These horse owners never raked up the clouds and clumps of shedding hair, and all of us wore some of that hair into the house on our clothing.

Since the horses also wanted to lose their thick coats, they rolled in the fields or rubbed against any handy post or wooden gate; soon they were once again shiny and sleek, with summer coats of short hair.

For Blue and future family horses, a friend of ours made four beautiful wooden saddle-racks and a closet for them just inside the back screen-door to the house, and I added a large bucket for currycombs, brushes, and hoof picks.

The pitchforks, shovels, wheelbarrow, and other such equipment were kept beyond the long shed in the white barn. Nancy and Danny did much of the horse feeding at that time, and they began using the pick-up truck instead of the wheelbarrow to carry the hay long before they reached legal driving age.

After entering the big horse show in Santa Barbara, Nancy and I concluded that smaller shows in the county would be a lot more fun. It hadn't helped that we observed a very young girl receive such a loud and severe scolding from her horse-trainer that she burst into tears. The little girl had arrived with several horses for different events, and the fine horses were obviously bought, trained, and outfitted with never a worry about cost. I could only speculate how much happier that child would have been laughing and enjoying an informal horse show, or maybe riding along the trails in some foothills. I noticed her family's long horse trailer with their stable name and address written on the sides. They had spent most of a day getting to the Santa Barbara show and, after showing for several days, would then spend another day getting home. This show was ostensibly for fun, but some of those who attended were obviously deadly earnest about winning. Expensive tack, clothes, and horses, endless training, and many hours of transportation to shows lasting several days, weren't what we had in mind.

I especially remember one informal show just south of town, when the whole area sparkled after a recent shower, and the arena was free of dust. A green field next to one side of the arena was full of horse trailers hooked to cars or pick-up trucks all spread out in random directions with tailgates down. The horses, thoroughly washed, brushed, and shiny, were tied to the trailers, where one serious boy and many excited girls brushed their mounts one last time before saddling and bridling them for the competition.

Blue loved the chance to socialize, and she arched her neck around to observe the other horses and whinny a few salutations. Nancy and her mare came in second in the Pleasure Class and Western Class. Then came the Trail Class. Rider and horse opened a ranch-type gate in the proper manner and with ease; then Blue had to walk over a small bridge, the likes of which the mare decided she had never seen before in her life. The bridge was a narrow, curved, wooden one with a rather steep pitch, and it was thickly lined with palm fronds tied to the railings on both sides. These green fronds were rustling and swaying in the breeze.

Blue, tense and frightened, arched her neck and, with head held high and ears pointing straight forward, stared at the bridge. She shook her head and mane and gave a few snorts, all the while dancing a few steps towards the apparition and then stopping and turning aside at the last minute while keeping her big eyes focused on that thing. After a few attempts to urge Blue across, Nancy had to turn her horse away and join the other riders, who were lined up in the center of the ring. There was no ribbon for Nancy and Blue at that event, and yet it was the greatest memory I've kept of all the shows I watched.

Blue was a beautiful six-year-old, rather small and a light dappled-gray, with a long, darker mane and tail. Nancy was wearing her show outfit of matching light pearl-gray cowboy hat, chaps, and pants, gray boots with dark stitching, and a long-sleeved blue-and-white-checked shirt. She sat tall and calm as she tried to urge Blue over the bridge. The sun shone brightly and warm in a sky as blue as Nancy's shirt, while the green of the palm fronds, field, and nearby hills added ever more color. It all made a wonderful picture. Time seemed to stand still as that scene was imprinted in my mind forever. With just a bit of healthy competition, there could be fun and social enjoyment from these smaller shows, even if the horses and kids did not always win. This day was one of the special, bottom-line reasons for all the years of mom and dad's endless work and shaky finances, yet few people could probably understand this. So many would just think, "So, a horse balked at a bridge. So what?"

A few weeks previously, Nancy and the mare had been through an incident of a very different sort. Blue was already an extremely well trained horse when we bought her at age five, but the one thing she still had trouble doing was changing leads smoothly and quickly. To force the horse to change quickly, Nancy put Blue into a faster gallop than her usual slow and gentle lope, headed her toward the fence at the edge of the barnyard, and turned her quickly at the last minute.

Blue was improving, and they practiced successfully for several evenings. Then Nancy happened to rein the loping mare too close to a small pile of gravel. As the horse made the sudden turn and changed leads, Blue slipped in the loose gravel and fell on her side. I was working at the kitchen sink and happened to look out at that very moment. Fortunately, Nancy's leg didn't end up under Blue, but she got a deep scrape on her leg from the gravel. Patient, kind, and worried, Blue made a fine decision. As soon as the uninjured mare got to her feet, she stood beside her mistress with the reins hanging loose to the ground, her feet perfectly still, and she turned her head around to watch Nancy until she was able to get a hand on a stirrup and pull herself up. Grabbing the reins and leading Blue, Nancy hobbled toward the house hollering, "Mom!"

Chapter 6
My Love Affair with the Rototiller

Once again it was time to create a large produce garden and green lawn. "All right, kids and Dad, each of you have got to give me a list of your twelve most favorite veggies. Write them down after you look through this catalogue. No, you can't write down carrots twelve times. I need twelve different ones."

Seed catalogues often arrived in January, and, as we had done with the old Sears-Roebuck catalogues that sold dreams, we dog-eared the seed catalogues while making lists of vegetables. This was my sneaky ploy to get everyone to eat vegetables—I knew there were no twelve vegetables they thought delicious or even tolerable; still, they observed my hard-to-believe enthusiasm and could hardly be snobbish toward the gloriously colored pictures in the catalogs.

The catalogues portrayed glamorous, perfectly formed veggies without a blemish on them, in colors as vivid as stoplights—plump beets and tomatoes glowed red, string beans and lettuce were pictured in shades of lime and emerald green, and squash came in marigold yellow and light and dark greens. All those packets of seeds, onion sets, and seed potatoes filled a big brown bag of promises and dreams.

The catalogues made having a garden seem like a cinch. They claimed such things as "Sixty days to harvest, plant 1/4 inch deep, plant

1/2 inch deep, plant seed two inches apart, and in full sun." I, too, began to make wild promises: "We'll eat like kings, and it will be as easy as duck soup!"

Then came the first installment in the treacherous untold story of those seed packets. I chose to develop a big new planting area on the east side of the house. The land was part of a field that cattle had roamed and it had probably never been farmed. As usual, this was the hard way, since there was a stretch of much easier land beside the lane near the house which had probably been used as a garden in the past.

Dan sputtered in dismay, "You're serious? You want to garden this much land? It's not even fenced!"

"Dash it, I do want it," I quickly responded. "My kitchen table must groan under platters of all kinds of ranch produce. It won't be too large if I plant twenty or more different items. Please?"

He was a kindly man. "All right, I'll help get it ready, but after that don't forget, it's your 'south-forty,' not mine."

Once again I felt that growing large red beets, orange carrots, and all the other produce from tiny seeds would be like a miracle—almost like giving birth. This food would be grown without store-bought fertilizers or insecticides, and the produce would be picked when ripe. I would freeze whatever we couldn't eat right away. Since we made frequent trips to see Dan's parents, it would be fun to just hear his frail mom rave over the bags of fruits and vegetables we would bring to her.

The arrival date of my first big piece of farm equipment wasn't far off. This wouldn't be a tractor, though the garden area was big enough to accommodate a small one. Instead, a large red rototiller was on its way. I could hardly wait. Some women long for fur coats or jewels, but I longed for this powerful plowing and disking machine. All my previous gardens had been too small to justify anything but a pick, hoe, shovel, and rake, although several of them could have been larger if I'd had a rototiller.

Removing countless rocks from the field was the first big job. I parked the pick-up nearby and started transporting wheelbarrow loads of stones and rocks—some almost too heavy to lift—to the truck bed. Then I carted them away. Everyone helped when they could, but with school in session I slaved alone most days. We took these pick-up loads of rock to the college dump; why we didn't dump the rock on the ranch somewhere I've never figured out. At the time, I just didn't see a good place nearby to stash them. The work went on for weeks.

Next, the huge area had to be carefully fenced. As Dan reminded me a dozen times, we had leased much of the ranch's grazing land to a rancher who might soon bring some of his Herefords to the property. However, with a rented post-hole digger, Dan and I dug deep holes and planted eight foot long 4" x 4" wooden posts. We stretched woven wire between the posts and used a stack of boards along the top of the posts. Dan promised that before long he would make me a gate between my garden plot and the lawn near the door to the kitchen.

After this, I set out sprinklers to soften this plot of drying land. I realized it would have been more ecologically correct to shovel the weeds into the soil, but instead I raked and hoed them all off because I craved a neat and pretty garden as soon as possible. Then, using a shovel, I sprinkled across the whole plot about forty or fifty wheelbarrow-loads of manure that I harvested from the old turkey sheds, cow corral, and the rabbit and chicken pens.

On the day the rototiller arrived, a lifelong love-hate relationship began between me and that monster. The gas-powered engine had a horrible rope starter that I had to pull and rewind and pull again until my arms were worn-out just trying to start the stubborn beast. The rototiller could plow, disk, and harrow, depending on how fast or slow I made it go, and on the condition of the soil. I walked behind it, gripping the handles firmly, rather like you would a huge lawnmower. The motor made the wheels and blades go around, but often the monster took off too fast across hard ground, or kept digging deeper and deeper in the areas that were too soft. I then had to lift the extremely heavy machine up and forward; the whole task was a bit like trying to drive a team of poorly trained horses in a perfectly straight direction, at a constant pace, and in a muddy field.

The blades simultaneously discovered a new crop of rocks beneath the surface and flipped them out with every turn. As the hours passed, the monster machine seemed to grow heavier and heavier, my aching arms and shoulders insisting the machine's weight had surely doubled or tripled. Not only that, but the rototiller still wouldn't go in a straight line. At the end of each row, I had to pull on a knob to reverse gears and pull on the machine to back it up and turn it around to begin the next row. It was a never ending battle.

I'd read that there's no such thing as a free lunch, but this was ridiculous. Late in the day, I left the critter sitting out in the middle of the field where it had run out of gas again. I, too, was out of gas. With blisters across the palms of both hands, a deep, pink sunburn on my face, arms, and legs, and my body bent over almost double, I stumbled to the house and ran water deep and scalding hot in the long, lion-footed bathtub. Tub baths usually soothed my aches, but this time every muscle in my body was sore. The family would have to get their own dinner.

The next day I carried off new rocks that the rototiller had brought up to the surface. Dan graciously offered to do the next tilling and start on cross-tilling, to make certain that all the land would be equally friable.

Surprising even myself, I blurted out, "No, let me do it. It's great. I love it, and the garden will be ready to plant by next week." This love/hate affair with the rototiller continued.

I continued to have a stubborn, persistent need to have straight rows of plants. On many trips up and down the state, I had been intrigued and delighted by views of the vast acreages on both sides of the highway—acres and acres of unbelievably straight rows of rich and varied crops marching off to hills in the distance. How could those farmers have gigantic fields with every single plant the same healthy green, the same height, and all in parade formation as far as the eye could see?

I quickly bought twine to tie to stakes to make my double-width seedbeds just as ruler-straight, and Dan helped one more weekend. At least the garden would be one place in my chaotic, messy family circus where something would stay orderly and straight! I hoed the dirt up toward the string on both sides of each bed. This made the beds somewhat raised and the soil less packed; watering would be easier, and poultry wire could be used if needed.

With the back of the shovel I whacked flat any clods remaining on the top of the beds, and then raked them smooth before using the end of a small stick to scratch a depression down the length of the rows. In these small troughs, I carefully planted the seeds by hand. The tiniest seeds would be covered with a thin layer of fine soil, and the larger seeds planted deeper.

March is a strange and uncertain month. It felt like spring—fresh and sweet with the sun shining. Yet, were those few clouds all fluff up there? Would darker ones follow, full of rain, and wash away all my seeds? Would some nights get cold enough to freeze again?

I attached the empty seed packets to small sticks and pushed the sticks into the soil to mark where each different kind of vegetable would sprout. There were beans, beets, Brussels sprouts, carrots, chard, corn, cucumbers, onions, parsley, peppers, radishes, spinach, tomatoes, three kinds of squash, turnips, cantaloupe, watermelon, and sweet potatoes. There was a flat of tomato plants to set out the following week. The tomato plants wore little white paper hats for several weeks to keep them from dying after any late frost.

Each day I ran sprinklers to keep the whole patch damp until the seed sprouted. If you let seeds dry out as they begin to sprout, you may lose them. Our primitive sprinkling system worked, the sun was bright, there was a quick late shower, and ever so soon, there was the thrill of a field of tiny leaves sprouting up from those dead-looking seeds. Then, at almost the same time, a complete carpet of weeds popped up. Lying dormant until the rains came, or until a lady with a hose and sprinkler arrived, these weeds were far thicker than the ones I remembered from my past gardens. The weeds in this bumper crop, sprouting up again and again, were not just the oats that had been growing there, but countless other troublesome invaders.

Where did all these wild seeds and plants come from? Probably many came from all the turkey and cow manure I'd spread, the same fertilizer that had caused my meek little vegetable plants to become so vigorous and healthy. Maybe birds passed by and dropped some seeds, while others may have blown in on the wind. The weeds were stronger than the vegetables which were sprouting, and they had to be conquered. I hoed, shoveled, or yanked weeds every single morning.

Long rows of bright green plants continued to emerge with shoots coming up in record time and leaves uncurling. I was thrilled at the sight.

Each morning after the kids left for school and the kitchen was cleaned up, I went out to admire and check on the beautiful sight. I stopped to pull out any remaining weeds, or just raked my fingers through the loam. I treated the straight, sturdy rows of new tiny plants with another light serving of fertilizer and gave them water to drink.

Then, suddenly, there was a disaster worse than weeds. Maybe I'd missed the first invasions, but there, where rows of lettuce, chard, beets, and so many other plants had been reveling in the sun and moist soil, many rows were now completely empty, with the remaining plants standing wilting and half eaten. Only a small area of squash, ripening corn, and some tomatoes, parsley, and onions remained. All the other plants were gone. Oh, catalogues! You don't tell the whole story!

This land that had been so welcoming had increasingly been giving food to armies of various hungry and relentless creatures; tunneling gophers, flying birds, crawling caterpillars, hopping rabbits, wiggling worms, and countless scurrying and flitting insects had all craved a salad! And to think I had worried mainly about deer jumping the fence! Sure, there had been grasshoppers, birds, and a few other invaders in my rural and town gardens in the past, but never, never had they caused such havoc!

Dan phoned at noon, and I gave him my tale of woe. "I try to love all living creatures, goodness knows, and for the most part I do, but the plants have so many enemies here that these uninvited guests have almost wiped out my whole garden. There continue to be more fresh gopher mounds out there, and I've seen lots of birds around that weren't here when we came, and the kids have seen several wild rabbits. There's no time to dilly-dally—I've got to replant right away! What else could I possibly do? Our gardens have simply got to feed us vegetables and salads each night for most of the year. That's my goal. I hate to say it, but I'm for putting chicken wire all around instead of the hog wire, and getting some traps and bait. The kids and I can make a scarecrow with that terrible old pair of jeans you have and your good white shirt that I turned pink in the wash. I'll have to keep the dog and cat out until the bait and traps are gone. Maybe we can get poisoned meal to use on the grasshoppers instead of pellets. It's got to be war!"

After the chicken wire was installed around all four sides, I sprayed, dusted, and trapped. Then I put up a whimsical scarecrow who flapped his long sleeves and gloves in the breeze (though the birds seemed to pay him little attention). I quickly replanted all the crops that had been destroyed, and I placed netting over the planted rows.

Since it was still early in the planting cycle; all the new seed had time to grow. Hooray! The corn grew tall, and the ears were tender and sweet. The tomatoes became ever so red and juicy, the squash ripened to the proper shades of yellow and green, and all the salad lettuce and other plants gave us bountiful produce.

However, there was one problem—it was Mom. By the time the second crop of vegetables were ready to be picked, washed, peeled, cooked, and served, who had the strength left to do the job? And at that point, who cared? I couldn't, and the plants didn't. With happy abandon, some of the squash grew as big as melons, carrots grew large and went to seed, the corn fed many happy worms, and a number of tomatoes eventually caught end rot. This is the rest of the untold story of fancy seed catalogues.

Yet, in spite of the gardener's fatigue, eventually many vegetables, fresh and full of flavor, did find their way to our dinner table for many years, while Dan began a long habit of reveling in farm-related jokes. One of his favorites was, "You know how the corn got here? The stalk brought it." Each year lots of farm jokes cropped up right on cue with my produce—the same jokes and the same produce.

The first year was hard, yet I couldn't help but comment later to the family, "There's a glorious big rototiller waiting in the shed, the ground will be more friable next season, and the rocks are mostly gone. Those destructive critters won a battle, but not the war. In the meantime, this house needs more than just bougainvillea and geraniums around it. Want to help me plant bulbs and fall flowers this weekend?" All heads quickly shook "No."

Still, the gardens, food, and flowers continued to provide more than baskets of vegetables and flowers: they became an oasis, a sanctuary where I let my mind slow down and drift while pulling weeds or putting a hose in a furrow to watch the water flow down to the far end. It was great—there was no one around and no phone ringing. If a cat joined me, even he knew it was time to contemplate, watch, and be quiet. Now I had two more escapes at Oak Hills Ranch: going out to the garden, or sitting on a plank in the ancient barn down the hill. Even a ten-minute break renewed my spirits.

Chapter 7
What, No Oysters on the Half Shell?

These years continued to be a time before there was an emphasis on serving lots of broccoli, skim milk, and egg-whites only. Most families ate much the same stuff, thank goodness. Fat, sugar, and cholesterol were still villains waiting in the wings. I was also not hounded to master the cuisines of Mexico, France, Italy, Greece, China, Japan, or Thailand. Better yet, no one seemed to feel deprived if we didn't dine out at places that served these foods. I didn't even make tacos, though my family thought they were delicious. We drank water straight from the tap and milk straight from the cow. The after-school snack-bar was usually on the kitchen counter, and it held little variety. Its menu consisted mostly of oatmeal cookies full of raisins and walnuts, a bowl of apples or oranges, and now and then a sack of leftover popcorn.

Evening meals were Early-Bird Specials long before countless restaurants featured them. Dan got home a bit after 5 P.M., and usually left again at 6:40 to teach his evening classes. In that time he changed clothes, rushed out and milked the cow, bathed, changed clothes again, and joined the family for dinner. Everyone had to appear for dinner at exactly 5:45 P.M., and each of the kids was supposed to relate one snippet of good news from the day. Special events, a good grade, or an idea of small proportions were shared, and sometimes there was time for a game of hearts after the dishes were done.

I aimed for dinners that were plentiful, hearty, and quick. Lots of meat loaf and chicken. Stews, made in a pot big enough to feed us for several nights, were full of a variety of foods: chicken, turkey, beef, dried lima beans, navy beans, potatoes, onions, and other vegetables. No oysters on the half shell, filet mignon, or chocolate soufflés.

As an only child, I had sometimes been lonely, and one overnight visit to a large ranching family, and a later trip north in 1940, had made a lasting impression on me: eight or ten people had sat down for breakfast in the family's early-California ranch house. I came down the stairs to a toasty kitchen, furnished with a gigantic black stove and a table that could have seated about sixteen. This family and their current overnight friends were full of laughter and congeniality. I watched a college-age girl, in the absence of her mom, cook and serve great platters of ham, bacon, scrambled eggs, biscuits, juice and coffee. Astonishingly efficient, she did it with ease, and I realized this kind of breakfast was an ordinary daily event in the life of this family. That was for me! Now, so many years later I served meals almost as large.

Another childhood friend had once invited me to stay a couple of days at her house, and her mother taught me a lesson of what not to do for a family. That mother had a family of six, and every one of them got up and straggled in to eat at different times. She stood at the sink and stove for over two hours each morning, acting as a short-order cook, letting each person ask for different things—eggs scrambled, soft-boiled, over-easy, or as an omelet. We could order crisp bacon, pancakes, or French toast, and hot cocoa, coffee, tea, milk, or juice. As the time wore on, this mom's shoulders began to sag, and she was one weary mom by 9 A.M. when she finally sat down to eat. Although I was only fifteen or sixteen at the time, I concluded, "Not in my future family! Never, ever daily meals made to order around the clock!"

On Oak Hills, the whole family got hot cereals on hot cereal days and cold cereal on other days, all served in small-sized mixing bowls, with milk or cream and a sliced banana or raisins on top. Bread came in one color—brown whole wheat. Orange juice glasses had to be left empty. No pancakes until the weekend. Everyone had to eat omelets filled with an assortment of leftovers like bits of meat, cheese, or vegetables. I was once falsely accused of putting lettuce in omelets. The one concession I made to individual ordering was on fried-egg mornings, when family members could order their eggs sunny-side-up, over hard, over medium, or over soft.

It was a bad diet for cholesterol levels, but ignorance was bliss. As a child, I had been served a breakfast of fresh orange juice, and bananas sliced over hot oatmeal or Shredded Wheat, so I kept that tradition alive. It's just that every morning, I added eggs, bacon or ham, whole milk, plus, on some Sundays, sweet rolls or waffles.

Sack lunches went out the door with milk, fruit, and sandwiches full of fatty ingredients: luncheon meats, cheese, peanut butter, jam, or tuna fish with mayonnaise. Dinners included entrees of marbled roasts, steaks, fried chicken with the skin on, pork chops, or hamburgers. The meat was accompanied by potatoes or rice, plus bland, boiled vegetables with butter, and salads with lots of dressing. Desserts were full of sugar, eggs, butter, and cream. Ice cream was churned, using thick cream in the recipe, and came to the table served in the cereal bowls. Again at night, all glasses were full of super-rich whole milk from the Jersey cow April.

It appeared to be O.K. to eat a bland, fatty diet when all six of us remained nothing but skin and bones. I'm not talking slender or lean, but emaciatedly skinny. A diet full of fat three to five times a day never put weight on the children. Of course, I now know even thin people should watch their intake of sugar and saturated fat.

My help-yourself salad bar consisted of a simple salad in a bowl, with a large serving spoon and a bottle of dressing on the side. To any plate that seemed to have an unusually small serving, I added another spoonful of the greens or edible produce from my home-grown garden.

Nothing came à la carte; everyone had to eat all of the main items, down to the last string bean. "Don't nibble like a rabbit—wolf it down or we'll be late," I often encouraged. "I'm not asking you to like it—just eat it." Only dessert was optional.

The kids now insist I was full of "the yummies" every day of their lives, right up to the present time. "Eat your turnips; they're yummy!" or, "One taste and you'll love it. It's yummy, yummy." They're probably right; I started early. I can remember smacking my lips and saying, "OK, now, open wide. Mmmm, yummy!" as I pushed the first baby spoons full of milk and Pablum into their mouths.

Such habits and training didn't always work. I served liver and onions, Brussels sprouts, and eggplant, and the children ate them each time they were served...but they've never eaten a forkful of most of these foods since leaving home.

Actually, I had improved my menu with the help of the garden. At first, store-bought salt and pepper were the only seasonings. Now I grew parsley, chives, sage, onions, and mint that grew like a weed around the faucet next to our garage. And the few times I remembered, I used seasonings like nutmeg, cinnamon, garlic, and lemon juice to bring out the flavor of dishes. Upon request, I even set out a bottle of ketchup or mustard.

It's strange to see some of the least expensive, most common foods from those years now dressed up and served in the best of restaurants. Fancy and expensive dining rooms that once served only items like lobster bisque, may now serve pastas, which used to seem in the same category as beans—served to fill us up and cost little. Now, crowds of hungry diners eat pasta in all shapes and sizes, dressed up with creams, sauces, cheeses, shellfish, meats, beans, and other leftovers from the kitchens, such as tomatoes to zucchini squash. Potatoes and beans have become fashionable and are now served in fancy restaurants, not just as chili beans, black beans, baked beans, and refried beans, but in salads, soups, and dips. Catfish is now acceptable on some fancy seafood menus, and there's even a shredded pumpkin soup.

I don't know what is happening to Mom...in less fancy restaurants, those featuring "Mom's Home Cooking" or "Family Style" are about steak, chicken, mashed potatoes and gravy, and vegetables. Now even some of these specialty places that serve tostadas, sushi, Greek salads, and such, are adding "Mom's Food." Cooking pots are becoming melting and merging pots, with specialty restaurants often adding fried chicken, baked potatoes, and green salads to the menu. Some stress "Healthy Choices."

Few left my diner hungry, and I often laughed, joked, and remained happy, even while staying open seven days a week, usually from 6 A.M. to 8 or 9 P.M. If I closed between Christmas and New Year's, it was probably to scrub down walls, ceilings, and floors, repaint, do end-of-year bookkeeping, and order more dishes and glasses. Not only that, but when schedules demanded it, the family could eventually order breakfast, lunch, or dinner at any time of the day or night.

Never should I complain about my workload, even if those moms in the commercial diners had many relatives and friends working with them. The "Mom's" name was often kept as the name of the restaurant even if hubby, uncles, sons, or cousins had taken over the workweeks that could be as long as ninety hours.

Several of our friends say, "We pick restaurants used by the Rotary Club (or Lions Club, Kiwanis, or Elks). The food is bound to be pretty good." What they don't stop to figure out is that the members of these clubs meet and eat where the room is large, the conversation is good, and there are plenty of chairs, tables, and servers. This does not necessarily mean that the food will be great.

Our friends report, "When we're on the road, we often eat where truck drivers stop. It may not be fancy, but those guys like to eat well and heartily." Again, it may be more the presence of a truck-sized parking lot and the chance to meet with fellow truckers. Or perhaps those friends are eating where the drawing cards for the truckers are hot showers, lots of soap, or long beds.

Restaurant owners are thinking more about the atmosphere, mood, decor, and catchy titles than they are about their chefs and what's served. They worry about the costumes of the servers, how dark they can make the rooms, or how to take orders while deafening "theme" music plays in the background. There are places with sawdust on the floor, mounted heads of longhorn steers on the walls, Santa Claus and Christmas themes displayed all year, full-size airplanes hanging from the ceiling, or maybe Hawaiian canoes. Mexican restaurants tend to have so much stuff from Mexico on the walls and floors that they could start selling knick-knacks instead of food. Other restaurants, trying to entice you to enter and eat, "do food" in fire stations, old banks, granaries, ships, trains, Victorian mansions, or Chinese palaces. You can probably top my list of funny places to dine. Some local bookstores sell food to be eaten as you spill gravy on new books you don't intend to buy. I say, if there's no good chef in the kitchen, go to "Mom's Place."

My Oak Hills eatery was sort of a "western ranch" style, especially aromatic and authentically ranch-like when under the table were six pairs of shoes that had earlier been worn by family members playing outside or cleaning and feeding all the animals. Restaurants in beachfront and lakefront areas often have signs saying, "Shoes and Shirts Required," but I considered having a sign saying "Remove Shoes at the Door."

Happiness was not big things, like a trip to China or a six-thousand-square-foot house; it was often the warm kitchen and mealtime. Of course, happiness also included things like rain on the tin roof of the barn, the lick and smile of the big dog Treve, and the reading of books each night to the younger boys: stories of pirates, horses, cars, ghosts, and sometimes of faraway places where the cooking might be 100% different from anything at home.

Chapter 8
O.J., the Throwaway Cat

One evening, just as Dan turned to drive up Prefumo Canyon Road toward our lane, he witnessed a terrible act of cruelty. Just ahead of him, a cat was thrown violently out of a speeding car full of young people laughing and blaring the radio. Left in the middle of the road was a slightly twitching, full-grown orange cat.

Dan got out, thinking he would have to find a rock to put the animal out of its pain. The car, now out of sight, had been going extremely fast, but the cat didn't seem to be bleeding, and, remarkably, he seemed to actually be alive. Although Dan was wearing a good suit, he knew he had to pick the cat up and bring it home.

Nancy, Danny, and I were still up when Dan came in and placed the unconscious cat on the counter. What to do? We finally decided to put him in the laundry room, which I was increasingly using to put up newly-acquired small critters. I laid the cat on a baby blanket on the floor and placed a saucer of water and a bit of leftover chicken nearby. He seemed to wake up a bit, but he couldn't really move and made no sounds. We shut the door and went to bed.

When I carefully opened the door the next morning, there was no cat on the baby blanket, and none of the food had been eaten. I found the cat hiding far back under the water heater in the corner of the room. There seemed to be no way to pull him out without hurting him or getting scratched. Surely the cat had to be badly injured! Each time I entered the room, he could see my shoes and legs as I ran the washing machine and carried the loads of clean laundry out to the clothesline. I just hoped his fur wouldn't catch fire under the heater!

The next evening, I again set food and water down, made up a litter box, and left the injured cat there. For several days he continued to hide just under the heater. I sat on the floor near the puss several times a day and talked softly to him, explaining that we were all pushovers for cats.

He couldn't have been too badly injured, because by the third night he was eating some of the food, drinking some milk and water, and using the litter box. Thank heavens the cat knew how and when to use the litter box.

A morning or two later I warmed up some liver and put it in his cat dish. I felt almost certain the aroma would draw him out; I had purposely fed him lightly the night before.

I got up extra early and sat quietly inside the room by the door. Soon, the big orange fellow slowly crawled out, watching me every second to see how great a danger I might be. This puss was going to be all right! Despite the bad treatment he had received, he wasn't totally afraid of humans, and after a few more minutes, when he decided I wouldn't move or hurt him, he ate most of the liver. However, when I was needed in the kitchen and started to get up, he flew under the heater with all his legs working—it was then obvious that none of his bones were broken.

Both he and my family were lucky. Wild, abused, or abandoned cats usually need many months, or even years, to trust people again; some never do. This beguiling cat became a regular member of our family within just a few weeks. He was lucky that Dan had found him on the road before. Miraculously, this cat seemed none the worse for that hard landing on the paved road; he had escaped serious injury, except for his fears and insecurities.

Humans have great advantages over animals; they have the power to say whatever needs to be said, make plans, take action, and band together in communities and groups for support. Animals, on the other hand, are too often completely at the mercy of insensitive or cruel humans, and are often terribly alone and in need of a caring human being.

One morning as I ordered "Come on, boys, finish your 'O.J.'" Doug suddenly spoke up as he emptied his glass.

"Hey, let's call the orange cat O.J.!" Suddenly the cat had a name.

Unlike Shandy, O.J. wanted to stay in the house. It was a refuge where he could relax in safety, and he checked out several hiding places to use whenever something frightened him.

Dogs are more introspective than they let on. Treve lay near me that morning and looked at me as though to say, "Why have you brought this cat into our house? Aren't I enough?" Treve wasn't above a bit of jealousy.

"Yes, Treve, but this guy was thrown out of a speeding car and needs a home. This is a poor, poor kitty; you be good to her, and don't you dare chase her!" This dog understood so well what I said that it was a wonder he didn't nod his head. Treve never hurt this cat or any others that we owned.

In fact, the time came when O.J. occasionally walked right under the chin of our dogs. This wasn't so bad when the dog was standing up, but when the dog had sat down, the cat let his tail and body drag right across the dog's mouth and nose. Talk about arrogantly showing the dog the pecking order! Treve just turned his head or got up and wandered off to pick another spot on the floor.

This orange puss never did become a lap-cat; instead, he would float in and out of rooms with no sound, then suddenly appear beside me and jump to the tabletop while I wrote checks or folded wash. O.J.'s repose was never quite the full, contented, and relaxed one of some cats, but he came a long way in recovering from the abused childhood I knew he must have had. He was obviously grateful for and content with the security of the house, and he liked company as long as no one tried to pick him up. He purred when I talked to him and soon liked me to scratch his cheeks and chin. He also followed me around the house and finally decided to do a bit of talking of his own, with "meows" about dinner or whatever was on his mind.

With minimal effort, our cats always seemed able to jump onto tables, dressers, and countertops and land on the exact spot they chose without knocking over anything. The dogs were never so accomplished; they jumped and jumped and often never made it to the top. Perhaps the dogs were only asking that I give them whatever smelled enticing, such as food, and they didn't really need to perch on tables or counters.

O.J. easily jumped to our kitchen counter and loved to sit there and watch me wash dishes. He was endlessly fascinated with water from the faucet, or seeing my hands and the dishes in the suds. Sometimes he would daintily put out a paw and hold it just above the water, but he never got a paw wet.

Because of what had happened to him on the road, I was overly indulgent with him, but I tried to keep him off the counters and put him outside when we had company.

Fortunately, most sunny mornings this docile and curious guy loved to pour himself out like taffy on the large bay windowsill in the boys' room. There he would bask in the sun, sleep, or watch the scary outdoors from the safety of the house. Like most cats, he slept a great deal.

O.J. continued to become more confident, and by happily waving his tail back and forth as he walked, he let us know that he had adopted us as his family. Cats do a lot of talking with their tails. The fur on their tails and bodies becomes bushy and full when they have to defend themselves, like his did the first time he met Treve. O.J.'s tail also increasingly jerked or twitched whenever his plate of food was too hot or not to his liking, as if he were saying, "This restaurant needs a cook that fixes better food." He would often walk off as far as the door and sit a minute or two before testing the meal again, hoping it would then be tastier or cooler.

Christmases and birthdays became perfect times for O.J. to make leaps of wild abandon into piles of wrapping paper, ribbons, bows, and string—tossing around everything with great joy. O.J. would roll onto his back, with paper clamped in his mouth and claws, and kick and shred the wrappings with his hind feet. Boxes and sacks made wonderful hiding places to jump in, and once he was inside them, he would peer out over the edge, waiting for the best time to jump out again and scamper into more piles of paper, toys, or containers.

As time passed, O.J. let me carry him outside, and he would stay near me while I hung the wash or did the farm chores. Finally, O.J. decided that this outside world might be somewhat safe, and he spent more time alone, investigating the barns, sheds, trees, and garden. Finally, he increased the boundaries and ventured out into the fields.

Even if much of O.J.'s behavior was instinctive, I was pretty sure he cat had been properly started out in life by his mother, with show-and-tell and learn-by-doing routines. He increasingly used a spot behind the garage for his bathroom, and began to hunt in the field near my vegetable garden. A few dead mice and a small lizard eventually showed up on our door steps.

Some days after breakfast he padded out to the sunny south side of the barn to sit and carefully wash himself and rearrange his fur for the day, eventually sleeping there for most of the morning. He was patient with the younger children when they came by to pet him, and he seemed to like all the family more and more as the years passed. It always especially pleased the younger boys that O.J. liked them, so they were extra careful to talk to him and stroke his fur in the right direction. For animals or humans of any age, there's tremendous power and chance for good and happiness when humans give just small acts of kindness—a touch or pat, a few soft words of encouragement or approval, truly listening and watching, or promoting some fun and laughter. Animals, like all of us, need to feel secure, successful, and part of a group or family. We never knew O.J.'s age, but he lived for many years, long enough to become a special and increasingly joyful family member.

Then came a morning when I was hanging wash and a young college-aged lady walked up to our gate. Crying, she told me that she had found an orange cat almost dead by the side of the canyon road, and that it had been run over by a car. Because she was certain it was in great pain and about to die, she had picked up a short, heavy tree limb and killed the cat. She wanted to know if the cat was ours.

I had to be kind to her, and she was probably right; the cat had probably been dying. Yet all I could think of was O.J.'s nine lives and his grim past before he joined our family. Had he truly used up all nine lives? Even if he had been badly injured, could I have rushed him to the vet and saved him? I would never know. I thanked her and told her she did the right thing. Later, Dan went down to the road to pick up O.J.'s body, and we gathered near the far side of the house to bury him facing the valley he had watched for so many years on sunny mornings from the safety of the large bay window.

Chapter 9
The Dump

With spring's arrival and the end of winter rains, I always began to think of new projects, which usually involved fixing up and repairing old projects. Summer would bring more time to fix, replace, clean, paint, and plant. Most of these projects required trips to the dump.

We had a long history of going to garbage dumps. Often they had more formal names, like Disposal Station, Waste Management Company, Refuse Station, Waste Center, Land Fill, or Sanitation Department Fill. Trips to the dump became a form of recreation, a chance to get away from the house and a change from the continuous round of our ranching and teaching. In the eyes of the boys, the dump was an exciting place, full of hidden treasures and interesting things. For Dan and me, the dump was a place that sometimes contained items useful on the ranch.

The best dump for us to use was one on the Cal Poly campus, up a hill to the right of a winding canyon road lined with some oak and sycamore trees. During those years, staff members were permitted to use the dump. Some faculty joked that perhaps they could use it because the school felt that free dumping privileges might help make up for low salaries.

One of the most important items Dan and I regularly took home from the dump was fencing material. Our horses were an ongoing destruction gang. The old turkey fencing was not ideal for them, even with a strand of barbwire installed along the top. The horses leaned over the fences with most of their weight to reach the grass on the other side of the fence (which in the case of the horses was really greener because they devoured every last wisp of grass on their side). The horses sometimes got a foot through the woven wire and became thoroughly tangled up in it. One season, I took the horses out of two of the fields to let the grass grow tall, and when I put them back in, they still stretched their necks across the wire to eat some of the dusty dried grass on the other side of the fence. I became convinced there must be something to the saying "forbidden fruit tastes twice as sweet."

Eventually, the barbed and woven wire we salvaged from the dump would make a return trip back to the same dump when the horses finally stretched and bent it beyond repair. Our wooden fence posts were eventually worn down to short pegs, and the gates and the siding of the barns were kicked, pushed to the ground, and chewed-on enough to be tossed in the "return to the dump" load.

In the eyes of the boys, dumps were always recreational places—places to find a treasure or something hidden, mysterious, interesting, or exciting. Almost always, our truck came home from the dump loaded just as heavy and as high as it had been when we drove it there, carrying a fresh load of goodies to be recycled one more time. Apparently, there was very generous state financing for the big agricultural school programs—we often found gates in one piece with the original huge iron hinges and latches, and useful barbed wire, woven wire fencing, lumber for siding, and posts (often perfect, except for the nails still in them).

While Nancy was off at college and Danny was not far behind, Doug and Jeff continued to bring home their own ideas of treasure, from a few objects from the faculty members' home trash to equipment and supplies from various classrooms and science labs. They collected countless small motors, lumber, wheels for go-carts, rope, and even some clocks to take apart and try to reassemble. Doug especially wanted to disassemble anything that had moving parts. He also found test tubes, beakers, and burners.

One Saturday when we drove up to park, there was a large, floor-model TV set in a satiny-perfect wooden cabinet perched on the very edge of the dump's cliff. It seemed to be hesitating, asking us, "Shall I jump over, or will you save me?" It was an easy choice to save it. I made the boys promise not to take the set apart if we took it home, for I thought I'd heard that TVs had some dangerous insides.

The TV came home with us, and Dan said he would ask a TV repair shop on campus to check it out. This truly was a "learn by doing" campus—over the years, they sold ice cream, meat, eggs, and other produce, operated printing presses, and ran a TV and radio repair shop.

On campus, the student worker for TV repairs decided he could fix our set for $35.00. That seemed like an awful lot of money, so I put it to a family vote. I voted "No," and the other five voted "Yes." The cabinet became a beautiful piece of furniture in our living room, and the TV, when repaired, had a large, clear, colorful picture and great sound. It lasted us many, many years.

Some months later, I invited a prof and his wife to dinner, and Dan and I happened to tell, in glowing terms, our story of the recycled TV. When we finished, there was a long moment of silence, and then the guests began to laugh and laugh. It had been their TV! After paying repair bill after repair bill on their new set, they had finally given up after about a year and bought another one. "We didn't want to give it to anyone we knew, since it would probably remain a lemon," they explained. "Yet, in spite of our great frustration, we couldn't quite bring ourselves to push it over the edge."

Soon after coming to town, I noticed that some of the college staff and their families seemed to feel that it was beneath them to personally take their garbage to a dump—proper and educated people don't go to dumps, and they especially don't bring stuff home from the dump. I only pitied friends and staff who thought themselves above such a productive and money-saving place.

Because of our loads, both coming from and going to the dump, the ranch began to look better and better. I bought gallons of white paint to improve the farm buildings and the posts around the fields. The heavy gates, hung by their huge hinges on sturdy posts, looked almost elegant under a fresh coat of paint. Finally, I painted the house yellow and trimmed it in white. All the fencing began to look newer and straighter as it marched around the horse fields and corrals, while the newly painted barns remained cozy and dry with fresh lumber and some metal roofing (acquired from the dump, of course!). The boys learned about building go-carts, about chemistry, about how small motors worked. A huge TV sat in our living room and poured out great music and episodes of the Little Rascals.

Because the owners of the Oak Hills Ranch property wanted to improve the house, plans were soon made to build a new living room adjacent to the dining room, since the original living room was still used both as the dining room and a small living room.

No dump-truck could get next to that side of the house, so to save the owners money I shoveled every pound of three dump-truck loads of fill inside the staked boundaries where the new room was marked off. A contractor built the room, and I painted it inside and out.

The room had nice window seats on both sides of a new second fireplace, and a big window gave fine views down and across the valley. We bought a used grand piano to replace the old upright one from Arizona days, and at last we had a special recessed place in the paneled wall for our bargain TV set. None of us used the new front door on the far side of the screen porch, but guests used it occasionally, and they were finally able to enter the living room without going through the kitchen.

Chapter 10
A Pony to the Rescue

Doug was becoming knock-kneed—his legs were developing an inward curvature that tended to make his knees knock together when he walked. I made long drives to get him to a specialist who decided that leg braces might help. The braces were horrible, ungainly things that attached to his high-top shoes and went almost up to his hips. The braces were made of leather and steel and each one had about twelve or fifteen straps to buckle. Doug was told to wear them at all times except at school—even for travel in the car, for naps, and at night.

It was torture when Doug wore his braces—he couldn't bend his knees at all and had to swing each leg out and around in a sort of circle to walk. Turning over in bed was almost impossible because the buckles and straps of one brace tended to get tangled with the buckles and straps of the other one. Soon I let him leave them off at night. I suffered just watching him and wondered whether making him wear them constituted child abuse.

As if that weren't enough, the boys and I suffered every time we went to see this doctor. I had to take little Jeff along, and the nurse never let anyone remain in the waiting room—instead, she would put all of us with appointments in a separate room where we waited and waited. It was two and a half hours one time, two hours another time, and over an hour other times. By the time Doug and Jeff and I got home we were completely exhausted, and the family was lucky to get cans of Campbell's soup or some cold cereal. It was no wonder that I began to plot an alternative treatment.

I finally asked Doug, "How would you like a nice fat pony to ride instead of these braces? If you rode him a lot, maybe we could throw the braces away." Riding a good round pony might just bend Doug's legs from knock-kneed to straight!

Doug had never shown any interest in riding horses, but we both beamed at the thought of never again going into the doctor's office; throwing away those braces would create a better celebration than the Fourth of July.

At the time I didn't remember that our friend Monty, who knew so much about horses, had never spoken well of ponies; I just figured that I might find a well trained one built like a small horse with good habits and personality. Each day I read all the ads in the paper under "Livestock for Sale," and Dan mentioned our need for a well trained pony to his ag classes.

Finally, Shorty, wearing an ever-so-thick chocolate-colored coat, came to live with us. As far as I could tell he reined well and was mild mannered. He had a strong and blocky build and hoofs the size of a horse's. He was strong enough to carry an adult and seemed very well mannered. He didn't seem stubborn and willful like I'd heard ponies might be, but was happy and cooperative when I cleaned his hoofs and rode him around bareback. He would back up, side-step, and go into an easy gallop—no rocking-horse lope, but fairly slow. A bridle came with him, but I wondered if I should buy a saddle. I wasn't sure what kind of pony he was, since there were quite a few breeds; I suspected he might be a Highland pony of some kind.

Shorty's feet were very much in need of shoeing, and the blacksmith who was coming to our ranch would be able to do the job. He came rather often to shoe Blue and the horses boarded with us. Cal Poly taught courses in blacksmithing and trained students to become farriers. Roger, the graduate student who did our horses, had a brisk business in our horsey county, and came with great horse and cowboy stories to tell our boys as he worked with his forge, anvil, and U-shaped iron shoes. Shorty willingly received new shoes.

Like Blue, the pony held his own just fine with the boarded horses. He was friendly, accommodating, and intelligent, but he kicked and nipped at any horse that came too close to his stack of feed. After getting out of the gate one day, the pony's gluttony extended to the grain room in the barn, where he left a partial sack of horse feed torn to shreds and empty. He must have had a tummy ache the rest of the day.

Doug was supposed to do lots of riding, but he didn't ride Shorty nearly as often as I'd hoped. His immediate big sigh whenever I suggested a ride was an indication of his lack of enthusiasm. Riding the pony was not much work, and we never even bought a saddle—we just put a bridle on him and rode bareback. When it was time for Doug to ride, Shorty usually made Doug and me chase him for a while in his field. Taking out a pail of oats worked fine, and the pony always came running back, but the other horses also saw the pail and they all arrived about the same time to step on my toes and try to get some "dessert."

Finally, I got up my courage and trailered Shorty out to show to Monty. To test his steadiness and training, Monty swung a leg over him bareback and bounced around on him while making him stand still, whirl around, back up, and gallop around the corral. Even he had to admit, "For a pony, he's not bad."

Nancy gave Doug some pointers about riding, and sometimes she and Blue would ride with Doug and Shorty. Other times, Doug and Shorty went out alone. Eventually, Doug's legs grew straight, but we never really knew whether it was from the riding, the braces, or just natural straightening.

In addition to not having their sister's passion for horses, the boys soon had a new reason not to ride a lot—the pony increasingly made all the decisions on where to go, at what speed they would travel, and when they would go back to the barn. Neither Doug nor Jeff was old or trained enough to keep him in line. With horses of any size, that spells disaster—horses should do what they are trained to do. Shorty discovered some low-hanging limbs on several oak trees and ran under them a couple of times, peeling Doug off his back and leaving him to limp back home alone.

Since Shorty seemed to realize he had to behave whenever a grown-up was riding him, now and then I rode the pony. However, it wasn't long before I refused to ride him near the fence line beside Los Osos Road, since several times people in passing cars honked their horns and hooted and laughed loud enough for me to hear, while pointing their fingers at the sight of a six-foot-tall lady riding a small pony bareback, knees bent up high like a jockey's in order to keep her feet off the ground while at the same time trying desperately to make the animal break from a trot into a gallop to catch up with another rider or two fast disappearing in the distance on real horses.

Chapter 11
Saving Like a Crow

My part time jobs of boarding horses, fixing fences and sheds, and growing vegetable gardens netted little cash to pay bills. Boarding horses turned out well, except that I didn't charge enough—the cash didn't cover much more than the horses' daily costs and gave nothing for labor and repairs. Dan's paychecks from the college increased at a very slow rate, and everyone seemed to send us bills:

- The service station companies could hardly send their bills fast enough.
- The phone company had to be paid so that the kids could continue to socialize for hours whenever the kitchen was empty of others who might listen to their conversations.
- The electric meter ran day and night, because only Mom turned off lights and radios, closed doors, and took hot baths in a tub less than full.
- The orthodontist wanted bushels of money for braces for each of the four kids for umpteen years.
- Income taxes were increasing with each of our jobs.
- Car and animal licenses consumed ever more money.

- Nancy and Danny soon needed huge funds for colleges and universities.
- The cow, horses, dogs, cats, and family members all lived to eat continuously, while the feed company, the rancher with the hay, and the grocery store clerks kept their hands out for my frequent checks.

All these expenses added up to no time to dilly-dally. Once again we were driven to revamp our schedules and think of more ways to earn money. It was time for a better solution. "What," we wondered, "can Dan add to a full week of teaching days and nights?" He'd long ago signed up to teach summer classes each year, be a department head, host the yearly three-day Farm and Land Broker conferences at Cal Poly, and produce the brokers' monthly newsletter. Time was tricky when one juggled so many jobs, but there had to be a way.

After a great deal of thought, I remembered the landlady we'd had in Tucson, Arizona. She never seemed to work at our pace—in fact, she never seemed to work at all—yet we knew that she was a wealthy woman, as she owned many houses and other real estate. "Maybe we should buy houses for students to live in," I suggested to Dan. "All we have to do is go to your credit union for state employees and see if we can get a loan—let money make us money!"

Maybe acquiring rental houses would be a way for us to get ahead and still get a few hours of sleep. Buying houses seemed better than buying dishwashers, clothes dryers, paint sprayers, or electric food mixers—especially since I seemed to survive on doing everything the hard way. We persuaded the local credit union to make us their first real estate loan customers, then set out to find a house.

Our first purchase was a small house on the south side of town. By the time our escrow closed, we realized we should have bought a house near the campus, so we turned around and listed the house for sale through the same realtor who sold the house to us initially.

Knowing nothing about real estate, but assuming that this rental house would be sold within three months, I discovered a five-unit apartment building to purchase closer to town, and quickly gave the owner half of the down-payment.

Suddenly disaster loomed. Our realtor wasn't able to sell the south-side house soon enough, and our deadline arrived for the second half of our down-payment on the apartment building. Panicked over the thought of losing all of that first deposit, I phoned and made an appointment for us to visit the apartment owner. The next Sunday morning, dressed in our best clothes and with all four kids in tow, Dan and I drove down to Santa Maria to meet Mrs. Nuss.

When we arrived at her house, Mrs. Nuss greeted us kindly and invited us into her house. We quickly laid out our predicament to her, telling her that we didn't have the funds, how we did not want to lose our down-payment, why we didn't have her money, who we were, and what our goals were.

Glory be! Mrs. Nuss smiled broadly, leaned back in her chair, and quipped, "Oh my, that's all right! I would actually prefer to receive more monthly income than to get the rest of the down-payment in one lump sum. Just take the balance of the down-payment and add it to the total of the first trust deed and make the same payments monthly. It'll pay off in not much more time. That'll be fine." Her gracious answer was the bail-out that saved the day.

After that experience we almost never did any more pyramiding, and we kept most of the places we bought. I would find a small house near campus or town, borrow the down-payment from the credit union, fix up the house (with the kids' and sometimes Dan's help), pay off the loan as fast as possible, start renting out the house, and borrow again as soon as possible to buy another place. The credit union head and staff soon knew us extremely well.

When we worried about extending ourselves in this way, we reminded each other, "At least our savings won't be in banks or stock certificates, for who knows when inflation will reach its breaking point and our world will tumble into another Great Depression!?"

Like the ranch's resident crow that carried off shiny treasures—pieces of glass, aluminum foil, and one of my silver teaspoons—to hide up in a corner of the old barn, we began to hoard houses. Collecting enough rent to purchase the next house was slow, but we figured people would always need a place to sleep and eat, and each year increasing numbers of students and others came to town and needed places to stay. We were seldom without renters for our houses.

Rental houses were interesting, and they always presented new challenges. It seemed strange sometimes: we wouldn't live in any of the houses we bought because we needed the rent from that house to purchase the next house. The only thing we ever bought on credit was real estate, and only because the rent usually covered the mortgage payments. Buying anything else on credit was against our convictions.

Since the kids and I did most of the physical work on the rentals, such as cleaning and painting, and I managed them and kept the books, Dan and I lay awake more nights plotting what else there might be that he could do.

"I could become a magician and do large conferences and meetings," he joked one night. "Or, how about my starting up a dance band group? I know how to do that." Dan enjoyed teaching and was busy setting up and heading a new department at the university, but he still wanted more. Our final decision was for him to go to the Adult Evening School office at the local high school and find out if the administrator would let him set up and teach some new courses on a variety of subjects—real estate, investment, finance, appraisal, principles, and law. The director of the Evening School thought this was a great idea.

Dan suggested to me, "The first course can be called 'Real Estate Investments' and I'll just ad-lib answers to questions, describe our mistakes and successes, and present a few principles of real estate. How about that?"

"Perfect! That'll make a great class," I replied. "Your students will love to learn about all the mistakes their teacher and his wife have made. Start out with that shaky night-time purchase of the house in Santa Margarita."

Dan got a license to drive a school bus and showed the first of many classes his first rural house-of-many-blunders. The story was short one, but it taught many principles of what not to do as a buyer:

"My wife saw an ad in the paper for a house for sale, and it sounded like it might fit our slim budget for a rental. We figured we could use Easter vacation to do any repairs and perhaps paint the place.

"Then I got to thinking that it was sort of far away from us to keep as a rental. What if we bought the place, fixed it up over the four days of Easter, and put it right back on the market and sold it for profit—making big wages for slaving for just four days? If nothing else, perhaps we could keep it as a rental until we could get capital gains treatment on it and then sell.

"The following Tuesday evening we drove up to look the house over. The owner had moved out so there was no electricity in the two-story house, and she held the only flashlight as she quickly led us through the rooms. She agreed to take a mere six hundred dollars for a down-payment. A bargain, we thought, and we immediately told her we'd buy it. She told us the size of the lot, but, since it was dark, we didn't even try to walk around the house or locate the boundaries.

"Early the next morning we signed the papers at the escrow company. Unfortunately, when we went back to the house that afternoon in the light of day, after the papers were signed, we discovered a row of gigantic eucalyptus trees hugging one side of the house, so close to the wall that roots were growing partially under the house and destroying the wooden foundation. It would take more than the whole down-payment just to have the trees removed and the foundation repaired.

"Inside, doors that had been welcomingly wide open the night before, would not shut and were almost off their hinges. We noticed a two-inch gap between the wall and the brick fireplace. Scratches and gouges decorated all the woodwork, and the second-story ceilings were water-stained—the roof had certainly leaked in the past, probably more than once.

"Over the next four days of Easter, our whole family went up there and scrubbed, sanded, spackled, painted, and cut weeds and shrubs. Each day we worked until we ached all over and sagged with fatigue, and every night both our pick-up and car went home with full loads of yard and house trash.

"Early the following Monday I picked up the first paperwork from escrow, and the next big bomb hit me. There was an acceleration clause in the deed which stated that all money still owed on the loan would be due and payable upon our sale to someone else. Since this house, unlike the other rentals, had been purchased with the idea of either selling it right away or as soon as we could get capital gains on it, this was a big blow. The house was not the type of place people would pay 'all cash' for, and it would be hard for a typical buyer to get new financing on such a house at that time.

"I suggest you students avoid mistakes such as these. See what you're buying and go over it carefully in the daytime. What kind of foundation is there? Wooden ones aren't the best. How old is the roof? Is there termite damage? Look carefully over the area, and ask yourself, 'Might it flood in heavy storms?' Find out the details of the present ownership, and whether there are any liens. Go to the city or county planning department and ask about any plans by the town or highway department that exist, or might soon exist, for the area. Never improve a purchase, like we did, until your escrow closes. And, for rentals, it's best to buy close enough to where you live so that you can manage and maintain the properties without a long drive."

Teacher had many more dos and don'ts for his classes by the time that house sold years later to someone who was finally able to get a new loan and would pay us all cash for our interest in it. In the meanwhile, the house had soared in value, the rent had easily covered the payments, and we could at last say, "All's well that ends well."

Like my friend who quit smoking by putting the price of two packs of cigarettes in a box each day so that she could save money to buy tickets for a trip around the world, we still banished all luxuries and non-essential items to buy rentals. It was hard for me to not become a real Scrooge. Would I ever take a trip around the world, or even to Los Angeles?

Meanwhile, Dan reported, "This teaching a class at night is actually fun, and it's working out well. It's nice to have all the students there wanting to learn and not just taking a class that's required in order to graduate. How about my trying some more classes, huh?"

"Yeah," I retorted, "maybe the kids and I can hang your picture on the wall to remember who you are and what you look like." But we both knew he had to forge ahead.

If Dan were to teach more classes in this field, a real estate broker's license would be desirable—not to sell or buy real estate, but to learn more and gain some credibility, since the night courses he was teaching were not in his own academic field. Thus Dan signed up to take classes in Santa Barbara every Friday night for ten weeks in order to prepare for the broker's license exam. The kids and I accompanied him on these trips south, and while he attended class we went to family movies in town.

Dan listened to lectures, practiced taking sample broker tests, and studied tests and textbooks at home for many weeks. Once he had the broker's license in hand, he began teaching most nights of the week, offering real estate courses at the junior college, the adult education school, and the U.C. extension. He continued to do that for the next twenty years.

At the time, Cuesta Junior College had none of the beautiful campus buildings it has today, and Dan taught his first real estate classes there in pre-fabricated Quonset huts dating from the World War II years. Cows wandered about, and students and staff drove over cattle guards to get onto campus. What the cows left on the grounds, plus the mud on rainy nights, made getting to class just like going into the cow corral at home.

Even with our heavier workload, there still remained a couple of evenings each week for more moonlighting. The Santa Barbara real estate classes Dan had attended gave us the idea of starting our own real estate school to prepare students for the salesman and broker exams given by the State of California. We drove to Los Angeles and convinced one of the Lumbleau Real Estate School owners to give Dan a franchise for Santa Maria and San Luis Obispo counties in exchange for a small fee. For fourteen years Dan taught Lumbleau classes every week in a commercial building we bought in downtown San Luis Obispo, and I hired secretaries to keep the school open during the daytime so that students could practice with sample real-estate exams.

Since Dan was at the university all day from 8:00 A.M. to 5:00 P.M., he couldn't deal with any administrative work in the daytime, so I took all the phone calls about the school and what was involved in becoming a licensed real-estate salesman and broker. Most calls lasted a half-hour or more. My dinners often turned cold while I explained the courses and invited any interested people to visit one of his classes the following week at no charge to see whether or not they wanted to enroll.

Getting enough sleep was another problem. While the animals all bedded down early, I turned into a bookkeeper at night. Increasing numbers of rentals, the real estate school, and ranch work, all made paperwork grow faster than zucchini, and my lists grew apace. The mound on the kitchen table grew too big to keep clearing off, with its endless to-do lists, half-written letters, business bills, and junk mail, so I gave up working on the kitchen table and transferred the mound of paper and record books to the cold and lonely dining-room table.

Every week-night, while Dan taught night classes from 7 to 10 P.M., I worked at the dining room table writing pads and pads of checks. At first the checks mostly came under the "Disbursements" category; those that came under the category of "Income Received" filled only a part of one page in my ledgers. However, gradually, the new ledger books multiplied. While never taking time to make budgets, I was suddenly the keeper of six separate large, black books: one for personal costs and income, one for real estate owned, one for evening classes at the high school, one for the Lumbleau Real Estate school, one for horses boarded, and yet another for the ranch records.

Each night, when I began to turn blue with cold, I left the clutter on the dining room table and returned to the warm, bright kitchen, where the kids were sometimes still doing their homework. I'd gulp a cup of hot coffee and hope that it would help me keep my eyes open— they always seemed to feel like they had sand in them about that time of evening. If the kids' schoolwork continued to cover the kitchen table, I often dragged out the ironing board to press shirts and dresses until Dan came home.

After the disparaging remarks I'd made in earlier years about people who stayed up late and failed to heed nature's sleep cadences, we were now turning night into day, and doing so for as long as we could keep our eyelids open. How could I go to bed with Dan still out there training more real estate brokers, salesmen, property tycoons, and the property poor? Once, when I was coming down with the flu, I collapsed into bed before he came home and was flooded with guilt. "No," I said to myself, "if he is going to work late into the evenings, I am too." When he returned home around 10:30, I was bent over the bills in the dining room—we were a yoked and plodding team to the end. Life never became full speed ahead; it continued in never-ending low gear.

Chapter 12
A Gopher Flies, and Other Happenings

Laughing uproariously, Doug came rushing into the kitchen with a fine tale to relate, but his uncontrollable mirth just barely let him speak. He had been wandering through the lower horse pasture, wondering if there were any arrowheads there, when all of a sudden, a few feet ahead of him, he saw a large clump of yellow mustard waving back and forth and sinking lower into the ground.

"I walked," he said, "as quietly as an Indian, and snuck up to the plant. I decided it must be a gopher chewing on the mustard or making a tunnel. I reached over, took hold of the weed down near the roots, and pulled it out as strongly and quickly as I could. Voilà! A big gopher came flying out of the hole along with a big clump of dirt around the mustard roots. The gopher actually flew up in the air!

"That gopher landed and blinked around, as though to say, 'Where am I?' and then ran off to hide in the other mustard weeds and grasses. I tried to follow him, but he disappeared too fast. Boy, I bet he'll never figure that out." The whole family laughed about that gopher for days.

One thing that both of the younger boys thought was hilarious, but that I didn't find funny at all, was a new "houseguest." Unbeknownst to me, Jeff and Doug had decided that the pony, Shorty, should be allowed to come into the new large living room and watch television. It had never occurred to them that the large room had brand new furniture, drapes, and wall-to-wall carpeting. One day, one of the older kids squealed on the younger boys and told me that the pony had come in quite willingly a number of times.

"Good heavens," I shrieked, "that pony can drink a tub of water at a time, and his body doesn't use much of it, except to pee! The whole house could have been flooded! Horses aren't permitted in the house!" Shorty was quite fastidious about his own quarters, but I was certain he would not have such consideration for someone else's floor.

To think that I had once worried about a kitty cat not remembering to make it to her litter box in time! Meaning every word, I put on a fine command performance of fury, with dire predictions of what would happen if the kids repeated their performance. I succeeded in effectively squelching any future attempts by the kids to invite Shorty past the threshold again.

Not long after this came two more exciting farm stories. One night, while Dan and I were away, Nancy was home baby-sitting the two younger boys in the living room while Danny was studying at the dining room table. Fog had drifted down the valley, as it often did in the late afternoon, and had deepened and enveloped the ranch, making the living-room very cozy, with no view beyond the windows. Suddenly the children heard heavy clumping sounds, as if someone in boots might be climbing the steps that led up to the unused front porch and to the door into the younger boys' bedroom. Living on an isolated ranch out in the country can be spooky at times, and these thumping noises terrified all the children.

Nancy asked the boys if they had ever unlocked that door to the outside, and one of them made the un-reassuring answer, "Well, I don't think so, but I think a key is in the lock."

Since there were no curtains on that glass-paned door, Nancy and Danny were afraid to go into the room—anyone at that door could look down the hall and observe them coming. The sound of heavy footsteps continued. "I'm not about to go to bed with that weirdo outside," Danny decided. Everyone agreed.

Nancy informed everyone, "We'll all just sit here and be quiet until Mom and Dad come home."

"What's happened to Treve?" Danny lamented. The dog that was generally so good about barking to warn of anyone who approached the house, hadn't made a sound.

When Dan and I returned home, all four children were still in the living room. They told us about the man on the premises, and we supposed, since our car would have been seen by whoever was out there, that the intruder must have known we were home. I went to the kitchen and flicked the switch for the floodlights in the barnyard area, and Dan and I went outside and walked the perimeter of the house. Halfway around, we found Shorty, loose and having a snack of grass on the lawn. This Peeping-Tom Pony had even left one of his calling cards up on the unused porch.

Nancy and the boys all wrote about "The Night of the Stranger" for English class compositions, and, with such a vivid memory of their fright, they must have written well—all received A's. I still wonder how that pony could climb the many steps up to the porch. Had he been taught by a former owner to do stairs, or was this just a lonesome pony wanting to get into the house and watch TV? Actually, the boys admitted they had never gotten him to look at any TV when they had brought him into the house through the back door, an easy two-step climb. Shorty had probably just wanted attention or a carrot or two.

The other story that was used for English compositions at school was about the day the boys had almost burned down the ranch and perhaps the whole Los Osos Valley. They all knew about what fires could do, and they had heard my mother-hen admonitions, "Don't ever play with matches!" However this fire wasn't caused by playing with matches, but rather by playing with a small model airplane.

It happened in late summer, when the oats in the front corner field of about thirty acres to the east side of the lane were tall, dry, and ready for harvesting, as was all the rest of the bone dry ranch and the entire valley. The day of the fire, Dan and I had gone to town. When we returned home, we found a large fire truck on the lane. Firemen and a number of other men in work clothes were putting out the last hot spots of smoldering cow dung and clumps of hay in a blackened area of about five acres of the large field below the house. Our boys, blackened, scratched, and bleeding, were helping the men.

Before any of the kids could speak, I exploded with questions, almost all in one breath: "How in the world did you get that fire stopped? Who did it? How'd the fire get started? Wait, maybe I'd better sit down to hear this." Between the place on O'Connor Way and the Oak Hill Ranch, we had lived in the Los Osos Valley about eight years, and this was the first fire we had ever seen there.

It turned out Danny had come home from college with the guilty thought that he didn't spend enough time with his younger brothers, so he took his little gasoline-driven model plane out to the barnyard to fly it with them. On one of its flights, the plane suddenly got away from him and crash-landed in the dry hayfield. In an instant, the hay was ablaze.

The boys had all raced for hoses and had screamed to Nancy to call the fire department. The boys couldn't reach much of the fire with the garden hoses available, but Danny remembered that firefighters sometimes put out flames with wet gunny sacks, so the boys took feed bags and soaked them, then climbed back and forth through the barbed-wire fence that bordered the field in order to get to the fire and try to beat out the flames using the wet feedbags. Each time they went over the fence, they scratched their arms and legs and shredded their shirts some more in their rush. Meanwhile, the fire was spreading rapidly.

Down the lane from the house and across Prefumo Canyon Road that day, a number of men were working to put in a new nine-hole golf course. Most of those men were "reserve firemen" of some kind. They all came running up the lane, grabbed the kids' wet feed sacks, surrounded the blaze, and then put it out by beating out the flames with the sacks. That golf course crew had the fire almost contained by the time the fire truck and the regular firemen arrived. We got home a few minutes later. If these reserve firemen hadn't seen the blaze immediately and responded so quickly, the whole ranch, the whole valley, and the Irish Hills and mountains along the back of the ranch property might have all gone up in flames. What were the incredible odds that knowledgeable firemen would be about a block and a half away at the very time they were needed? The sky didn't fall that day, but it was close.

Actually, I was a terrible sky-may-fall mom, like in the story of the Little Red Hen. It started with the birth of Nancy, and I worried the rest of my life about a million perils—dangers seemed to lurk everywhere.

"How could I keep my babies covered, yet not let them get smothered in a blanket?" I bought big safety pins to secure the four corners of the sheet to their cribs, leaving the bedding loose on the sides.

"How could I keep Arizona's scorpions away from the baby's crib and playpen?" I set the legs of the crib in small cans full of water and sprayed insecticides everywhere. On Fowler Lane, our first little farm, I probably almost killed us all by spraying far too much DDT, as well as other poisons of the time, all over the house and yard.

Certainly there are seldom lightning and thunderstorms in the Los Osos Valley, but at the first clap of thunder, I made the kids come inside, away from trees, metal roofs, and the car, and insisted that they avoid bathing until the chance of lightning had passed.

I insisted that handles on the pots on the stove had to be turned toward the wall, and that only grown-ups could light the oven, which required a match.

I came by all my apprehensions with good experience, as I had grown up as a fearless "tom girl." Years later, I realized that I was lucky to be alive after all the reckless acts I'd chanced. I have several particularly chilling memories of my careless daring as a youth. One day I climbed down a burned-out water well on the charred rungs of an old ladder still in place adjacent to an ancient barn. Some of the rungs broke off as I stepped on them to climb out. The water was deep in that well, and no one was with me. If I had fallen in, no one would have found me for a long time.

Another frightening experience occurred while I was riding a friend's overly fat and seldom ridden horse. In the middle of the ride, my out-of-condition mare suddenly decided to lie down. I barely missed being sandwiched between her thousand pounds and the dirt road.

Not much later, while riding with a friend along an unfamiliar road across town, we failed to see a cattle-guard ahead, as it was covered by the soft dirt and oil of a newly laid surface. We galloped our horses full speed across the metal bars, which were spaced to prevent animals crossing it. My friend's horse fell against mine, then regained his footing and made it safely across the grate, but my horse fell on his side just as he cleared the far side of the cattle-guard. By some miracle, his hooves never went down between the metal rails into the shallow ditch below, for he would certainly have broken a leg, or legs. I landed clear of my horse's body as he went down. My horse and I both got up, bruised and covered with the oily dirt but miraculously free of serious injuries, and passed through a nearby gate to return home.

Twice I was nearly caught in dangerous waves in a stormy ocean. The first time was in heavy winter surf off the coast in Ventura, California. I was with a school friend named Mary. She was a poor swimmer and having serious trouble making it back to shore due to a strong rip current. Luckily, my dad saw the problem developing and ran to the only two people sitting on the beach to ask for help. One was a strong swimmer, and he was able to get to Mary and pull her to shore, though only after she had swallowed a lot of water; the second fellow and I barely made it back to the beach on our own. Another time, lifeguards in Montecito became alarmed when they spotted me and a friend having trouble getting back to shore from a floating dock. They swam out to help and saved the day.

Of course, the kids inherited many of my genes, and as the older children began to borrow the car, I worried where they would go and at what speeds. Clearly, they were experiencing the double thrill of being more independent and of having just obtained driver's licenses. Still, my worries continued to float around them no matter what their ages or how far away they were from home. Even today, at the end of a visit, as they're getting into their cars, I urge them, "Let us know when you get home."

Chapter 13
Smoochie Comes to Stay

While I was at the pet store buying dog food, rabbit pellets, and hamster food, the owner of the store seemed to have something very much on her mind. "Do you still have a cat?" she finally asked. "I gave a home to a beautiful cat to be boarded for a week, and the owners have never come back. That was two months ago. He's still at my house, but his time's up—I'll have to take him to the pound if I can't quickly find a home for him, but he's just too fine a cat to end up at the pound! The owners just called him Puss, but you could easily name him something else and he would be happy with it. This cat would be perfect for you. He even loves dogs."

I had to admit we were without a cat, but we were still bereaving the loss of O.J. "How old is this cat?" I asked the store owner.

"He's a nice young cat," she answered. "Maybe one or two years old. I'll bring him to the shop tomorrow if you want to come and take a look at him. He's such a beauty and so loving that it breaks my heart to think of him not finding a good home."

I was hardly the type to choose a cat for his appearance, but I was a pushover for an animal needing a home, especially if the animal was happy and affectionate. I promised I'd be back the next day to see the cat. I had lingering concerns, though, for I knew that we would never know anything about the cat's past.

While I always insisted that beauty was only skin-deep, I found myself struck by how lovely this cat was to behold: long, long pearl-gray fur, four white paws like little gloves, and a delicate, rather round face with solemn, big green eyes that looked both friendly and curious. He was a large cat and had obviously been specially groomed for this introduction. Much of his size was probably in his thick and long coat. I wondered how I could keep his hair brushed and clean after he started roaming our fields full of stickers and burrs. Oh well, many years ago I had managed the hair of another longhaired gray cat. I could do it again if I had to, and maybe this puss could be a mostly indoor cat.

I picked him up, and he immediately settled down in my arms and started to purr and lick my hand. What a charmer! I thought cats were reserved and shy of strangers. He was definitely not a haughty, one-person cat. This puss would love all the family, and with his abundant affection, he would make each of us feel special.

At home, the children took turns gathering him up in their arms, and each time, he seemed right at home and didn't struggle to be put down. After meeting the family, he began a leisurely stroll of discovery, checking and sniffing every piece of furniture in every room, and jumping up on the sofa, chairs, and even the piano. Clearly, he knew why kitchens were special, and he ate supper without complaint.

During the evening, he snuggled in Dan's lap and later climbed up to drape himself around Dan's neck. While Dan laughed and then tried to remove the cat from his shoulders, he made the comment that this cat was a real "smoocher." Right then and there the family agreed that Smoochie would be his name.

Dogs seem to learn their names right off and come when called, or even when you're thinking about calling them. They'll try to do whatever you want whenever you ask. Cats, on the other hand, will seldom oblige you. If they are to come when you call them, they need to like both you and their home, and, most of all, feel like coming. Cats constantly use much editorial control over not only their name but also over the whole household. The family agreed with me when I observed, "Smoochie already knows somehow that he has a real home now and that he won't have to go back into any cage." Later, he sprang lightly onto my lap and became a heavy, velvety lump of purr. He could express what life is all about, and in doing so made our family richer again.

The owner at the pet store had made a big sales pitch, insisting that the cat liked dogs. At the time this seemed a likely story, but it soon became apparent that this cat had definitely not been reared with any dogs. When I invited Treve in to meet the new family member, poor Smoochie was petrified. Although he tried to jump out of my arms, I held him tightly as I sat, first on a chair near the dog, and then on the floor, and told Treve very firmly this cat is family; Treve immediately went to sleep. A number of times I woke Treve up and asked him to come closer to see the kitty. The cat continued to growl and hiss, but gradually he gave up his struggle to get out of my arms. Treve thought I was crazy to keep waking him up to see a cat that didn't like him. "It's bedtime. A new cat? So what?" Yet, gradually, as the weeks passed, these two became the best of friends and raced each other to the kitchen whenever they heard the refrigerator door open. Both were moochers, especially the cat!

In fact, I soon realized that I had brought a thief into the house. This dear cat snitched meat every chance he got as long as he lived, and this was a cat who lived to be extremely old. He stole meat from kitchen counters, the table, and even the stove when the burners were off. He even jumped to the top of the refrigerator where I often put meat out to thaw. At first when I caught him in the act of stealing food, I grabbed him and placed him out on the screened porch. Eventually I added a small slap and dropped him outside the house each time he became a thief.

Smoochie only learned to be more ingenious. He knew opportunity arrived whenever I was called outside or when I walked to another room. Like a sleight-of-hand artist, as soon as family members were out of sight, he used the few moments to snatch a chicken leg, a hunk of hamburger, or a slice of beef or bacon.

This became more complex for him when the dogs learned to team up to rush Smoochie. Again, the cat improved his act to outwit the dogs. Several times I came in to catch him in the middle of his new strategy, which involved carrying the meat to the washroom or under one of our beds, where he could eat his loot at leisure.

I think this cat, with more cat-love for us than Shandy had shown, felt very secure and loved. He knew he could risk my wrath. Banishment out the screen door only lasted until the next time the door swung open, which was never long on Oak Hills Ranch. Unlike Shandy, Smoochie had no desire to leave; he was almost always back and sitting beside the door by suppertime.

However, Smoochie grew to love all the animals on the farm, and it was a wonder he was never rolled on or stepped on by the cow or one of the horses. To keep him from sleeping near the larger animals, I encouraged him to stay inside the house at night: consequently, this puss never received dinner until he was home and inside the house. Of course now and then someone left a door open and one of us would find the cat asleep with the horses again.

There was one great contradiction to Smoochie's love of people and the farm animals. Certainly cats are complex creatures, with many private thoughts and a long history of certain behavior, but it was still a big surprise to all of us to know that this loving, huggable, fastidious cat liked to kill mice. I suppose most cats like to hunt both rodents and birds, but, this puss specialized in killing mice, especially mice out in the fields.

Padding out to monitor his secret routes, he flowed like water between and under the tall yellow oats. Cats have great patience and persistence, for how else could they use just feet and mouth to catch their prey? Smoochie could spend a whole day out in the fields without tiring of the hunt. Only by seeing the slightly swaying oats could I sometimes detect his stalking trail. Soon, feeling safe enough to roam the hay barn and, eventually, the distant fields, he was bringing back an endless number of dead mice, a couple of big rats, and once a little rabbit. He always deposited them on the back steps, where I suppose we were expected to admire them. He also began to watch the wild birds with great concentration, seemingly puzzled and startled that they could fly. I was thankful that he continued to specialize in killing mice.

Back inside the house, Smoochie kept me laughing. He had ever so many variations to his voice, and he liked to talk. There was the insistent, refrigerator voice, "Please feed me now; you're at least five minutes late." In case I didn't understand, he sometimes stood on his hind legs, with his front paws braced on the refrigerator door, and begged more stridently.

There was his happy voice, saying, "Hello. My, I'm glad you've come home safely!" There were insistent, impatient yowls, clearly heard all over the house, that said he was crouching at the door and wanted out, though he had a perfectly fine bathroom in the laundry room. There were even tentative, soft meows saying he was bored and really didn't know what he wanted. These we could usually cure by playing a game of hide-and-seek or ping-pong with him.

Smoochie's best conversations were the lovely purring and cooing talk he started the minute I or anyone else picked him up. Those purring conversations, or songs, were good for all of the family and sometimes I just stopped working and sat down to hold him in my lap. He seemed to have no worries for the future, not even tomorrow—only this moment mattered. He kneaded my lap with his white-gloved paws and hummed his dreamy thoughts. If he was on the rug, he often made me laugh by lying on his side and covering his eyes with one paw to snooze with wonderful contentment. Sometimes a little sigh bubbled out as he began to sleep more soundly.

I complained to Dan, who, like this cat, slept easily, day or night, "Why can't I relax as completely as Smoochie, at least a few times each day?" Even at night I never slept with such total oblivion.

Play was another thing Smoochie tried to teach us. His games didn't have to take a lot of time, but they had to be done wholeheartedly:

nothing could interfere, not even the phone, and there were rules. I never did learn all the cat routines, but I saw some of the rules observed when Smoochie played with Bogie, a visiting cat.

Bogie was a huge orange cat belonging to our son Doug and his family. When they came to visit, Bogie usually came with them. Like some big humans and big dogs, Bogie's very substantial size was accompanied by a gentle and amiable personality. Very soon after greeting each other, both Bogie and Smoochie were ready for rather violent games. They wrestled and boxed each other with great concentration and mock fury, yet one never tried to bite hard or to hurt the other. They chased , stalked , or hid and suddenly jumped out and tried to frighten each other. Such games ended quickly when one cat just walked casually away or stopped to clean his face. Smoochie occasionally played with their children, but I know that for games, he much preferred Bogie, his cat friend.

Not all cats "like to walk alone," as I'd once read. Except for Shandy, our felines loved companionship and attention. I gave a lot of thought to the personalities of our animals, and knew how terrible it would be to ever hurt a defenseless animal and make one afraid; they can't understand cruelty, and they don't forget it. Many animals who are punished with force become timid and fearful, often high-strung, unloving, or even vicious. All need to feel secure and understand they'll have constant and dependable caring and love.

I had once seen in a restaurant parking lot a medium-sized white dog restrained with a heavy chain and collar in the bed of a pick-up truck. As a friend and I walked by, the dog pulled back his lips and showed every tooth in his mouth as he went into a vicious, snarling, barking frenzy and tried to break loose from his chain. The friend who was with me exclaimed, "What a terrible and vicious dog!" I found myself thinking of Littlefoot, the kicking and biting horse that a horse trader had once sold us, and of other dangerous animals I had seen.

"No," I replied, "the dog is dangerous, but he's to be pitied. Some cruel owner has probably made him this way, and this dog is probably very fearful, thinking that all people are mean. Now he may be trying to please his master by overdoing his protection of the truck." Gentle and

loving Smoochie had probably never been mistreated, other than by being abandoned at the pet store, and he always accepted us with love and
an obvious desire to be with us. He followed us on all our walks, even
to the far end of the ranch. He watched and followed me as I weeded
the garden, hung the wash, or fed the horses. Smoochie often stopped
to roll around in a nice dusty part of our parking area. This meant I had
to grab him and brush clouds of dirt out of his fur before he could go in
the house. We both grew to know and love such routines. How could I
have not known how much I needed another cat in my life?

Chapter 14
Paint It Yellow

As soon as Dan started taking on additional jobs and my spring garden sprouted, I continued a lifelong career as a house painter. I had painted two small farmhouses in Arizona a snowy white, as well as several back in California, but now, my very soul yearned to make things yellow with white trim. Don't ask me why—I should have gotten enough of that color with the relentless yellow sun on the desert lands of Arizona.

Fortunately, the timing was right. The owners approved since there was very little paint remaining on the outside of the ranch house, and my color preferences were in vogue, with many yellow-with-white-trim homes blossoming across the country. Still, I promised Dan, "If I get to live in my yellow and white house, I promise to paint the barns and sheds all white."

Before I could paint this home on the hill, I had to do a lot of prep work. After cutting huge bougainvillea bushes away from the sides of the house, my arms and hands had enough scratches to prompt some friends I met in town to ask, "What did you do? Try to stop a cat fight?" Next, I brushed and scraped off all the loose, flaking paint. This gave me a second round of cuts and scratches. Finally, after much sanding, I painted the trim and the house itself. When I finished the job, the ranch house sported a coat of primer and then two coats of a wonderful lemony yellow with white trim around all the doors and windows.

On many painting days, I'd become almost as yellow as the house or as white as the trim, and from then on, my jeans and shirt, with their heavy overlay of paint spots, were designated as my painting uniform. It was a mystery to me how most professional painters paint for days with nary a spot of paint on their white pants and shirts.

My next painting targets were the long sheds and the hay barn, but I kept my promise to Dan and left them a conservative and safe white. With all the fresh paint on the house and the several outbuildings, and the fields then green, Oak Hills was becoming amazingly like the visions I'd had of a "real ranch."

I left the work needed on the inside of the house for last; the sky and land had always won hands-down over ceilings, walls, and floors. While the sun burned bright and warm outside, interior work, lit by dimly burning bulbs in always somewhat chilly rooms, couldn't entice me. When I finally began to paint the interior of the house, it was often as a closet painter at night while Dan taught his evening classes or went to meetings. Every room in this country house had extra high ceilings and lots of woodwork. I had to constantly move furniture back and forth and remove all the clothes from the closets. Since it was so much work to paint a place that was already being lived in, I made a decision: the inside walls and ceilings would be "Bone White" or "Antique White," then and forevermore, on hundreds and hundreds of rooms, both ours and those of present and future rental properties. Keeping to one color made touch-up jobs easier, and kept to a minimum the cans of paint we needed to use and store.

When we began to acquire some quite old rentals, I finally lamented to my brood, "All right, I'm crying uncle. You've all got to give me a hand and paint with me on this big project." When our high-ceilinged, two-story rental with five units needed paint, Dan, Danny, Nancy, and Douglas all helped. The building was so tall that, in order to paint its side next to a somewhat steep driveway, we parked the truck in the driveway, placed a thirty-six-foot extension ladder in the truck bed, and leaned the ladder against the building. Of course, the colors we chose for the apartment building outside were butter-yellow with bone-white trim.

As soon as that rental's down-payment was paid off, I raced off to the credit union and borrowed again to buy four old houses on two lots not far from campus. One was so old that the newspapers in the kitchen cabinets read 1903 and 1904. The kids and I took a wheelbarrow and garden hose into the kitchen and hosed off all the walls, ceilings, and cabinets, inside and out, with a power sprayer before we scrubbed and scraped the room with cleaners and filled the cracks and holes with spackle.

We cut and trimmed high trees, Bermuda grass, and shrubs, and picked up loads of old wood, cardboard, cans, and other trash. The seller, then about ninety-three years old, had personally built two of the other three houses on the property and had left much of the leftover cement and other construction materials there in the yard all of those years. Three of the four houses became yellow and white.

One stranger, walking down the sidewalk in front of one of the houses, saw my skinny kids, with the boys stripped to their waists on an extra-hot day, and came over to me to whisper, "Looks like you have a skeleton crew working for you, and all of them over six feet tall!" He laughed and laughed. He was the kind who might have added to his remarks by saying to me, "And, how are you doing, Shorty?"

All I could do was nod and reply, "Yeah, and you'd never believe their weight if you saw the meals this crew wolfs down about six times a day."

Soon we bought a small two-story house, again on the road to the campus. It, too, would be painted—yellow and white. The members of my crew learned to work at an early age—Jeffrey was now able to work with us, even though he put a new, high-topped, white shoe in a roller pan of the yellow paint his first day on the job. With Jeff taking up a brush and roller, I became the unpaid contractor, with four unpaid helpers. They were weekend and summer "subs," and they slaved alongside me until they were old enough to leave for colleges faraway enough to make them unavailable for any more paint jobs.

We also bought and painted three houses which weren't far from the swimming pool at the high school, where the two older boys were taking summer swim classes. I took the hose and a washcloth to their arms and legs to remove paint before they dashed off to swim, but several times I missed some of the paint, and Doug reported, "The coach blew his whistle at us and warned that every speck of paint has to come off or we can't swim there any more. Even when the paint on our skin is dry, it peels off as we swim." The swimming instructors were not amused when oily white and yellow paint floated on the water and attached itself to the other swimmers and the sides of the pool since there was no easy way to get the bits of paint out of the pool. When the pool's strainer became gooey with paint, I bought the school a new strainer, and I began scrubbing the kids' skin until it, too, almost peeled off.

The pick-up truck I now had as our second car carried all the ladders, paint, hoses, plaster-patch, sandpaper, and other such items, as well as my painting crew. Once in a while, we got careless about loading the truck, and early on, an almost full can of yellow paint fell off the truck's tailgate onto Los Osos Valley Road and spread over a large area. The paint stuck to that asphalt surface for years and years, and we saw it daily when leaving the ranch. Since the kids disliked the color intensely, it was something I wished I could erase, but I never found the time to paint over it with some kind of dark asphalt-colored coating.

With such long summer workdays, I granted all of us a fringe benefit of eating junk food at noon. One of our group was chosen each day to walk a few blocks to a fast-food store and bring back our orders for greasy hamburgers, wieners, fries, donuts, and other items that were almost never served at home. I packed and brought from home Cokes, jars of juice, and apples. We would try to sit on the floor or steps of a sunny porch—all of us talking, laughing, eating tons of the tasty, usually forbidden food, and drinking the sixteen-ounce bottles of Coke. We all decided there could have been much worse ways to pass the lunch hour.

After it became too dark to paint, the next reward for slaving all day was an informal dinner at one of the local Chinese restaurants. This was the cheapest yet tastiest and biggest meal in town for us. With no time or energy remaining, and without a good way to clean up as the sun went down, we washed our hands and faces under a hose or faucet beside the house we were painting and, as soon as Dan arrived after a day of teaching, headed for the restaurant. We usually still had paint on our hair, faces, arms, legs, clothing, and shoes, and I always worried that one of us might track paint into the restaurant. Our choice from the dinner menu never varied—it was always "Combination Dinner for Four," split six ways.

Dan and I went back to that restaurant not long ago, and even without four kids in tow and without our being spotted with yellow and white paint, that nice Chinese family still remembered us after ever so many years. The minute we walked in the door, the two owners almost doubled over with laughter, clapped their hands, and walked towards us with hearty hellos.

Chapter 15
Fireworks and More

Because we repeated our painting routine summer after summer, "How I Spent My Summer Vacation" could have been written once as a school assignment and then copied each September as long as they were required. But although our summer routine seldom varied, there were a few holidays that we tried to treat as mini-vacations at very little cost.

The main one was probably the Fourth of July, which our family, along with a number of our friends, celebrated by going over the Cuesta Grade to Atascadero Lake as long as the youngest children wanted to go. The large crowds reminded me of those at a county fair, with many arriving in family groups, dressed informally and ready for a good time. People spread out crazy quilts, blankets, or sheets on the grass bordering the lake, or sat on the wall rimming the lake and picnicked as the sun went down.

Children were everywhere, running with abandon, yelling, laughing shrilly, and lighting sparklers and other "safe" fireworks. Adults poured drinks and unpacked containers of fried chicken, salads of all kinds, pickles, buns, wieners, and beans. Some of the men set up little grills to barbeque meats. Often a baby lay asleep on a quilt as others ate and ate.

One year, as we picnicked on the wall beside the lake, I managed to let a silver serving spoon slip into the water as I passed the potato salad. "Doug, you'll have to save the day and get my spoon. Take off everything but your under shorts, and dive for it."

In Atascadero's afternoon heat, half the folks there were barefoot and scantily clad, but Doug was horrified. "Mom, I can't strip down to just underwear. No way!"

I only owned a couple of silver serving spoons, and this one was part of a set. I gave the ultimate-or-else, stern order, "Get that spoon!" He got the spoon, and I wonder if he doesn't still remember this incident as if it happened yesterday.

I suspected that for some folks, the evening of the Fourth of July, along with visits to the nearby County Fair in Paso Robles, were the best outings of their year. The members of different generations—parents, children, grandparents, aunts, uncles, and cousins—could enjoy just being with one another. Young lovers sat quietly, usually down beside the water. The crowds, young and old, watched the sky intensely and waited for a darkness that seemed to take forever to arrive. After the sun went down, people pulled sweaters over their sundresses and shirts, and finally put on shoes.

Meanwhile, across the lake, men unloaded the fireworks from a couple of pick-up trucks and arranged the staging area for launching the display. Finally, with everyone's patience running out, the sky darkened, and nature's own prologue of bright stars filled the sky.

The evening's main entertainment began with an explosion of big firecrackers and rockets, and the people in the crowd clapped and tilted their heads back as the first meteors rose high in the sky, then burst into kaleidoscope flowers of red, blue, yellow, green, white, and purple. Streamers and sparklers quickly fell in showers above the lake. The dark, still lake reflected the bursts of color, while the tall trees on the far shore became a black-silhouetted backdrop. A great chorus of "Ahhhs" and "Ohhhs" rose from the satisfied crowd every time the sky brightened with a burst of color. The final explosions boomed like cannons amid a number of extra-lovely, colored rockets, and then the sky became dark, and the night was suddenly quiet again. Extra quiet.

The audience, sleepy and content, gathered up their children, picnic baskets, and quilts. With little talk, they trudged slowly down the slope and sometime alongside the lake, heading for the parking lot.

Even though probably only a few of those who attended stopped to think of the struggle for our country's independence, this was a special and lovely evening. Families seemed close and happy; couples held hands or kept an arm around each other. I mused that it was the exact same thing every year in most towns all over America. "Kids, in addition to the Declaration of Independence of your country," I suggested "this can also be a picnic with friends, a celebration of family and community together, of summertime." I knew this was a wonderful tradition and that we'd come again with thechildren.

Halloween was one holiday I wished I could skip, right from day one. This was too bad, because all of us except Dan were costumed for Halloween most of the time. Tennis shoes were held together with string substituting for shoelaces and were worn even after the shoes lost their tongues. We put cardboard inside the soles to hide holes, and plumber's tape across the toes. Jackets and shirts had usually been outgrown the previous year, and the kids' faded jeans always had frayed holes. Most of the time we could pass as scarecrows, country bumpkins, beggars, or tramps.

Halloween gave me a horrible guilty feeling that lasted from one year to the next, because while other mothers created elaborate costumes, I could neither sew nor create any costumes that would rise above the limits on my time and lack of talent. The boys usually left home as ghosts, wearing bed sheets and paper bags over their heads with holes cut out for their eyes and mouths.

We lived too far out in the country for Halloween visitors to come for treats, but I transported the children to some of the nicest neighborhoods in town, where the candy pieces were reported to be bigger, with more sugar and more wrappings—there were even five-cent candy bars and candy-coated apples. Each year the kids always had the latest scoop, directing me to the best streets, where I parked and waited.

With about a pound of candy inside each child by bedtime, they often came down with mean colds a few days later. These were the first colds of the season, and I was always suspicious, right or wrong, they were brought on by the volume of candy the kids consumed on Halloween. So much for that holiday.

Valentine's Day was deeply felt but low key, with homemade cards for the kids' classmates and relatives. These cards involved using lots of red paper, white doilies, bits of ribbon, scissors, paste, and colored pens for sentimental messages. My own feelings about Valentine's Day were ambivalent, and Dan always insisted he didn't want me buying him a thing. We eventually decided that there would be no cards, and a pound of candy for each of us.

Nancy and Danny also struggled to find perfect cards as they grew older, and that brought back a memory of my early years. When I was in fourth grade, a little classmate gave me a huge fold-out card. It was larger and higher than a three-layer cake, and was such an elaborate creation that I was totally confused. I knew this boy came from a poor family. There followed parent-teacher talks about where he could have found the money, and what I should do. Confused or not, I remember that I kept the fancy card, and it sat on top of my tall dresser for a couple of years.

Easter, too, seemed low-key, with our attendance at church followed by an egg hunt in the house and the hay barn for the younger two children. Even after we no longer did the egg hunts, we still colored several dozen eggs, until the year when I tried to veto the egg-coloring activity. Even the older children were horrified. "Honestly, mom! We kids will color the eggs from now on. In a pretty basket, they can decorate the table for a few days, and then we can eat eggs for lunch." Without my realizing it, this yearly egg-coloring had become a family tradition.

So much has gone out of truly honoring and celebrating the special dates of the country; people increasingly find these days good for sleeping late, doing home chores or projects, and going to sales at the malls. Some holidays have had their dates moved to Mondays or Fridays, making it possible for people to have a three-day holiday. For instance, George Washington and Abraham Lincoln's birthdays were lumped together as a general Presidents' Day in February. Memorial Day in May is a huge day for store sales, as is Labor Day in September, and Columbus Day in October. Veterans Day, in November, was once called Armistice Day, but now it just means a big shopping opportunity in the pre-Christmas rush. Thanksgiving more often than not only represents a ton of food. And so much of Christmas is now Santa Claus, parties, and a buying frenzy, with the celebration of one special day expanded to include the whole holiday season through New Year's.

Every year, for each child's birthday party, I panicked at the idea of not having enough entertainment and games to last until the parents arrived to pick up their kids. I bought bottles of bubble stuff for the boys to blow through little wire rings, and handed out small airplane gliders made of balsa wood. For several years, we took all the children for a boat ride around the harbor in Morro Bay. Even with the nice cruise, I fretted that the boys might become bored, so again I handed out bubble jars and wire rings, and bubbles floated in the breeze behind the boat.

The most memorable birthday party of all time was an overnight slumber party for Doug and Jeff in the barn. Shortly before the party, the barn had been filled with a year's supply of oat and alfalfa bales, which were stacked in tiers almost to the ceiling. Fortunately, no one fell to the cement floor during the long dark night of tag, ghost stories, and food fights. Dan went out to the barn several times to see if the wild boys would sleep just a bit. One weary reveler must have finally conceded, because the next morning, we found him sound asleep in his sleeping bag beside the gate to the house with Treve lying close beside him. For most of the year we continued to find some reminders of that sleep-over: soft-drink containers, candy wrappers, flashlights, unmatched socks, party favors, and a couple of tooth brushes.

Dan and I skipped celebrating most of our birthdays; neither of us has any memory of just the two of us ever eating a gourmet meal "out." During the ranch years there wasn't even a bottle of champagne opened. I had no need for special clothes, dark glasses, or luggage for any vacations. Since Dan taught both summer school and night school and put on summer conferences, the only time off we had was when we "dressed up" in bathing suits and "vacationed" at Avila Beach, even when the waves were icy cold in the winter months.

Tennis was a sport that all of us played once the kids became old enough. It came naturally to Dan and me, since we had grown up in the

Ojai Valley, north and inland from Los Angeles, which back in those early years had hosted the nation's best players in the first-of-the-season big tournament each year. It was glamorized with all-white tennis clothes, tea, and fresh Ojai orange juice served in a "tea-tent" near the main courts. The tournament ended with a formal dance in a local hotel for all the players. Those courts are still used for tournaments.

Now, many years later, we played as a family on courts in San Luis Obispo. No fancy country clubs, though—we played on the high school, junior college, or university courts. Because our balls often went flying onto the other courts, regular players groaned when they saw us coming. "Those Chases should play at six in the morning, or after dark," we thought we heard them say one day. "Is this our ball or one of theirs? The Chases play with any brand of ball, so there's no telling." Actually, they could tell at a glance—our balls were the oldest, grayest, least fuzzy, and most dog-chewed ones. Still, it was fun, and all the kids played and often won on their school teams as they grew older. Holes in their shoes never seemed to hurt their scores.

Neither Dan nor I cheated on "sick leaves." I had only one person to "call in sick" to, but Dan couldn't come home to care for me unless I was at death's door. In twenty-five years of teaching at Cal Poly, Dan lost only two days of work to illness. Because of this, the universitiy gave him an extra year of retirement credit when he finally retired. I'm not sure we were very smart. It would have made a lot more sense for him to play hooky and feign sickness now and then. There were a few "family emergencies," but they had to be "lulus" to have him take even a few hours off.

Christmas was always a lovely holiday on Oak Hills Ranch—a special time with a big wreath on the door and the splurge of a ceiling-high green tree with a fresh, foresty fragrance. I sent long letters to friends, made long-distance phone calls without watching the clock, and we always visited Dan's parents. There were school programs to attend, and as all the kids learned to play carols on the piano, while we gathered around it to sing enthusiastically loud and off-key. In addition to clothing and practical gifts like toothpaste and pens in their Christmas stockings, each child received something he or she actually wanted.

For a lifetime, Dan and I mostly repeated, "I don't want anything for Christmas. Please, please, don't buy something I can't use!" Actually we both wanted a lot—another rental house, a new car, a bigger horse trailer, or a check that could put four kids through college and grad school. A new coat or jeans might have been nice, but I would wait a few more years, since clothes many decades old still hung in the very back of our walk-in closet. It was too bad clothes couldn't melt or dis-integrate over time: some of my high school- and college-era coats and dresses were still there on hangers, "perfectly usable."

I said there were no real vacations those years, but I don't know how to classify a trip we took "to the snow" one long weekend. When the kids went with their scouting or Camp Fire troupes on trips to the Sierras, they had always returned with glowing reports. Twice as a teenager, I had spent six weeks at a summer camp beside Huntington Lake in those same mountains, and I still remembered the wonderful singing around big campfires at night, the fragrance and the murmur of wind in tall pine trees, the horseback riding, the boating, and the hearty meals.

Now the kids mounted a campaign for a family trip to Yosemite National Park. I wasn't sure why they chose that park, or why they lob-bied with so much fervor. Maybe they realized it wouldn't take much convincing or pleading?

"Mom, let's go for Thanksgiving weekend," the younger ones pleaded. "Nancy and Danny will be away. You can rent us a tent cabin and not have to sleep on the ground. Maybe we can build a big fire, or maybe it'll snow outside. They rent skis up there, you know."

Thus, it came to pass that we went, accompanied by Treve, to the Sierra Nevada's Yosemite Valley. We wore only tennis shoes, light sweat-ers, light jackets, and blue jeans. We didn't have much clothing in re-serve in the few bags we took.

In the cabin, the evening was icy cold, and the little fire in the stove only flickered and then went out. All the firewood was damp, and soon the room filled with smoke, until we finally gave up on the fire. The cabin's amenities included only two double beds, with two twin-sized blankets, one for each bed, plus thin cotton spreads. The boys dressed Treve in an extra pajama top and convinced him to sleep on the bed with them. As long as a dog is with his loved ones, he can be a happy canine-camper almost anywhere. We dressed for bed in all the clothes I had packed for the weekend—the additional cotton shirts, sweaters, and lightweight jackets. Still, we all shivered until dawn.

The next day, there was just enough snow on the trails to make hiking difficult, so the trails we climbed could not be the high ones with the magical views. This, too, was a bit of a disappointment.

The second night, the camp staff brought us dry wood to build a fire, and our mood changed. Dancing firelight, the heady fragrance of the pine trees, and eggs and bacon frying properly on top of the stove the next morning made up for the difficulties of the first night. However, the decision to go home a day early was unanimous. The dog in pajamas and all of us awake and shivering all night became just a funny story after enough years passed, but was this a "real" vacation?

Horseback riding, tennis, and the beach became the main substitutes for vacations to faraway places. Horseback rides were hard for me to schedule, but I crammed in a few each year, usually on Blue. Treve thought those times were wonderful. He always went ahead of us to roust out whatever small game he could surprise, while racing over the golden hills or up into the denser chaparral of the hills. No one ever saw him catch or kill anything, but he felt complete joy in the chase, and with tongue hanging out, sides heaving, and tail waving high as he raced along the trails. He didn't stop his "work" until he saw that it was time to follow us home for chore time.

We had a number of friends who traveled all over the world, and we always marveled at the postcards they sent us from faraway places. But it wasn't hard for me to postpone long trips. Life was still centered on Dan, the kids, and the various critters. Occasionally we took a short trip by foot, car, or horse, and traipsed around the Irish Hills or the nearby seashore. Very nearby places can be a key to happiness, even when a pony visits your living room.

Chapter 16
In Sickness And In Health

I never had time to schedule an illness, especially for things like a broken big toe, which I duct-taped to a Popsicle stick to hold it rigid while I continued to work barefoot or in open sandals. Strep throat, the flu, or a slipped disk, were another thing. As these situations came unannounced, I caved in easily and made the most of my time in bed. They were my rare type of "excused" vacation. I devised numerous schemes to turn such times into a plus: get meals in bed with foods I especially liked, have books stacked high about me, and have family or company coming in so I could relate all my real or fancied symptoms. The vicious germs and viruses were usually brought home from school by the children, and the germs usually infected each of the kids, one after the other. Before I could get the last sick child back in school, these bugs sometimes decided to take on one more close-at-hand victim, and laid me low.

However, I couldn't blame some back surgery on the kids. Once, in one long day while Dan was out of town on behalf of the college, I removed all the clothes from Nancy's closet, covered the furniture with newspapers, and proceeded to paint the entire room, including the walk-in closet and the trim around the windows. After finishing the paint job, I re-hung the clothes in the closet, and re-hung the curtains, Nancy's pictures, and her bulletin board of horse ribbons.

Feeling like a limp dishrag by the time Dan came home, I still joined him on a short horseback ride early that evening. I was riding Blue, who at one point slipped down a small bank beside a stream and then, instead of walking through the water, suddenly made a big jump across the creek bed. I wasn't ready for her leap, and wound up with a slipped disk and a good vacation in bed before getting surgery. Down in Santa Barbara, Dr. Reeves called me his Chicken Every Sunday Gal, because with every visit, all the family went with me, and we filled every chair in his waiting room. After surgery, he only laughed and warned, "Now, please don't lift the dining room table for a while."

Most animals are just the opposite from me. When they're sick, instead of craving attention, they want to be alone, really alone. Twice stray cats crawled under the house when they were ailing. I was flirting with danger when I crawled under the house two different times in search of a sick or dying cat.

I tried this the first time with a stray white cat. Smoochie, with some halfhearted yowls near the entrance to the crawlspace, had let me know this intruder was under the house. Smoochie didn't relish the idea of facing an injured or ill cat any more than I did, but he wanted that cat dislodged and removed from his territory.

I put on an old glove on one hand to avoid getting scratched, set Dan's tennis hat on my head, and carried a gunny sack and a flashlight in the other hand. In the darkness of the underside of the house, I tried to avoid black widow spiders hanging above, prayed nothing lethal lived on the ground, like a snake or other spiders, and hoped to grab the cat and wiggle back out to safety.

It would have been easier with six hands: two to crawl with, one to hold the flashlight, two to hold the gunny sack open, and one to grab the frightened, suddenly wailing stray cat, who was lying there trying to hang on to one of his nine lives. I dragged him into the bag. Desperation to save a cat's life helped me get that cat out and I quickly drove the poor cat, still in the gunnysack, out to the pound.

The second time, it didn't take Smoochie to let me know that an animal, probably the gray cat I'd seen in the barn, was under the house. The stench became worse and worse. He had probably lived on a diet of just mice and birds too long, or perhaps had some disease. It must have taken a final burst of bravery for him to get past the dogs and under the house. Getting the dead cat out was a job about as pleasant as my struggle with the first cat. All the while, I though how horrible it was for anyone to abandon their pets to unnecessary suffering like this. He had probably been abandoned on the canyon road at the bottom of the hill.

Horses and cows also distance themselves when they don't feel chipper. Several times I found them at the far end of the pasture or barn, heads down and drooping. I always quickly called the vet, and I let him deal with the big animals. Twice, the emergency was due to Shorty getting into the storage room of grain and eating too much. Several other occasions arose when a horse bloated on too much green grass.

What got me thinking about all this, was the death of Treve. One morning I found him dead on the lawn up against the house and under our bedroom window. He had come as close to us as he could possibly get, making it extra-heartbreaking because I had no warning that he was ill, even though he had become an extremely old dog.

With the increasing numbers of ranch animals, giving pets pills and other medicines successfully soon became our lot. The dogs and cats instinctively seemed to know we had something ready for them that they wouldn't like. Dan and I usually worked as a team: I held the critter, sometimes between my legs and with both hands, while Dan pried their mouth open with one hand and we got the pill or liquid way back on their tongue and then held their mouth closed. With the animal's head up and back, Dan would then stroke its throat, saying, "OK, now, down the hatch." Sometimes we hid pills in a bit of hamburger, yet all too often we'd later find the pill on the kitchen floor, and then we'd have to resort to the two-person pill-giver approach.

Cats, especially, feel insulted and violated when force-fed medicine, and ours spent a long time moving their tongues around, trying to remove the taste. After being force-fed a dose of medicine, cats gave themselves a long period of grooming, while continuing to also send me beady-eyed, severe looks. The obvious remark and body language was, "Why in the world would you do that to me?"

.

Chapter 17
Pepper

The next spring, with the thought of another long school vacation approaching, my desire for another full-sized horse greatly increased, and I started a daily search for available horses by watching the livestock section of the daily paper. June was a lovely month for riding in the valley. The hills were still green, my garden was in full bloom, and daybreak came early, often with soft gray fog from the west that usually burned off by ten or eleven. Evenings arrived late, giving more time to be with the animals. In the early dusk, bats and swallows swooped and darted between the barns, sheds, and house to catch gnats, moths, and mosquitoes; later, the mockingbirds often sang. Robins, doves, and sometimes quail, kept busy early in the morning on the lawn and up and down the lane, perhaps getting an early start on breakfast. Having another horse would make it possible for two of us to enjoy the trails and birds before or after work without one of us having to scrunch up our legs to hold them high enough to manage riding Shorty.

The horse I finally found in the north county was an old but wonderful animal, with easy gaits, sensitive playful moods, and a keen mind. Pepper was his name. He was a large and majestic horse, over sixteen hands high, with a proud head and large dark eyes. His mane hung thick against his long and slender neck, and his body was white but with a lot of black hair mixed in, as his name Pepper implied.

Pepper scrambled quickly out of the trailer in the barnyard, snorting his disgust at having been cooped up. He was immediately a thrill to watch as he danced around with the rope and halter on him. I hoped our fences would be high and strong enough to hold him. Still, he wasn't pulling on the rope; he was just excited and happy. Pepper was probably fifteen or more years old. Yet, like Monty, the very old white horse I'd been given when I was a gangly twelve-year old in the little town of Ojai, California, Pepper would be full of spirit and the joy of life as long as he lived.

I wondered, "Do you think the couple of sedate and serious mares we're putting him with will catch his enthusiasm and lighten up? We should all be like him."

Everyone was watching the newcomer, and no one answered me. Dan asked Nancy, "Think you can ride him, honey?"

"Sure, I already like him a lot," she quickly replied. "He'll calm down."

Nancy and I led him to the smaller field where the serious mares were kept, and off he galloped, snorting and blowing air out through his nose, head high, ears pricked forward, and his long mane and tail flowing out behind him. Right away, the other horses began to tear off around the field with him. His long legs seemed to be full of springs, his feet linghtly touching the ground.

Pepper had been someone's pet, and that person had surely loved him, for he very shortly trotted back to us and put his head over the fence, probably hoping to be given a sugar cube or a piece of apple. I knew that Blue would always be first in Nancy's heart, but I also guessed that this huge, responsive, irrepressibly upbeat horse would be loads of fun for her as she rode him out over the hills, and that he, too, would be deeply loved. Pepper would always be ready to charge, whether there were bugles sounding or not. The word "horsepower" came to mind. He had lots. Joan of Arc could not have ridden a horse looking any more heroic and commanding.

I had been proudly told by the previous owner that Pepper could "do tricks," but no one ever asked or figured out what tricks, or what the magic words or commands were to produce them. Now he did a beautiful job of taking center stage by just being himself—a rollicking, lighthearted fellow. I didn't think Pepper would miss the applause for any special tricks he had been taught.

Unlike Blue, with her slow hobbyhorse lope or gentle canter, Pepper almost continuously pranced with excitement while out for a ride, and he often came home in a sweat. Since he was light on his feet and his joy passed into the mood of the rider, we gave up trying to settle him into the role of a sedate, calm walker. I was quite sure he had always danced a lot.

Eventually, our all so-different horses—Blue, Shorty, and now Pepper—were moved to share the field that included the old wooden barn down the hill. This separated them from the boarded horses—a good thing, since our horses had often nipped, kicked, and snorted as they lunged toward the boarded horses at mealtime. This was disruptive, as it made the newer, boarded horses square-dance around in a rush from flake to flake of hay.

Pepper was so big, he easily put up with Blue and Shorty and their tricks for getting the largest flakes of hay. Pepper didn't bite or kick, he just swished his tail, shook his head, and stayed in place to eat his own serving of hay. I've always believed the biggest creatures are often the most gentle and show the most empathy for others.

Since Blue had never perfected her biting and kicking, she quickly gave up and ate her own flakes of oats or alfalfa. She, Shorty, and Pepper soon became good barn-mates. Shorty and Pepper adopted Blue's talkative neighing whenever any of us came in sight, and even as we left them. They probably just wanted more food, but it did seem as if they enjoyed seeing us and were saying so.

Blue and Shorty were always ready to enjoy their food, and were usually too plump. Pepper, on the other hand, needed to gain weight. As soon as he began losing his winter coat, I realized he was very thin and needed more nutrition, so I kept a halter on him, and most days I led him up the hill to the hay-barn to feed him a supplement of grains. My other remedy for his condition was to have his teeth worked on; horses' teeth wear down unevenly, especially as they grow older, so I had Pepper's teeth filed when the vet came several months later. The vet had explained that horses have to grind their food, and when their teeth get sharp edges, they can't successfully do this. The veterinary term for filing a horse's teeth is "floating." The floating seemed to help—Pepper finally began to put on some weight over his ribs and backbone, and we decided to have the vet also do Shorty and Blue's teeth every year or so.

Moods are contagious, and none of us could stay sad or grouchy while this dynamo of a horse found so much fun all about him. And why go through life on idle or at half-speed when it's more exciting and challenging to go along at a full gallop? Life is often what you make it, and this bubbling-with-life fellow knew how to live from morning until night.

More than Blue, when any of us rode Pepper, he seemed to sense there was nothing wrong with a bit of goofiness, and he loved to act astonished or fearful of anything along a trail or road, whether it was a paper caught in a bush, a bird moving in the grass, a puddle of water, the breaking of a twig, or the roll of a stone down the side of a trail. He arched his neck, kept his ears pricked forward, and intently focused his eyes on the "thing," while he pranced in a wide circle around the object and often tried to break into a run. If our new dog Boomerang came too close in front of him, he quickly tried to get his head down to nudge or nip at the dog. This was all for fun; when it was necessary, he reined easily and obediently.

As I had hoped, having the second horse made it more companionable and fun to ride with Dan or Nancy up the canyon road and off on a couple of trails bordered by oak trees and chaparral.

An especially joyful day involved Pepper and Blue some months later. A little riding group that Nancy and her father belonged to planned a ride along the surf and sand out on the strand in Morro Bay. Dan didn't ride very often, yet he and several other fathers, who also didn't ride, got pressured into helping establish this riding club and taking their daughters to the meetings. One year, Dan even had to be president, and a doctor who had never even gotten on a horse was roped into being vice-president.

The club was composed mostly of young girls, and I rode with them along the beach north of the town that day. Both the open ocean and the sky were a deep blue, and long rows of white waves constantly rolled in towards the beach. The brilliant sun made the sea sparkle, and the wet sand near the edge of the water was smooth and firm—perfect for riding. Nancy had given Pepper a soapy bath the day before, and his long tail and mane were as white as the waves. She rode Pepper and I rode Blue. Both horses were excited and exuberant with this new experience and enjoyed the sociability of being with other horses.

In addition to the visual appeal of the scene, there was the good scent of salty sea air, my sweating Blue, and her squeaking saddle leather. There were also the deep booming sounds of the multiple rows of breaking waves, and Blue's occasional snorts of excitement—perhaps wishing she could gallop faster. Finally, there was the happy, high laughter and chatter of the girls riding ahead that came drifting back to me from time to time.

I continued to watch Pepper as he pranced and galloped down the shoreline with Nancy his delighted, carefree rider. Nancy wore her light gray boots, cowgirl hat, plus a blue shirt and green jeans. After so many lessons, she rode beautifully, as one with the horse and his easy gaits. Pepper, obviously counting his blessings on getting this special outing, was very willing to get his feet and legs wet, and galloped and splashed along in the foaming water as the waves reached shore.

Blue's gaits were easy, and even she soon loped and galloped along in the shallows, while I found myself grinning until my jaws ached. We took no photos that day, unfortunately, but that ride was a feast for my soul, a sort of celebration of life. I still remember it as vividly as if it happened last weekend.

Chapter 18
Dress-Up Parties?

I bet you keep your motor running even when you're eating and sleeping. Can't you manage to try even harder and work twenty-five hours a day? You guys need to take vacations—sit back and smell the roses. Do you even have dress-up clothes back in your closet?" So spoke and questioned a good friend, who actually worked almost as long as I did each day.

She made me think a bit more about our no-time-off routines. My social life, with only slight variations, revolved around a seldom-home partner, four kids home less and less, exchanging a few words with shop owners and clerks in town, and visiting briefly with a brown cow, horses, a dog and a cat. Maybe Dan and I could plot vacations between our having to be home to milk April around 6:00 A.M. and again about 6:00 P.M. The cow didn't quit making milk on weekends; this was a seven-day-a-week job for about ten months each and every year. There must be some sort of short-time vacations that I could organize, plus a lot more nonsense and laughter.

Most weekends we stayed home and attempted to catch up on ranch projects that were never ending, including such fun-filled activities as patching fences, repairing floats in watering troughs, and replacing fence boards kicked out by the horses.

Finally, as time went on, several outings became more frequent as food on the table became more plentiful. There was a drive-in theatre south of town, and with the coming of our big station wagons, the children insisted that going to the movies could be fun and easy. Since we were a squirrelly and squirmy crowd, with four to six in the car, movie-going was never an easy or a completely happy experience. Just as a show would become slightly interesting, too often a voice from the back seat of the car would pipe up, saying, "I've got to go to the bathroom, Mom."

Still, besides our own home-show productions, the drive-in was the only show in town for us. Fortunately, Dan and I didn't have to spend all the show time in bathrooms.

I mentioned in an earlier book, better outings also meant trips to several swimming, fishing, and picnicking beaches after we moved to this coastal area. At first, this had meant putting baby Doug, and later Jeff, in a cardboard box lined with a blanket. As soon as the babies could crawl and sit up, I took along a fold-up playpen—sandy beaches and babies are not a good mix.

In addition to swimming and picnicking, as soon as they were old enough, all four kids began to enjoy ocean fishing. We would load everything into the station wagon—fishing poles, spreads, towels, jackets, caps, sacks of food, sun glasses, one or two dogs, the kids, and sometimes one or two of the kids' friends. This was such a job that we only went fishing on weekends when Dan was able to go along. The best fishing piers for us were at Pismo Beach and Avila, while the swimming beach was almost always Avila Beach. Favorite picnics spots were farther south in beautiful sand dunes below Pismo Beach or, now and then, along the strand north of Morro Bay.

Dress-up clothes for beach parties were never smart "resort wear," but old shorts, shirts, and jackets, usually with a bathing suit underneath. We always took jackets, because the fish bit more often in the early morning or the late afternoon, when it might be cool and sometimes windy.

Dan and I "fished" by spending our time untangling fish lines, freeing hooks that became imbedded in the wooden pilings of the pier, and re-baiting the younger kids' hooks. The bait that seemed to catch the most fish—usually perch, but sometimes rockfish, small bonito, shark, or halibut—were pieces of mussel, and in those days the bait shop sold mussels still in their tight black shells. Dan and I pried them open with a heavy-duty knife, or used pliers to crack them open.

The younger boys only watched at first, but soon they learned to use "drop lines" and often caught large fish just as often as we did with fishing poles. Long after the playpen was no longer used to restrain Doug or Jeff, I constantly felt like leashing the younger two with a harness. As they fished, they could have fallen over the edge of the pier, especially the sections with no railing.

The result of the kids' success at often catching half a bucket or more of fish, was a reward that went to Dan and me. This prize entailed having to clean the fish. If we were on a pier that had running water plus a wooden trough, we could scrape off the scales, cut off the heads and tails, gut the fish, and then wash them. If we were on a pier without cleaning facilities, I did the smelly job at home in the kitchen sink. However, that still didn't end my delight in fishing.

Back at home, I dipped the fish in egg batter and seasoned flour and then fried them for supper. Conversation for the entire meal became, "That's my fish! Mom, why did you give Doug my fish?"

"No, it's not your fish," Doug would reply. "You caught four teeny, tiny ones and only one this big."

"Mom, he's eating my fish. Doug, give it to me!"

Even if there were dozens of fish that had since been reduced to small, broiled pieces, each child thought he knew all his catches by sight.

If the outing was just a picnic with no fishing, the dogs accompanied us. It was a given that food would have sand kicked or blown into it before it reached our mouths, and that we'd need warm jackets and sweaters in the late afternoon air on some cooler beaches.

The spectacular stretch of shoreline south of Pismo had a car ramp to the beach at that time, with sand hard enough for cars to drive on. We always arrived with two boxes of firewood, an old oven rack to place on a circle of rocks around the hot coals, and enough meat, corn, salad, and beans to give everyone two platefuls, plus plenty of marshmallows to toast on the dying coals for dessert. Sharing the beach sometimes with the sandpipers racing along the water's edge, we drove south on the sand for about a mile to our favorite dune area.

I liked bringing grape juice on picnics. The dunes were a perfect place for spills, and once we were there it didn't matter if we spilled the juice onto the sand or onto our decrepit clothes. Grape juice became one of our picnic traditions.

To get some protection from cold sea breezes, we usually carried the picnic makings and firewood away from the surf and into the soft, snowy-white, fine sand of the sand dunes. There was always a special perfume in the higher dunes with their coverings of plants such as sage verbena, mock heather, ice plant, and dune grasses. Small birds, including doves and sparrows, often flew out of the bushes as we arrived. And always there was the wonderful roar of the often large breaking waves not far away.

More often than fishing, picnics, and barbeques, we would enjoy a weekend day-at-the-beach back in Avila with the children, where the only entertainment involved swimming in water 50 to 65 degrees cold. Very few beach-goers swam in that ocean ten or eleven months a year, as we did, and those who did usually had far more fat on their bones to keep them warm. Still, our swimmers always rushed into the water to meet the white waves, hoping to catch them at just the right moment to body-surf to shore. When Nancy or Danny took a wave successfully, they always emerged at the shore and quickly glanced up to Dan and me sitting on the sand to see if we had noticed their skill in the white waves. In wintertime, these waves were sometimes huge and strong, and we learned to dive deep under them when not in the right spot to ride them to shore. Whether the day was cloudy, cold, or rainy, we still swam and shivered.

As soon as I left the water, I began a shouting match with the roar of the surf. "Get out of the water, will you? You're turning blue and shaking all over."

"Aw, Mom, just one more wave."

Ten waves later, my voice rose higher, "Get out this minute or you'll go sit in the car 'til we leave!"

In other seasons, when the sun made the sand nice and hot, we usually stretched out directly on the sand instead of the spreads or towels. Sand then coated the inside and the outside of our wet suits, forming a caked shell as it dried, only to become fine sand again in the car and on all the floors at home. With so much baking in the sun, we stayed dark as scorched toast year after year.

At noon, the kids ran hot-footed races over the burning sand to small fast-food shacks and cafes across the frontage road next to the beach, and brought back sacks of greasy French fries, hot dogs, tacos, and hamburgers "with all the trimmings." I then brought out a bag of carrot sticks, oatmeal cookies, potato chips, and juice from home.

Yellow jackets, with their intense cravings for both food and liquid refreshment in open Coke bottles, often joined our picnics by flying around in close combat formation. More than one of the nearby families usually fled to their cars because of a particularly bad wasp invasion. We always stayed, and dad proceeded with several coping strategies. His main battle-plan involved folding up a napkin, waiting for the second a wasp landed on a plate, and then clobbered the unwary insect. His second method was to pick up the unwary insect with a napkin and then press the napkin firmly together with his fingers. His last solution was to insist, "If you'll all just ignore them, they won't sting you!" Even when we waved them away, for some reason, those beach scavengers never actually stung us. So these picnics progressed, with sand in the food and yellow jackets flying reconnaissance above, or practicing take-offs and landings on our fries and wieners and dive-bombing into open Coke bottles.

Too often those years it appeared as if so many people were grasshoppers—traveling, taking part in many sports, playing bridge, and going to other social gatherings—while Dan and I were merely ants, working seven days a week. Still, it was grasshopper time for me and other family members on those brief beach escapes, and such days were our "vacations" for years and years; with seagulls crying and the surf pounding, it was mental and physical heaven to stretch out flat on that hot sand, relax weary bones, swim in the salty ocean, eat junk food, or just sit on a pier with our legs dangling over the edge and fish. Often I would think, "Who needs to go to Bermuda? In more ways than one, we're there while staying here."

Chapter 19
April and the Christmas Calf

April, our beautiful doe-eyed Jersey cow, continued to furnish us with lots of milk for many years. Each year she was artificially bred. We always sold her female calves, and kept and raised the males. Each year we also bought a couple of day-old calves in order to use up all of April's extra-rich milk. Later we sold some of these animals as yearlings.

Often during those years economists came to the university from the Washington, D.C. office of the Agency for International Development, or A.I.D. One day, after meeting one of them who was at Cal Poly for the day, Dan insisted that the visitor drive out to Oak Hills Ranch and join us for dinner. The Washingtonian still had on his suit and tie when he arrived at the ranch, but he followed Dan out to the corral when Dan went to milk the cow.

Right away our visitor, who wanted to be called Dewey, started laughing and asked, "What in the world are you doing milking a cow, Dan? That doesn't make any sense at all. You could be spending your time a thousand better ways. Economically speaking, she's not worth all this time and feed."

Dan had to agree that economically that was true, but that it was only part of the picture. "Dewey, I'm with great numbers of students from eight in the morning until I hit the hay at ten-thirty or eleven at night, if you count all my adult night classes. When I milk a cow at dawn and dusk, it's the two best times of the day; I can be absolutely alone with my thoughts and this nice quiet Jersey, and usually a few other creatures. Birds sing, the dog and sometimes the cat come out here with me. It restores my soul and relaxes me all over—I go back in the house whistling a tune."

What Dan failed to mention, but probably didn't have to add, was that a wild gang of a wife and kids, all wanting to talk his head off, were waiting in the kitchen. Time at home could often be just as frenzied as days at school. Cow-time for Dan was like my time spent down in the old rustic barn with my only company a large owl sitting on a rafter.

Yet, Dewey had a point. We never did find an easy way to bring April inside the hay barn to milk her, and when it rained it was brutal. I have no idea why we didn't find time to make at least a shed in the corral.

However, April was growing rather old, and I finally decided to keep one of her sweet little heifer calves and raise it for our next milk cow. The dairyman, Mr. Righetti, agreed to take April back the next time she was dry. The new beautiful baby calf, looking like a miniature of her mom, was born the day before Christmas, so her name became Noël. That brown calf soon grew big enough to enjoy chasing Boomerang, as well as any cat that took a shortcut through the corral, and she dashed up to me each time I arrived with a bucket. Noël was such a cute tomboy of a calf that Doug and Jeff actually offered to feed her now and then. It was always hilarious to watch the calf drink from the pail. She would try to get the last drop by nudging the bottom of the pail with her nose, while constantly dancing around on her dainty, tiny, black hooves, with her tail and velvety ears wagging back and forth. But time goes quickly—it wasn't long before Noël grew up, was bred, and gave birth to her own Jersey calf and became a friendly and beautiful milk cow like her mother.

Besides the man from Washington, D.C., there was another couple during that period who were transplants from the East coast and felt that we were crazy to be living on a farm. This new-to-town faculty couple came out to have lunch with us one Saturday. It was soon obvious that they were the sort who gave a highfalutin' sneer over anyone going to a dump or milking a cow. I'm not sure that they had even been on a farm or ranch before. Within a few minutes, the wife even said, "I don't see how you don't lose your mind out here—so far away from everything!" None of us mentioned that town was only about four or five minutes away by car.

These two were negative people, whether talking about ranch life, the lack of large department stores in town, the limited number of plays and musical events available locally, their less-than-perfect rented house, or their need for a more careful house cleaner.

By the time they left, after changing into our old clothes and cleaning up the kitchen, none of us felt like settling down for the rest of the day. Such company had depressed every one of us. "Kids," Dad said, "those people are programmed to always feel like victims and to complain about everything they can find lacking. When that husband can find another teaching position, I bet they will leave this area, only to find things just as bad, or worse, wherever they go."

"Right now," he continued, "we need a diversion, something good to erase the taste of their dreary outlook. Since the moon will be up early this evening, let's finish eating the leftover pieces of pie and then go on a trail ride and breathe some cool fresh air." The idea was a good one; negative vibes faded away as we climbed on the horses bareback and a couple of bikes and went for a long country ride on the main ranch trail to the west.

The horses made tentative, low snorts, as though saying that this was fun and most unexpected. Even the dog and the cat followed us up the hill and over the well-worn trail to look and listen for any night creatures that might be hiding beneath the grass and brush. It was overwhelmingly lovely, and it surely made each of us feel warm and contented. Before we returned to the barn, the moon came up over the far hills and painted the whole ranch with a clear, creamy glow. I reflected again how sad it was that our guests were incapable of understanding how wonderful life really was out here. All was fine in this place beautiful and tranquil place, often called the "Valley of the Bears".

Chapter 20
Just Say "Yes" and Don't Look Back

I should have been the leader of this pack of kids, at least when Dan wasn't home, but it didn't work out that way. Since I'd given birth to two children in close succession and then had two more nine and ten years later, it was hard to keep even the simplest basic rules and decisions going my way. Since Dad was seldom home for our battles, it was I who often found myself outmatched in voice, votes, and influence. Plus there were always too many priorities, different schedules and other "wants" floating around. It was often harder to be decisive and give a "Yes" or "No" on small stuff than on big decisions. Since Nancy was away at college, and Dan Jr. soon would be, it was sometimes two or three to my one vote. Three different "wants" can lead to a real free-for-all; my authority waxed and waned with the kids' well planned, often exuberant proposals. Each one of these precocious kids would have been a great snake-oil salesman. It became obvious my life would be easier if I just went with the flow and said "Yes."

Doug and Jeff didn't always have real "wants." Sometimes I couldn't even figure out what their demands really were for, and maybe they didn't know either. Demands to do something "fun," or to "have friends over," could fill a boring, out-on-summer-vacation day. When the kids demanded more fun than cleaning their rooms, perhaps they reckoned the talk with me would escalate into a fine battle that they could win or at least enjoy fighting. "Did you boys eat enough breakfast this morning?" I sometimes asked. "Maybe you're just hungry."

Occasionally there was anarchy, but at least I had age and size on my side. Teddy Roosevelt once advocated, "Speak softly and carry a big stick"? Well, I'd get no work done if I carried a big stick around, and I could hardly talk to them softly when often I didn't even know where they were on the range. It usually took yelling just to find them on our seven hundred acres.

When home, the older two always joined the fight against me, questioning my authority in many devious ways. Over and over they scolded, "You never used to let us do that—those little guys are getting away with murder. Why don't you make them behave? You treat them like a grandmother would."

That really did me in because the charge was partly accurate. Although I was not going to accept that I was grandmotherly, I was getting older, day by day, and I had relaxed a number of rules with the hopeful thought that the two younger kids might turn out just as well if I became mostly blind, deaf, and forgetful about small, trivial infractions. Would my laxness really matter ten years later?

I should have at least bargained and bribed each supplicant by demanding they do more work. Finally, after a friend of the boys visited and remarked to them about how messy their house was, I created a scene and shouted, "It's much more fun to be a doer instead of a whiner. Blast it, look at this house! I'm not the janitor and maid for this whole chaotic place! What you've got is new management here. From now on, every Saturday morning, all of you at home are to clean your rooms, change your sheets, and hand me your dirty wash before you even think about any movies or trips to the beach, and that's final! Haven't you ever noticed how often I scream as company drives up the lane, 'Stall 'em outside, don't let them come in yet!' while I gather up newspapers, dirty glasses, dishes in the living room, and a thousand other things you've spread around? My Saturday crusade demands that we clean until noon and then have the treat of a fun afternoon.

It didn't end there. The younger two kids began to pull the same tricks as the older ones and put their own spin on requests. Jeff and Doug would ask, "Why can't we go see the movie? You're letting the big kids go." Or, "Yes, we are old enough to go to the lake alone," or, in the voice of a demand, "How come they get to stay up until ten and we have to go to bed at eight?"

The ending comment that I disliked the most from the younger two was "You like them better than us." I developed a suspicion that the kids sometimes willfully prolonged debates just for cheap entertainment while I sputtered and babbled.

Often I wondered where I missed learning all the ways of saying no that many parents normally parrot. Most people have a whole drawer full of replies that really mean no but aren't technically no. They avoid the little word and pull out gems such as:

…well it depends…
…maybe later…
…perhaps for Christmas…
…let's get the Consumer's Guide…
…where would you put it?…
…it's too much money…
…I just don't know…
…I'll ask your father…
…it would make too much noise…
…you're too young…
…I'll think about it…
…your dad will have to think about it…
…we'd better find out the pros and cons….

I called these the "Impact Report people." Since they didn't like to make decisions or take action, they seldom did. By the time they finally decided, if indeed they ever did, they had often missed the boat: the kid who wanted a chemistry set was now forty years old. Delaying mechanisms were often safer, and the people who used them didn't make many mis-takes. The only mistake they made was missing out on the excitement and fun of taking thousands of chances—big ones, such as falling in love, exploring the world, and fulfilling dreams—or little ones, such as trying a new recipe for dinner or exploring a nearby mountain. Even some wrong turns might have been the best decisions.

I fell into the, "Let's do it now" extreme, and so, fortunately, did my partner. No research, no Impact Report, no procrastination, and, especially, no time to lose. It was always time for the show to begin, to go straight to the heart of the matter, to buy the rabbit and then make the hutch, to try adding one more job and see if there's still a way to get several hours to sleep, and to always try to say "Yes." If it doesn't work out, learn from the experience, but say "Yes" again right away to something else.

No one's perfect. I decided it took a bigger brain than mine when Doug came to beg for a large chemistry set. I procrastinated and finally told him, "Go ask your father." Dan, however, was often worse than I at saying "No"…

The younger two kids decided that the ranch, with its almost mall-sized parking area out back and its long easy trails over the lower hills, would be the perfect place to zoom around in a go-cart. Like their older brother Dan, Doug and Jeff now wanted wheels, not a horse. This re-quest didn't seem too extravagant to me, as I knew nothing about go-carts. The trouble was that their daddy found a special one for them that had been made by a creative college prof for his son. That son now drove real cars, and the prof agreed to sell the go-cart to Dan and the boys…and it came with no ordinary motor. This little red number had a huge engine behind the seat, and could hold Doug and Jeff side by side while flying recklessly fast up and down the lane, roaring over the hills, and doing "wheelies" around the parking area.

"Don't worry, Mom," they said in a comforting tone. " It's a great go-cart!"

"I can't help worrying," I quickly sniped. "And since you guys keep me busy days, I do all my worrying from 10:30 P.M. 'til 5:30 A.M. See these circles under my eyes like dark, deep craters?"

In the meantime, older brother Danny improvised a different (and safer) version of summer fun. He and a friend named Roger found an old car they could have for free, including free delivery. They intended to take it completely apart to learn how cars work and how they are made; they were even given the mechanic's manual for the old vehicle. Proceeding very systematically and carefully, they disassembled the car's motor, labeling every part with cards stuck on with lots of duct tape and then placing all the pieces on bed sheets beside the hay barn wall. Both boys became oblivious to everything around them except their car.

After working most of the summer, Danny and Roger finally put the car back together, and the engine actually started...sort of. The boys asked brother Douglas to steer the car down the lane while they stood on the running boards and studied how the many parts of the engine were behaving.

Roger and Danny didn't notice that Doug had to either sit very tall in order to look out the windshield through the steering wheel, or scrunch down to reach the brakes with his foot and not see where he was going—he couldn't do both at the same time.

As soon as the car reached the end of the parking area and the beginning of the hill, it started rolling down the lane. With its increasing speed, Doug managed to keep it straight for a bit without swerving, but then careened off the lane and into the shallow side-ditch and horse fence just before they reached Prefumo Canyon Road. Fortunately I had the station wagon up at the house and was able to help the boys tow their wreck back up the hill. Just before school began that fall they actually sold their car for fifty dollars and laughed and laughed about the car they'd "made and sold for a profit."

Danny probably never realized that I also got a lot of mileage out of that car project. Too often summer vacations were boring blank slates, with few town or school activities for the kids. That summer, Danny was completely content to hang out at home. For him and Roger, the car became like an addictive big-kid Tinker Toy set, while for me it became a hassle-free time. Not once for the whole summer vacation did my oldest son whine, "There's nothing to do," or, "Let's go somewhere—anywhere but here."

Chapter 21
Hunters and Their Prey

As the saying goes, "We all march to different drummers." When our friends John and Helen came from Oregon to visit us for a few days, it wasn't long before we understood what that saying really meant. They were traveling around California on vacation, and John, determined to go home with a deer, had immediately bought a hunting license for our state. He had inquired at two sporting stores in town about places to hunt, and one of the clerks had mentioned Prefumo Canyon, the same area where John and Helen were staying as our houseguests! Consequently, John spent much of the first day of his visit hiking the steep terrain of Prefumo Canyon by himself.

The following day, John asked me if Dan and I would like to go see the pretty spot he thought would be an excellent place to shoot a deer. It had a small pond and a tiny stream flowing from a natural spring, and a nearby copse would serve as the perfect blind, allowing us to sit quietly and wait for the deer to come and drink.

At first I said no, that we didn't like to hunt, and that we preferred shooting with a camera to shooting with a gun. John did not find that amusing. "Aw, come on," he said, " Dan will be home in time, and Helen can fix dinner and watch the kids."

Suddenly, I crafted a sneaky plan and told him we'd go. I had resolved to show this nice couple a good time, and we were all going to Hearst Castle the next day, but there was no way he'd be shooting a deer on our ranch if I could help it. As soon as Dan opened the door, I quietly filled him in on my designs.

Just as John described, a short way up the canyon in a sheltered spot on the lower right side of the hill, there was a little spring feeding a shallow pond. The pond was surrounded by moss-covered rocks, and a stream trickled down from it to a creek below. A host of oak trees, thick brush, and green grasses stood watch nearby. John showed us a faint trail he expected the deer would use and pointed out some deer tracks around the water's edge.

Dan and I carefully hid near John on the other side of the trail a short way up the hill. I subtly removed a fistful of small stones from my pocket, put my two hands on the ground behind my back, and set the small stones there. A number of other pebbles were already beside me in the grass.

With John and his gun in front of me and a bit to one side, I carefully made a fist around a stone, and, while keeping my hand behind my back, I tossed it up the hill. Every three or four minutes I tossed another stone and prayed that it would create enough noise for a deer's keen, velvety ears to hear. Only once did John give a quick look around at the slight plunk. Finally the sun set, and it became too dark for us to stay. Either there were no deer nearby that afternoon, or I had sabotaged John and granted a deer another day of running free in those mountains, drinking the cool spring water and eating the green grass beside it.

During hunting season, a number of hunters routinely scurried up the canyon road in cars or on foot, and we often heard the echoing sounds of deer rifles. The wild birds near the house instinctively sensed danger. We, too, always felt a bit uneasy, both for ourselves and for our animals, about the stray bullets of unskilled hunters.

I guess the hunting instinct is somewhere in the genes of some people. After all, during much of the known or surmised history of man, he was primarily a hunter. Dan and I must have evolved from berry pickers and seed gatherers—and if not that, perhaps an ancient sea-faring people, since our love of oceans, rivers, and lakes was almost as deep as our love of the land. We were surely given few predatory genes.

Though we weren't hunters, there was always the question that John and other hunters brought up—what's the difference? They would argue, "You raise animals for slaughter, and your family eats meat." Well, the big difference in my mind was that domestic animals were usually killed instantly, whereas wild animals were often horribly wounded and died slow, excruciating deaths.

Besides that, there was a question of motivation. Quite a few of the hunters here were city folk, with brightly colored plaid shirts, vivid caps, new hiking shoes, and brand new hunting licenses in their pockets. Many hunted just for the "sport" of killing, not the need for food. Of course, guns don't really give their targets a sporting chance. If a hunter is going to kill a living creature for sport, that animal should have an equal sporting right to shoot back and defend itself.

I was quite sure that nature knew how to do her job far better than government agencies, who assumed they should decide which species were expendable, which should be decimated, and which should be enlarged. Politics take over, and decisions are influenced by the gun lobbies, which have their roots in a more primitive era.

Now, pressures to destroy animal habitats for additional human purposes—lumber, mining, cities, homes, factories—are intensifying. The whole world is imperiled, with living creatures, forests, deserts, fertile lands, and even clean air and water disappearing on an increasingly greater scale. All living things are interrelated, and government agencies and others just don't know or understand all the billions and billions of pieces to this increasingly intertwined planet. Maybe it's time to let nature once again have more say and try to restore the wild, natural areas. Where possible, let the only hunters be hawks, owls, coyotes, foxes, wolves, bears, and the countless other animals that help keep nature in balance.

And while cruelty to animals is on my mind, let me also mention the debate over fur coats and other daily acts of unbelievable cruelty to animals. Fewer people now buy fur coats than in years past, but this remains an extremely cruel way for a human to keep warm or to display wealth. A mink coat requires the fur of dozens of wild mink caught in leg traps or "domestic" minks raised in cages to suffer until killed.

The responsibility for a compassionate world falls on every human being, at home, in the immediate neighborhood, and wherever a person finds himself or herself, to act, even in small ways, to lessen needless suffering. Write letters, vote for the more humane and well trained candidate, pick up stray dogs, stay away from circuses and rodeos that use animal acts. May the time come soon when all people understand animals' capacity to feel pain and suffer and when all people will treat creatures kindly. Animals have only one life to live, and as said before, it's people who determine what their precious lives will be like.

Chapter 22
The Wandering Prince

Though we needed time to grieve after Treve's death, the fact was that we needed to find another ranch dog rather soon, since shortly before we lost Treve, a large, unfamiliar truck with high wooden sides had chugged up to our barn door on a dark night to steal either hay, saddles, grain, or all three. Treve's urgent barking had prevented the theft by waking us up in time to turn on the barnyard flood lights and watch Treve fulfill his self-appointed duty of escorting the two men and their rickety, rattling truck back down to the end of our lane and out to the road.

The memory of the potential theft prompted me to suggest, "Let's get a German shepherd this time—they're intelligent, and they look like they mean business."

Dan felt the same way. "Not a bad idea," he replied. "You and the kids would be a little more protected during the day and when I'm out teaching at night. Life isn't getting any safer. Why don't you check out the pound today, if you have time."

As always, the pound had a huge assortment of animals. Almost every dog was barking at the top of his lungs as I moved up and down the walkways between the rows of cages. Dogs at the pound almost always bark this way, obviously shouting, "Please save me! I want out, and I want to go home." Dogs of many sizes, shapes, colors, and personalities jumped at the wire gates or stood on their hind feet with their noses against the wire to try and reach me.

There were no German shepherds in any of the cages, and I should have gone right home and come back in a few days to make my choice from a mostly new crop of strays. However, a gigantic coal-black dog locked eyes with me, and I stopped to let him lick my fingers through the wire mesh. The card hooked to his gate gave his age as three. He was named Prince and had been given up when his owners moved to a new city. He had been in the pound for over a week.

I quickly pondered, "Wouldn't this dog's color, size, and big-dog voice deter intruders?" He was clearly a friendly, sweet, and playful guy, and I immediately decided he was very intelligent, though I couldn't say on what basis. He certainly had room for lots of brains in that enormous head.

I asked to use the phone. Happily, Dan was in his office, and he readily agreed I should give Prince a home. The pound's information on Prince stated that he was a very fine purebred Newfoundland, but I didn't care about his pedigree. Of course, he was almost pony-sized, but how could I let such a stately, obviously intelligent black beauty be executed? I filled out the forms, paid for his release, and stroked his surprisingly soft coat.

Prince was delighted to jump into the station wagon, whose entire back seat could barely accommodate him. This debonair fellow's head came almost to the ceiling! All the way to Oak Hills he slobbered all over the back windows as he pushed his nose out to sniff the air, perhaps an attempt memorize the route to his new home.

I decided that a rope might not suffice to keep him in the yard, since those large teeth of his could probably chew through a rope in no time, leaving him free to make an almost effortless leap over the fence and roam the land at will. Instead, I left him in the house and went to the barn to get some goat chains we had used years before. As I untangled the chains and fastened several lengths together out on the lawn, Doug and Jeff came up the lane from the school bus. I warned them not to let "the big guy" out as they made through the yard for the house, but when they tried to open the door "just a crack," Prince bounded out and frolicked around them, licking their faces and treating them like long-lost brothers. Both boys dropped their books and laughed as they tried to keep him from pushing them over. Finally, picking up his books and scattered papers, Jeff declared, "This dog is no German shepherd. He's the size of a pony, and he almost knocked me flat!"

Prince's wild and loving exuberance actually made me pause. It's fine that dogs recognize the possibilities for joy in life and that the present moment looms large in their minds. It's also wonderful to have a dog that enjoys humans, young and old. But would this majestic, slightly disheveled, long-haired fellow not greet burglars and other strangers the same way—no discrimination and no pause for evaluation before demonstrating total acceptance and love?

Smoochie sat frozen and breathless upon seeing this black giant come galumphing up to him suddenly in the back yard. Not until the dog got close, wagging his tail with so much enthusiasm that he ended up wagging his whole body, did the cat rise and lash out at him with claws and warning growls. The guy just wandered past the angry cat and inspected the rest of the yard.

At first, Prince spent the nights and part of each day in the kitchen because I didn't want him to take off in search of one of his former homes. The rest of the time I chained him to a strong clothesline post or walked him around the sheds and barns. It was immediately obvious that the dog thought cats were great and that he would try to make friends with Smoochie. For a few days Smoochie stood still, fur on end, and swatted at Prince. Eventually, though, the cat decided that Prince was just another dog—albeit a very large one—and that he meant no harm. She even let Prince lick her occasionally.

This huge bundle of energy couldn't be chained up forever, yet as soon as I turned our new family member loose, there were problems. Prince had never been around livestock, and he kept hurrying out to the pasture to chase and try to play with the horses as well as the cow and her calves. A couple of swift and fortunately off-target kicks from the horses, plus my angry yells, convinced Prince to find other friends. Still, he remained curious about these large, foreign animals, as though he wondered if there just wasn't some way to get these even larger monsters to play.

One thing I never kept him from doing was jumping into the horse watering troughs, which were still the three old bathtubs we had found at the dump. Prince jumped in the tubs, lay down, and then rolled around, splashing out most of the water and wrecking the floats that we used to keep the water at the proper level. If the day was warm, Prince took these baths a number of times, since after each of these baths, he could roll in the dirt, weeds, and prickers of the horse fields or in the straw and dung of the corral. His long, luxurious hair immediately became a wet, tangled mass of stickers, burrs, dirt, and manure. Shambling up to the house, long tail wagging and body wiggling, he would smile and pant at the same time, clearly declaring, "I'm a bit tired, but I've had the most marvelous morning!"

Tub baths in the house are one of the things I remember most vividly about our rowdy black Prince, probably because he had to be washed and brushed so often. At least two of us had to join forces for the job. Then, before Prince could shake himself after he jumped out of the tub, we had to throw multiple bath towels over his back, rush him down the hall to the outside door, and chain him outside.

I continued chaining him in the yard and letting him loose only part of the time, and he continued to sleep in the kitchen at night, because when he stayed outside too long, the chain sometimes became tangled in the large trumpet vine against the fence. However, my feeling that Prince needed to roam free part of the day became a fact and soon led to some wild escapades in the lower reaches of the Valley: Prince's adventures soon made me reluctant to even admit that I knew, much less owned, this drifter. If you went down to the end of our long ranch lane to the Prefumo Canyon Road and turned left, you'd come to the Los Osos Valley Road. If you turned right onto Los Osos Valley Road, you would reach what is now called Madonna Road, and on both sides of that road, subdivisions were being built. Laguna Lake was on the western side adjacent to some of the new houses.

Prince decided that enthusiastically greeting the builders and potential buyers of the homes was a delightful pastime. Unfortunately, this was usually after he'd had a good swim in the lake. Most dogs seem to like to shake water out of their dripping coats, often upon any nearby people and will even go out of their way to do so...Prince was a happy and vigorous shaker.

As landscape people for the new houses installed new lawns and sprinkler systems, I received more and more furious and frantic phone calls. I was soon well known as the owner of the monster from up on the hill.

"Your dog just made my lawn look like a plowed field with a pond in the middle," came one complaint. "It seems he tried to find the best place to create a dog-sized lake, and then lay there under the sprinkler, got covered with both mud and new grass seed, and then finished the job by rubbing himself off on our new back screen door and the wall of the house."

Globs of mud were tracked all over many new sidewalks and driveways, and I began to wonder if those callers would ever regain their composure or get the mud stains off their walls. With each phone call, I tried to understand why no one was furious or demanded money for repairs, though one lady gave a clue—"I can't just shoo him away; he's too sweet, happy, and friendly, and it's such a hilarious sight to watch him lying on his belly or back and rolling in all the soft, cool mud. However, I'd better get out there and hose down the house and walkway before my husband gets home. Once he plants our lawn this will have to stop."

I ordered a nametag and collar for Prince, but our vagabond managed to slip out of the collar a couple of times and take off, leaving his chains tangled in the trumpet vine. I also tried hard to make Prince a house-dog, but he felt it a prison and was terribly bored following me around from room to room. With the comings and goings of a family of six, it was almost impossible to keep the porch and kitchen doors closed tightly, and Prince increasingly managed to escape to far off places.

When he left the tract houses before I got there, days and days sometimes went by before I could find my tramp. Soon I began to have to bail him out of the pound, and that was not cheap. Neither was the time and gas I used driving all over town and countryside looking for him. Once, the owners of a hamburger drive-in south of town let him stay for most of a week and never tried to phone us about our charming man-about-town, even though our phone number was clearly displayed on his tag. Obviously, he had been in hamburger heaven the whole time, and everyone had enjoyed him…and fed and fed him. I was told that many customers had bought him his own wieners, hamburgers, and French fries, and even made us sure he had water to drink.

I had to face it: Prince would never agree to be a full-time ranch dog. Since he wasn't allowed to chase the cat or the livestock, the children were in school all day, and mom and dad were too busy to spend much time with him outside, this thinking dog had decided to find his own diversions.

Prince never seemed to seek a girl-friend. His passions were water, lots of friendly people, fast-food, or, perhaps, a longing for one of his former homes, if it might be found. What kind of homes had he had? One of the staff members at the pound finally confided to me that several owners had "brought him back to them," but the staff weren't always told why. Having had multiple homes might have taken away his sense of place and his loyalty to a single family. He enjoyed many loose bonds of affection and friendship, but he had no sense of protective loyalty to just one person or household. For Prince, perhaps it felt normal to have one nice foster family after another.

In an earlier era and a far more rural setting, such as the Ojai Valley, the town of Dan's and my childhood, perhaps this enormous, bright, and social dog could have survived, become a mascot for the whole community and visited countless people, since many lawns were old, and the doors and walls of houses far from new. That wouldn't work on our ranch, and I was finally at the end of my rope. Dear, amiable Prince had a final tub bath, a good brushing and combing, and another ride back to the pound. He greeted the staff happily, like they were old buddies. I left him there after getting their promise not to put him down—that I would come and get him if they couldn't find him a home. In spite of all the Princely problems, I drove off with tears in my eyes.

Miracles do occur, and this is a true ranch story that had a wonderful ending as far as I know. The pound boarded him for a few extra days, and finally he had another chance. As reported to me by a staff member at the pound, it sounded grand. She said, "Prince was finally given a home by a lady newspaper reporter who owns a topless red car. She told us she would remove the goldfish from her garden pool so that Prince could use it as his own spa. And one of our staff has seen her several times, driving about the county in that red car with the gigantic black dog sitting beside her, his ears pinned back by the wind, and a big grin on his face."

I liked to believe that my intelligent and wandering Prince continued to take a leading role with that lady reporter. He had a commanding presence with his awesome size, thick and long black coat, friendly bright eyes, and smile. Always enthusiastic to meet new people, travel, and sense the intelligent conversations around him, my charming Prince probably helped the reporter get more than one hard-to-land interview, and, just perhaps, Prince did some of the interviewing himself by judging the conversations.

Chapter 23
Boomerang

After Prince left, I had to go once again to the pound and get a "good ranch watch-dog." And, once again, I came home with a big dog who possessed no known traits of being a watch or guard-dog. However, this one would become one of the all-time favorites of the family throughout his long life.

He was a large dog who looked a lot like Treve, and the pound had listed him as a "two-year-old shepherd." The fellow had a collie's white fur ruff around his neck and chest and a thick, orange-beige coat over the rest of him. His big brown eyes seemed to absorb every detail of these surroundings, the pound staff, and me. Certain that this dog would be similar to Treve in reasoning and high standards of behavior, such as tolerance, loyalty, and a million other fine attributes, he came home with me.

At first, he was so relieved to be rescued from the pound and so happy to be with a house and family, that it seemed enough. As I let him out of the car, he pulled me toward the house, as the kids opened the door to see this new member of the family. His past life must have been satisfying, because he immediately showed a friendly, confident, and trusting view of all of us.

Like many of our animals, he also came with a number of uncertainties and some sadness. At first he seemed to be thinking, "I simply can't understand how I lost my family and ended up caged with all those wildly barking dogs. And the place had bad odors, even frightening ones." But somehow, he quickly figured out that this was now his permanent home. And it took but a short time before all of us felt our new family member was almost human, and we loved him as much as he loved each of us. Lady Lu was still with us, but, as I've mentioned, she never really was "all there." Her beauty shined brightly, but not her brain. She wasn't even affectionate.

Some dogs just seemed to get the feel of the family, our thoughts, wishes, and moods, better than others. They then try to match those moods, whether it is with excitement and action, lighthearted and happy fun, or sad and quiet times. Like Treve, this dog was sensitive yet enthusiastic, and quickly blended in with the family.

He needed to. Dan had a warped sense of humor in dealing with dogs, and made a lifelong practice of teasing them. He would make funny faces at them, pucker up his lips like a fish, grin with a wide-mouthed growl or glare, and call to a dog, "Here kitty, kitty." He tousled their hair and patted the sides of their jaws back and forth. I was sure it confused the dogs, yet, for some crazy reason, they all loved him dearly and greeted him like a long-lost friend each and every day when he came home.

The pound hadn't had a name for this dog, so he must have been picked up as a "stray with no collar." When he began to come back so often and quickly after chasing a tennis ball or exploring the nearby fields and barns, we named him Boomerang. We felt certain that he would never leave and fail to come home, as Prince had done.

I don't believe Boom thought Lady Lu was top dog, in spite of her being present when he had arrived, but he didn't seem to want or care for the top position. I think he soon believed Dan and I shared the position of top dog. He would be next down the line in the hierarchy, since he clearly wanted to protect and befriend the kids and help me keep track of them and the whole ranch. With his intelligence and love, he became a great watchdog.

If Nancy came home and went riding, Boomerang went along. He enjoyed exploring far ahead of her as they went, but he was always right behind her and the horse when they arrived back at the barn. If Danny went out hiking or started working on a car, Boom stayed with him to keep him company. He worried about the younger boys and tried to figure out how to manage them when they fired up their over-powered go-cart or climbed the bales of hay in the barn with friends.

This dog also shared my love of the barns, especially in stormy weather. Thunderstorms were rare, but seemed louder and more scary when not mixed in with buildings, streets, cars, and buses in town, while lightning sometimes came in awesome, blinding flashes. These infrequent storms often came up the Valley from the south. A wind picked up force and rattled the tin-roofs of the sheds and barns; it blew tree limbs around, and made any oat fields that hadn't been grazed into beautiful "waves of grain." This was especially true of the big field below the house and to the east. The man who leased the ranch for cattle seemed to forget about that field, and the oats there stood tall until he finally brought some of his Herefords to graze the yellow oats during the fall months.

On the other side of the oat field and lane, dark clouds would gather and the wind increase. All the horses seemed to know when a storm was coming, and with heads high and their manes and tails flying, they raced around and around their fields in play, snorting, whinnying, and kicking up their heels.

One evening, with lots of rain on the way, I told Boom, "It's going to be a horrible job to milk and feed the horses and cow tonight. I think I'll feed the horses in the shed right now, even if it's earlier than usual." The dog got up when I did and followed me out as I put flakes of hay in the wheelbarrow.

Although the small shed next to the corral provided little shelter for them, the calf and the cow were also in high spirits. Dan would feed the cow later, but I gave her a bit of alfalfa. When finished, Boom and I dashed back into the hay barn to sit on a bale of hay, side by side. He seemed to rejoice at being with me as we watched the first rain fall and heard the glorious sound of the drops as they began to come down faster and harder on the big tin roof. Sitting like that in the barn and listening to the music of the rain made up for the fact that in the house, we scarcely heard the rain at all—somehow, the house's heavy slate roof deadened the sound, and only the rain gutters at the corners of the house gurgled the good news of rain.

During a downpour, Smoochie was usually there in the barn too, staying warm and dry, and often hunting mice. The cat found any wetness distasteful, and always tried to put off going back to the house until the rain passed. Both dog and cat seemed to enjoy my talking to them, and Boom soon learned to understand many of my words and short sentences, such as: "I'll feed the horses" "Let's go" or "Where's Danny?"

However, we all soon realized that Boom wasn't a water dog and that he didn't even like to get wet in a rain. He also wasn't used to the ocean and became crazy with fear for our safety when all of us waded into the waves and swam out beyond the breakers at Avila Beach. Since the whole skinny family swam in that cold ocean about ten months of the year, the first few times we took Boom he frantically barked and barked and finally dashed into the surf and swam out to "save us." Boom was actually a pain in the ocean, because his front paws had sharp nails, and he came up to us with paws flailing as he tried to herd us back to shore. I never found out whether he would have pulled on an arm or whether he just wanted to turn us back toward shore, because we always swam away from him as quickly as we could.

However, to be sociable and, perhaps, to please us, this was soon eating all kinds of foods, especially those proffered him by the kids. "Look, Mom, Boom is eating a piece of my pear!" Boom seemed to enjoy eating everything from spinach to string beans—often sneaked to him under the table at dinnertime. Since he appreciated and wanted to promote or share any silly nonsense, I'm sure he ate some of the food just for the laughs and attention it brought.

This dog was also a great companion and listener, with the ability to make each of us his special friend. Again, as it had been when Treve was with us, I noticed that gallon-sized cookie jars emptied frustratingly fast when one or two of the boys sat with Boom on the back step, an arm around his neck and holding a fistful of cookies to share with him, often while relating their woes at school that day. Boom would lick the boy's face, and he probably wished he could say, "You'd feel better if we went for a hike."

Other times, Boom just sat across my feet in calm fellowship when I sat down to write checks or fold wash. He was just too human to not get invited into the house whenever he was dry and fairly free of dirt or mud.

Most of all, Boom had a daily wish to enjoy life and tried to make the most of any glimmer of fun or laughter. He knew happiness was in the here and now. With his quick insight, if I laughed, he would all but laugh with me and try to prolong the lighthearted times, wagging his tail and watching my face. Living up to his name of Boomerang, he would also fetch a stick or ball whenever anyone took time to throw one; or he sometimes just rolled around on his back in hopes one of us would scratch his tummy or wrestle with him.

When dogs are a close part of the family and are loved, petted, talked to, and have a varied, chance-to-learn existence, they, just like children, become more confident and knowledgeable. Boom dearly loved having adventures and just seeing and doing new things. He visited friends with us, went to the ocean or a lake when we did, and when the car would remain cool enough, just came along with me while I ran errands in town or transported kids to or from their activities.

Going out to the pound or Animal Control center is always such a sad experience, although it can become great if one finds an animal to give a home to. On the trip when I found Boomerang, I acquired a wonderful new family member who needed saving, but many dogs end up there because their owners never should have had a dog in the first place. Buying a "cute" puppy and then not caring for the dog as he becomes an adult or gets old, is inhumane. So is buying a purebred dog as just a possession, like a fur coat or an ornament. Pets are completely at the mercy of humans, and too often face cruel neglect.

More and more people are also buying or getting "guard dogs" at the pound, and these are often among the most abused and pitiful. We met a man and his wife who bought a German Shepherd because they wanted a "theft-deterrent." He kept the dog chained and completely alone, day and night, in the back yard. The dog suffered, and burglars just broke in the front door of the house and stole a valuable coin collection and many treasured antiques. If the dog had been a family member, whether in the house or loose inside a fenced yard, he might have saved their belongings.

On one occasion, we went to buy some fruit trees, and in the owner's orchard we saw a lonely, scared Doberman, recently acquired from the pound and locked in the orchard "so no one will steal my nursery trees." As I knelt down and hugged the Doberman, I could see she was ever so thin, shaking like a leaf, and had no water. She, too, was kept in her lonely, frightening jail both day and night with no idea of what had happened to her family.

I've seen other dogs tragically left to guard car lots, big estates, and industrial buildings. Too often they are kept on twenty-four-hour daily duty and never receive love or companionship. Those dogs, chosen by their owners to be guards because they were thought to look like guard animals, would have done a far better job, more intelligently and willingly, if they had remained in a family circle, even if for only one shift each day. Boomerang became a shepherd of his flock—his family—and would guard us even if his life were at stake, but it would be through love, loyalty, and caring. I plan to work with a well run Humane Society if I ever find the time—most can use the extra help for the proper placement of their animals in kind and loving homes.

Chapter 24
An Apple a Day

September was a summer-like month on the central California coastal lands, and the apple crop was being harvested in the orchards in See Canyon. Apple-buying day almost always became an all-day affair with a beach party at Avila first, and I always picked a weekend day when Dan could go with us.

We trudged back to the car about mid-afternoon, somewhat pink from the extra-long day in the sun, and with damp, tangled, sandy hair and wet bathing suits, and no showers available, we pulled on shirts and jeans over our suits, tried to find our sandals, and then drove to See Canyon. On both sides of the canyon road, orchards of trees were decorated with apples, like red, green, or yellow Christmas tree ornaments. The fruit hung so heavy that many of the limbs had been propped up with wooden poles. We soon located our favorite farm and stopped. A number of large boxes, piled high with apples for sale, were waiting on wooden tables and on the ground beside a shed. The farmer or his wife always greeted us and handed each of us an apple to "test" for its juicy sweetness and crispness, while we tried to decide which two boxes looked the most fresh and full. The boxes were then taken to the back end of the station wagon, often beside our current dogs.

Each year, after buying the apples, we had a big discussion: Should we go home the rest of the way on the slow but beautiful route through the rest of See Canyon, over the mountains, and down to Oak Hills Ranch on the other side, or should we take the quick and easy way and drive back toward Avila and get on the freeway? By then the whole clan was pretty itchy with dried salt water and sand on their skin and hair, and the sun had disappeared behind the mountains to the west. About three times out of four, the vote was for the quick route home on the freeway.

Everyone then helped unload—shaking the sand from clothes, spreads, and towels, carrying empty Coke bottles, picnic baskets, and fishing poles to the screened porch or the kitchen, and Dan then carrying the heavy apple boxes to the long kitchen counter.

About half the apples, which I judged to be almost perfect and extra large, were set aside on the screen porch for lunches, after-school snacks, and for cooking. The rest would go into the huge deep-freeze in the form of apple sauce, Apple Betty, and apple pies ready for baking at a later time.

The air became thick and sweet with the fragrance of apple peelings, cores, and seeds piling up in the sink. The scent was accentuated by the cinnamon, nutmeg, and sugar added to the big stew-pots on the stove, pots almost full to the top with bubbling "plop-plop-plop" apple slices. In addition to the scent, I could almost taste and smell the apple air in the hot kitchen. Jars for the applesauce lined the counter, and shallow glass baking dishes waited for the Apple Betty or apple pie desserts that would be put in the freezer. Even with the days still warm and no snows on the horizon, it became a nice ritual on a fall weekend for each of the twenty-five years we lived on the Central Coast of California.

"Give me a simple, somewhat rustic life!" Fall was a good time for such shared thoughts, and in that season I found myself thinking more about our lack of "luxuries," our plain living and emphasis on family, kids, and animals. I seemed to flourish in this Spartan life and almost always welcomed the lack of any ostentatious or fancy things. However, in the county's booming economic times, it was becoming harder for the children not to have their endless "wants" gratified. They noticed classmates with more and more, and on TV they saw a world of goodies constantly displayed.

The kids should have made the same decision that our dog Treve had made when he saw a couple of dogs eating on the TV screen. He walked up to the screen, couldn't find the dogs, carefully looked around both sides of the TV set, and then tried to reach and investigate the back of the TV. He made the sound decision: there was nothing there—certainly not anything concrete and of value.

But what is enough? I certainly valued most things I had acquired, and I could easily have been called a pack rat, as many long owned possessions seemed OK to me. Those things were usually belongings that might come in handy "someday" and that were functional…like the two extra frying pans I kept in a closet along with a two-slice toaster and all kinds of old ranch jackets. At any rate, my agricultural work, and the feelings of self-reliance and frugality it inspired, seemed to make sense. There was no need to keep up with the neighbors or anyone else. Buying boxes of apples and having a day beside the ocean still made for the best of times.

Yet that day of apple-buying and apple-cooking actually helped make up for a rather unfortunate time several weeks earlier. Danny had read in the paper that field-workers were needed to help harvest string beans down the road near the town of Arroyo Grande. He had some purchase in mind that would take extra funds, and he asked Nancy and his dad if it wouldn't be interesting to go pick beans for a few days. Dad agreed, thinking it might be a rather good learning experience for them.

The three of them slaved as hard as they could the first day, had their picked beans weighed, and couldn't believe they had worked all day for something like six dollars each. All three had painful backaches. Nevertheless, they wondered if they couldn't do better, and they decided to try one more time. Their total income the second day was no higher than the first day.

Coming home by way of the Edna Valley, south of town, an exhausted Dad became careless and let the right wheels of the car drift off the road. The car wasn't going very fast, so they all said, but the car tipped over in some soft gravel and came to rest in a shallow ditch. A sheepish and very apologetic father called to ask me to come and pick them up at the local garage. No one was hurt, but two days of bean picking for a few dollars resulted in car repair bills of over four hundred—a fortune at the time…and they didn't even bring home a bag of beans.

Chapter 25
The More the Merrier

The dogs often slept in the kitchen on stormy nights, or when they had to dry off from soapy baths. I tried to make the newly clean dogs feel better about their scrub by suggesting, with great enthusiasm, "Oh, don't you look all shiny and clean—you're beautiful! Come, stay in the house today and tonight." Ranch dogs usually didn't stay inside the house at night, and, at times, they were too muddy to be inside during the day. Often they slept in the barn, in the open garage, or on the front porch, and, with their keen hearing, they did a bit of work by watching over the ranch and the livestock at night. If anyone came up the lane, or if a horse or calf got loose and was wandering around in the yard or on the lane, they barked until we awoke. Boomerang even came around the house to our bedroom window to bark. I don't think Prince ever barked, but the rest of the animals seemed to enjoy their "guard duty."

About then, the two younger boys suddenly decided they weren't satisfied with having only large dogs share our family life, and my two pint-sized negotiators came to say, "We have an idea" (Jeff and Doug said that only when their idea was either going to cost money, take a lot of my time, dirty the house, or all three). Bingo! This was an "all three." They presented a well-organized and well-thought-out proposition, said in such a rush by Doug that he finished their proposal before I could interrupt.

"We've been thinking—wouldn't it be a good idea if all of us could have a little, 'ol house dog'? You know, one that could be in the house all the time and not get all dirty. A puppy would be fun. He could sleep in our room, and we'd only let him out on the lawn during the day. Can you take us out to the pound and see what they've got? We have some money saved. How much does just a little puppy cost? How about it?"

At first, I tried a little collective bargaining, though I realized I was being skillfully manipulated. "Who's going to feed this dog? Are you willing to take it outside when it has to piddle? Puppies have to piddle ever so often, both night and day!" I finished by asking, "Boys, tell me, just how much money is 'some money'?"

Actually, their request sounded reasonable to me. It was true that the big dogs were usually full of dirt and burrs, and there was always some mud around the watering tubs. Mud dried between the pads of the dogs' feet, only to come off later in the house. All the dogs got lots of pats and hugs, but they weren't like a "clean little cuddly dog on a bed." They won. They had a point and I didn't need to let them down.

Since I found no little dogs at the pound, each day I read the pet advertising section of the paper to the boys. Finally, there was an ad boasting "Small, poodle-type puppies, $35 each." I took the boys to see them. Even I could tell this litter wasn't all-poodle. Father had been some other small breed, but the mom was a small poodle, and the puppies looked as if they would probably stay small enough to be house dogs. One of them was ever so lively and kept trying to climb up on the boys' laps while they giggled and sat on the kitchen floor to play with them. These puppies had been kept outside and had been brought in only for showing and a sales pitch. I pointed out to the boys that the price was about double what they'd brought, and that I had little to spare that month.

"How about our washing the car for you to earn the rest? It's pretty dirty," Doug suggested.

"You can try washing the car, but puppies are a lot of work morning, noon and night. And he'll have to have his shots and some other attention at the vet." Oh well, I had been dreaming when I had thought the demands for additional pets would diminish as the kids got older. It didn't, but at least none of the boys craved horses.

The puppy came home with us. I knew very well who would take the guy out most of the time, fix his meals, and feed him. Puppies and puddles come as a package, and I would have to take him outside several times a night for a while or by morning there would be a large wet spot on the hall floor or dog blanket.

Fortunately, our cats arrived already housebroken by their mothers. One had insisted on going outside, and the others used the litter box in a laundry room or another "least public" place I could devise. No puppy ever came trained, and this one needed my almost continual help, patience, and attention. Still, the dining room carpet already needed replacing before long. Actually, I would have liked to purchase a new patience, as well as new carpeting. I had to add one more eye to the other eyes tackling the day's chores in order to grab the puppy the minute he looked like he was ready to puddle. Snatching him up suddenly usually frightened him into leaking as I lifted him, even if he hadn't planned on "going." It was worse than toilet-training the kids. Puppy buyers, beware—momma dogs leave this big job for you.

The nine-week old puppy, all curly black fur and bright dark button eyes, did seem a bit like a French poodle. I don't know if I or one of the older children thought up the name of "Jacque," but Jacque he became. Nothing had ever come of my dream of having unique, catchy, clever, historical, or literary names for the animals, but this name seemed to fit. Of course, the kids named a few and some arrived with names, but all of them had such unique personalities and behavior, they deserved better. It didn't help that everyone, including mom, wanted animals named within minutes of their joining the family.

This puppy was never daunted by the big dogs. While still a baby he gave a funny high-pitched growl, snapped his jaws, and tried to attack them. Boom and Lady Lu merely turned their heads and walked away with a studied nonchalance, or sat down to lick one of their paws, as though Jacque didn't exist. Smoochie also refused to run from Jacque and hissed and swatted him with both paws and claws out. After standing her ground until he stopped, she then wandered off to sit in a window sill and bake in the sun. Poor Jacque could never find out how to be top-dog or even get the animals to play with him. Fortunately, for quite a while, he had two boys who tossed balls and sticks and told him he was one good buddy.

With this going on I had forgotten that Jeff and Doug were still keeping two mud turtles tethered with long, small size chains fastened to small holes near the outer edge of their shell and at the other end to stakes in the ground beside an outside corner of the house where there was both sun and lots of shade. The turtles had a small muddy swimming hole that the boys made by sinking an old roasting pan in the ground, and they lumbered about on the lawn now and then, but mostly chose the shade and a wet spot. Living mostly on leftovers from the kitchen and garden, they chomped and munched salads of lettuce, celery and such, but I feared it might be because they were starving. It was hard to tell if they were becoming skin and bones inside their shells. Since part of a turtle's diet must be protein, had they eaten mostly creeping, flying, or swimming things down there in their mud hole by the lake?

Better late than never, I began a campaign to convince the boys to return the turtles to Laguna Lake and set them free. "You kids have little Jacque now," I explained. "You've taken the turtles to school for 'Show and Tell,' and you know they aren't eating right. How about taking them back to their real home today?" Finally they agreed, and Danny and his younger brothers escorted the turtles on a trip of kindness back to the edge of the lake.

Still, other family pets were always arriving with Doug and Jeff, and I became den-mother to them all. These included creatures such as frogs, tadpoles, huge moths, grasshoppers, and butterflies. I had once taught the older kids how I had caught fence lizards with a noose made from the top of a stalk of green oats when I was a small girl; now I taught the younger boys. Lizards seem to adjust to sitting in the palm of a hand and being stroked and can look quite comfortable there.

To catch a lizard, I stripped the oats off the stem and then made a slipknot noose at the small end. The brown lizards on the ranch fence posts and rocks seemed to like the feel of the little piece of grass moving across their bodies, so it was easy to put the noose over their heads. For an hour or two, there was often a lizard houseguest in a glass terrarium that the boys had brought back from the dump. However, finding flies, spiders, and insects that lizards would eat was a chore I refused to do, so these little lizards were carefully returned to the old barn wall or a wooden post soon after being caught—at least in time for them to catch their own dinner.

Goldfish, in both nice, large bowls and tiny bowls—both of which I considered cruel—showed up off and on as all three boys grew up. It was an era when businesses, like stores, fairs, and even filling stations, sometimes gave a small bowl of water holding one little goldfish for some promotion or when customers purchased something, like a tank of gas. These fish are supposed to be able to live for many, many years, but the boys never had them that long. Several bowls and fish had to be given away to school friends after I insisted that mom had cleaned the bowl for the very last time.

However, one day, when I went to collect the boys from school, they came out to the car oohing and aahing with excitement while carrying the biggest glass bowl I'd ever seen, and in it were several large goldfish. Their classmate buddy lagged behind them carrying a large box of fish food. Peter was moving to another state, so he had brought the fish to Show and Tell after his Mom had insisted some school chum would give his fish a home. The bowl and these fish stayed for a number of years on the dresser in the boys' bedroom. This time they were forced to help on clean-and-change-the-water day because the bowl was so heavy. Still, I didn't mind too much most of the time—those fish were rather fun and relaxing to watch.

Rodents came next. Not mice, thank heavens, for they were already all over the barns and in the fields. Mice are not odorless, by any means, and I would have no mice in the house, even a cute tiny field mouse, very much alive, that Smoochie brought to me one day.

Yet before long, three more different small pets became part of the family until they died of old age. The first of these interesting little animals came before the boys' little dog Jacque was even full-grown. The boys discovered some hamsters in some feed or pet store. It was the old routine over again. I got a little bear-like hamster to care for. However, this time, "he" or "she," whom Doug and Jeff named "Guy," had to have a good-sized cage, little watering and eating dishes, and proper food. He looked like a little bear and, I think, was called a Golden hamster. True to his name, he wore a nice golden coat with a white underside. The one they chose had bright and dark button eyes and seemed more alert than his brothers and sisters.

Fortunately, the clerk in the store assured me, "These guys are solitary animals and don't need a social life—it will be fine to have just one of them. Even when hamsters live wild, they don't live in communities and only come together to mate. Momma hamsters only stay with their young for several weeks." The clerk also mentioned hamsters like to sleep days and don't like to be disturbed. "They wake up about dinner time for food and a social evening." That must have been true, because he immediately made the food being prepared toward the dinner hour the major interest of his life; Guy would wake up, give a big yawn, begin to groom himself, and decide he was starving as soon as I started to fix dinner or he saw me in the kitchen.

It wasn't that I starved him, but, in addition to his special hamster food, he liked bits of greens, carrots, rolled oats, apples and even a nice red strawberry. He also liked to store all sorts of food away for a rainy day. Hamsters have pouches in their cheeks where they can put food to take to a secret pantry, or they can leave it in their pouch to eat at a later time. The back corners of his cage became little storage pantries. I grew to like him and actually found myself buying treats for him like sunflower seeds and unsalted nuts. Guy grew to be quite tame, and the kids tried to keep him in the palm of their hands or out on the lawn with a little leash of twine.

The hamster's cage was on the floor of the dining room just beyond the door to the kitchen. Fortunately, the rug was only under the table and chairs. I've since read that these critters should not be kept in a drafty place, but none of the small animals we kept in that cage near the door ever caught a cold or got sick as far as I could tell. Since the barn was full of alfalfa and oat hay, I made a thick bed in the bottom of the cage with hay. With no "hamster house" provided, he made tunnels under the hay and slept near his extra food supplies. Since the hay had to be changed almost every day, I began to feel like a rodent-hotel maid.

It was a good thing that Guy slept days, because late afternoons and evenings were when all the family became noisy and ran and walked back and forth dozens of times through the doorway next to him. He seemed to have lots of curiosity and liked the activity. Guy only lived several years before he began to get thin, seemed less interested in life, and died one night. Even with all the extra work he made me, I missed him and wondered just how old he had really been when we brought him home.

The cage wasn't empty long. The next occupant of the cage-for-small-creatures, was a large, friendly white rat. Though not nearly as pretty as the hamster, he was a lot smarter and often calmer. He was also a ham actor at times, especially when he tried to entice the dog to chase him or when he jumped back and forth over my paper work on the table. I grew very fond of this bright and happy pet, who was given to us by a friend of Doug's whose family was leaving for the summer and told him, "No more rat in this house when we come home!" Smarty was the name the rat came with, and it fit him well.

Wild rats are a terrible problem throughout the world, and deservedly so. They destroy food supplies, spread diseases, and chew up all sorts of things—one had once gotten into my laundry room and destroyed most of the washer's wiring. Tame rats, though, have been given a bad reputation without cause.

The tame versions have saved countless lives as laboratory animals in the past and are still saving them. From helping us find cures to diseases, such as polio and cancer, to enabling us to learn more about arthritis, nutrition, vitamins, heredity, psychology, behavior, and much more, these very inquisitive and affectionate animals have helped humans. The white kind of rat the boys were given are popular as pets, and somewhere I once read that they are as intelligent as any dog!

Smarty, with his soft white fur, bright pink eyes, and quivering nose, quickly learned we were all friends, and he only looked concerned when Jacque or the cat walked by. The rat had the right idea—some farm animals hunt rats and mice and are not safe as a trusted friend; although in different situations I've heard of cats and dogs accepting rodents as part of the family instead of part of dinner. Of course, in the comics of the time, Garfield and a mouse got along in a most unnatural way.

He soon recognized that the cage kept him safe. We fed him little bites of much of the food we ate, and I just tried to keep the kids from feeding him junk food. Smarty often sat up on his hind legs to eat little pieces of celery, apple, cheese, meat, salads, bits of sandwiches, grapes, seeds, and some of Guy's leftover hamster food.

Because he was smart enough to stay on table tops, beds, and shoulders (sometimes even in a shirt while the boys studied), he was out of his cage a lot more than Guy. This white fellow was both resourceful and athletic and loved to play on the floor with a Ping Pong ball, a couple of heavy golf balls, or some marbles, which he batted around in great form. Smarty thought it was great when Doug or Jeff threw the Ping-Pong ball so that it bounced several times toward him. Even Nancy gave him a tiny plastic doll and some little metal bells when she came home to visit, and those gifts intrigued him for a long time.

However, Smarty hated meeting new people and tried to avoid being picked up by Doug and Jeff's classmates. Probably in his previous life he'd been handled by some rough young children he wished had never touched him. There's just no way a tiny animal in a cage can screen those who can snatch him up to hold and carry around and no clear way to say "Ouch!" (though he slightly bit one school friend of Doug's who tried to turn him over and hold him on his back).

The little fellow knew all of us by sight and sound, came when called, and took a smart interest in everything that went on around him. Smarty lived only a couple of years—rats only have a three to five year lifespan. With his long tail and short hair, he wasn't quite as cuddly as the hamster, but he was still loveable and by far the most interesting, bright and fun animal outside his cage.

The last pet in the cage was a beautiful, orange and white, long-haired, guinea pig, with short little ears and no tail. While she wasn't as smart as the rat, she is the rodent the family seemed to remember best.

As you may know, these animals are not from Guinea and are nothing like a pig (although ours loved to eat). She came as a youngster, once again in one of the common ways children acquire pets: the boys saw a bunch of them in a pet store window. Because she soon cried, "Sweet, sweet, sweet" in a high feminine voice every time the refrigerator door opened or I began to fix supper, she received the name, "Sweet-Sweet." I've never known a real pig, but perhaps Sweet-Sweet's frequent call for food sounded a bit like a small squealing pig.

Like rats, guinea pigs have long been used as laboratory animals in university settings, private and governmental laboratories, and in an endless number of industries, from the drug companies to cosmetic companies. That is probably where the phrase, "Used like a guinea pig," originated. By knowing Guy, Smarty, and her, it hurt to think of all the horrible suffering that their relatives, and untold billions of their kind, had endured over the years throughout the world, much of it for un-needed, duplicative tests involving every pain conceivable, and not always for solid new research to save lives. It helped some that these small members of my family came along when I had little time to reflect.

My days were still turning into about hundred-hour workweeks, yet, to this day, I wish I had taken the guinea pig and other pets outside more often or let them run around in the house more frequently. At least I did the daily janitorial work of the cages, and their diet was varied, fun, and plentiful. They had store-bought food, plus a long list of foods we ate, like bits of apple, pear, orange, melon, berries, carrots, celery, let-tuce, nuts and seeds, bread, and rolled oats. I believe the hamster had less variety, but ate greens, carrots, celery and chewed on the hay.

With lots of our alfalfa and oat hay for bedding, Sweet-Sweet also had the fun of burrowing tunnels under the hay. It was a time when Doug and Jeff had increasingly more to do: homework, scouts, piano lessons with practicing each day, school sports, and ranch jobs, especially feeding the horses. More and more, it only became frequent meals that entertained the small creatures.

I did try one thing new with Sweet-Sweet. I let her enjoy the time I spent cleaning and cutting up vegetables. I set her down in one side of the double sink where I put the tops of the carrots, celery, broccoli peelings, and such. She inspected it all carefully, took a few nibbles, and jumped around to see what would show up next. Better choices for her to eat came to her dish later, along with commercially prepared and balanced food in pellet form. She seemed to know this, except when I gave her a cherry tomato or something juicy that was better eaten in the sink than in her cage.

Dan didn't think having a rodent of any kind in the sink was a very sanitary thing to do, even on the "trash side" of the sink. He was probably right and only caught me doing it once. Sweet-Sweet continued to visit the kitchen and investigate the vegetable trimmings; I just scrubbed that sink a little harder and returned Sweet-Sweet to her cage before he got home.

All three animals were tidy and neat, spending hours grooming themselves, and only using a certain area of their cage as a bathroom—or for storing food in the case of the hamster. I had read that guinea pigs can live longer than hamsters and rats, and she seemed to stay plump and healthy. Still, Sweet-Sweet died about four years later, in spite of a number of visits with me outside on the lawn,

I later felt somewhat disturbed that I didn't know more about the care of these special animals who became, for such a short time, a fun and happy part of our life. Many pet stores now have wheels, perches, ladders, and other interesting things for their exercise and entertainment, plus rodent-sized, elaborate, comfortable sleeping quarters. These small creatures returned far more than they received with their friendliness and amusing antics.

Meanwhile, little Jacque wasn't becoming a loving, people-dog. He received lots of attention and affection from Doug and Jeff, especially the first years, but it was either in his genes or, as a knowledgeable "dog-person" suggested, "He may have had no handling and affection during his first nine weeks of life. This is a special development period, and maybe he was taken away from his mom or brothers and sisters too soon." That wasn't his problem since I bought him when he was nine weeks old, but for whatever reason, Jacque was not an affectionate dog.

With both younger boys attending school longer hours, I eventually decided that Jacque shouldn't have to remain a "house dog," and increasingly he joined the big dogs outside and enjoyed the ranch or tried to join the boys in their games. I seldom found time to clip and comb him, and his hair often grew long and matted. Yet, like a much earlier dog who had the same indifference toward human attention, Jacque soon became a happy hunter of gophers in the fields and mice in the barns, even if we never found a single one he caught.

Chapter 26
Eric and His Visit

Several times I tried my hand at taking in another child to live with us, either while a parent suddenly had to work some extra long days or take an extended trip. It must have been Eric's first time away from home when he came to stay with us for six weeks, beginning on a Friday afternoon.

This lad, an only child being raised by a loving but busy working mom, was just four years old. Missing his mom would be bad enough, but he had also never had a pet larger than a goldfish. As his mom carried in his suitcases and several stuffed bears to his bedroom, Eric, with a shy smile, but close to tears, slowly followed her. With their arrival, the back door was left open, and Boom, Lady Lu, and Jacque wandered in. Suddenly, Eric had to meet these other members of the family. He raised his arms up above his head, and hurried past them, then looked back to see if they were going to follow him, but they had stayed in the kitchen. Clearly he was frightened and overwhelmed.

Yet his coming began a delightful time for me. Often children only think of themselves, but for some reason, during those six weeks all bickering in the house stopped. When at home, all the kids seemed to sense

Eric's fright and sadness, and all wanted to show him how Boomerang, especially, only wanted to love and kiss him.

They showed him Sweet-Sweet and told him what he'd say when they opened the refrigerator door. The guinea pig, on cue, called out his, "Sweet, sweet, sweet." It all seemed such a revelation and joy to the boy to be surrounded by family and animals, that it encouraged all the family to continue to treat him with kindness.

Nancy, home for a quick visit, also volunteered to read him a bedtime story. The next day, everyone was determined to show him every bit of Oak Hills ranch life. With a couple of the children holding his hands and Boom close behind, they took him around to pet Blue, Pepper, and take a quick ride on Shorty, feed the cow a bit of hay, and give the rabbits pieces of carrot. Eric's barriers of reserve and loneliness began to melt after just a day or two.

It had been terribly hard for his mother to leave him, but she had no choice. The worst part for her was that Eric would have his fourth birthday with us. She had left a wrapped gift box with cowboy boots, and I gave him the cowboy hat he'd wanted and a birthday supper. On his special day, Nancy led him around the yard on Blue, and Doug set up the train set that his brother Danny had kept packed away for a number of years in his room. Eric, Jeffrey, and Doug stayed up later than usual running the train around and around the tracks. Since the kids and Dad and I always hugged and kissed our goodnights, Eric got kissed or hugged by everyone in the house at bedtime. That night the hugs included wishes of "Happy, happy birthday, Eric."

When his mom came for him, she immediately asked him about a large scab on a knee. My new little buckaroo, wearing his cowboy duds, shrugged and more or less repeated one of our family-style descriptions when getting "owies," "The sidewalk tripped and bit me, but momma-C said I was brave to pick myself up real fast and not cry." He pushed his cowboy hat firmly on his head, grabbed her hand, and insisted she had to go outside to see every animal and be told their names. He especially wanted her to see him ride Shorty, but his mother had to return to work. The lad left the ranch a happy and rather cocky little guy. I never saw Eric again. I think they moved east. But in that very short time, I sensed both he and all of us had profited from his visit.

His coming had highlighted one aspect of country living I hadn't noticed as keenly before. There are more sounds and even smells at night, to be identified as I lay in bed. On a whole ranch that was slumbering peacefully and without a sound, I still fretted: was there the smell of smoke? Did the dog bark? Is a horse loose and clattering up and down the lane? What woke me up? Or, why is it so quiet? Of course, I had been an insomniac presumably from birth, and a non-sleeper or a light-sleeper ever since, but with another child to care for on a twenty-four-hour basis, my mother-hen instincts had risen to new heights. I listened even harder to all the sounds of the house and ranch.

In addition to listening for any coughs or a cry for "momma," the old frame house had always spoken with many voices—floorboards squeaked whenever anyone walked down the hall. Bedroom doors stuck and creaked when opened, pipes under the house clunked, windows rattled, and strong breezes caused the bougainvillea outside my window to scratch across the glass.

It was about then that the sky would begin to lighten to the east. I began to hear the soft low snorts of the horses, and the bathroom door opened and closed several times. It was then early dawn, too late for me to go back to sleep. I sighed and wondered what it would feel like to always sleep like a rock. I never knew.

However, at that time a bevy of doves would coo softly, perhaps on the lawn or parading up and down the lane, maybe even hanging out with the horses. These gray doves, who hunted for breakfast by parading up and down the lane or hanging out with the horses in the early dawn, got up about when I did, and their talk was delightful. Then, as the sky became lighter, the horses did more and more snorting and neighing, anticipating their breakfast. Not much later, with the clink of the milk bucket and the screen door shutting, the cow and often a couple of calves mooed more stridently, hoping to catch a glimpse of Dan going out to feed them and milk the cow.

School mornings were the only time the children's voices seemed muted and thoughtful as they began dressing. Then, all too soon, came loud symphonic kitchen sounds revving up while I prepared breakfast. Nancy or Danny hurried out to feed the horses and then reported if there was anything I should know, like a scraped leg on a horse, or a watering trough that was running over. Everyone ate a big breakfast and then scrambled to find books and papers, fixed their lunches, told me their daily schedules, and raced out the door at the last minute.

Immediately, the house became ever so still. Dishes were all over the counters, table, and in the sink, and a high stack of laundry sat on the floor beside the laundry room door. As soon as I finished those tasks and drank my mug of cold coffee, my job would be feeding and watering the dogs, cat, and rabbits—just another ordinary day of senseless work.

Chapter 27
A Glass of Water, Please

While it was still dark, the first words I heard that Sunday morning were screamed from the bathroom, "There's no water! Mom, there's no water!" I believed I knew why even before we could go to investigate.

This was one of those years when a good portion of all our annual rainfall came in a period of about two months. A flood of water from the storm had been tumbling down the Prefumo Canyon creek, overflowing the banks in spots, and had probably managed to damage the pump or rip out the pipe that carried our only supply of water to the house. The well and pump were down in the meadow on the far side of the swollen and fast-moving stream that for much of the year was just a dry creek bed.

There was also a large water tank nearby at the top of a hill beyond the barns that filled, by gravity from a spring farther up another higher hill, but that water could only be used for irrigation. Birds and rats had had to be fished out several times after somehow drowning in that tank. I wouldn't want to even try boiling that secondary source of water to use in the house.

Dan hurried down the lane that had pretty much become just two gullies full of water. He soon discovered that the pole which held up the water pipe across the creek had fallen over with all the mud, rocks, and fast moving water swirling past, and the pipe was no longer attached to the pump. There would be no water in the house until the pipe could be reattached and put back in place.

I was having three couples and several children come to dinner that night. Dan knew how much work I had already done for the party. The whole house hadn't been so clean for months, and the pies and some foods were already sitting on the counter or in the refrigerator. The biggest emergencies always seemed to occur at such times.

It was always a worry, as now, when Dan said during any crisis, "I have an idea that might work." Now he firmly added, "Yeah, I think this plan will work.

"You've got to have water; in fact, all of us and the animals have to have it. The plumbers in town will be swamped for days after this deluge, and I can't stay home tomorrow to fix anything.

"I'll find all our ropes and tie them together. I'll then tie one end around my waist and carry that new eight-foot two-by-four with me. I can throw a wrench and a shovel across the creek. You and the kids can stand up above the water at the edge of the road and hang on to the rope in case the current starts to pull me downstream. I wouldn't ask you to help and get all wet, but I saw no trees up the hill to tie a rope to. Don't worry, we'll get water."

That was another statement I feared. "No cause to worry" usually meant there was lots to worry about. Instead of patience or prudence, it was always "can do" right now. It didn't help that I had this same impulsive tendency. Also, the memory of my best childhood friend's relative immediately came to mind—a relative who had drowned in a creek probably one no bigger than this one, during a similar winter storm in Ventura county. I mentioned this, but his plan had already taken hold.

The storm seemed mostly over, but a light rain still came down like an icy shower. As the kids and I braced our feet and hung on to the long rope, like a tug of war game on a school playground, Dan barely forded the swollen creek as he kept stumbling on rocks he couldn't see beneath the muddy water. The water came almost to his waist, and, for a few moments, it was all we could do to hang on to the lifeline. He planted the new post in the old hole after removing the mud and rocks; then placed a large number of rocks and mud back around the new post, and then fastened the pipe to the post with baling wire. Finally, he got the pipe reattached to the well fitting.

Meanwhile, the kids and I were shivering and almost as soaking wet as Dad, and I was becoming increasingly frightened. Even with the children's help, would the rope tear out of my hands when he crossed again? Coming back across the raging current, Dan wouldn't have the "two by four" to balance him like a ski pole. Fortunately he made it through the racing water the second time, but the waters claimed one of his rubber boots and the wrench he'd tucked in his blue jeans. The kids and I continued pulling and hauled him up the slick and mushy slope to the road.

"You're quite a guy," I told him, "but I vow that next time I'll counter your 'I've got an idea' with more than an idea—it'll be a full-fledged plan to hire the job!" Later I began phoning repair people of all kinds to get a long list of competent carpenters, plumbers, electricians, and water well repair experts, who at least said they would be willing to travel out to the ranch for a job in the rain, and I stapled the list inside the front page of the phone book.

During my company dinner that night, I tried to describe Dan's heroic or stupid act. "You folks almost had nothing to drink tonight except unlimited good wine that friends who live in the Fresno area have given us and are stacked up in the tack room closet." City people can seldom clearly picture country living, and some don't care a bit for it. Inside the house, with the warm fireplace blazing, all of us could still hear the boisterous water of the swollen creek, and rain again rattled and gurgled loudly down the drainpipes. Still, our guests didn't seem that impressed with either Dan's success in getting water running in the pipes or with the storm's lovely music wafting through the room. The men fidgeted and one of the lady's eyes glazed over, wanting to get the conversation back to their coming spring vacation. If water is turned off in town, a regular army of city workers goes out with their yellow slickers and heavy equipment, and soon the faucets work again. I, on the other hand, would never forget the picture of Dan, up to his waist in racing water—not with mirth, but rather like a living nightmare.

Chapter 28
Snake and the Spotted Kids

There's a dead snake in the gutter," came voices from the back-seat. "Please stop, Mom. Stop! Stop! It was really big and neat. Stop! Stop! Can we have it?"

After finishing my dozen or more errands in town, plus the week's grocery shopping, I could only protest, "Just hold your horses, please. It would smell awful and be full of all kinds of bad bugs and germs. Anyway, it's late and I've got to get back."

That didn't stop Jeff and Doug. "I bet it won't be there tomorrow. We would keep it outside. You could still go back. Mom, we need it."

I continued to say things like, "We have no box to put it in, and probably we and the whole car would reek forever."

Several weeks later the kids were still talking occasionally about that dead snake, but they were now home with a bad case of chickenpox. I left them to bring dad home from work, and he chose to drive on the trip back. Suddenly, just as he swung the station wagon onto our dirt lane, there in front of us was a very large and long, snake, sleepily soaking up the sun and stretched straight out, right in the middle of the road.

While opening the car door and jumping out, I yelled, "Brake, brake! Stop the car. I've got to catch that snake." In addition to seeing this long and large snake, I also visualized the two miserable children, all covered with spots, up in that house on the hill. My next vision was that I could now redeem myself in their minds and do something heroic. I continued to look very, very carefully at the end of the snake's tail and saw no sign of rattlers.

There was no time to explain the whole story of the snake in the gutter to Dan, even if I could have made him understand the boys' passion to have the snake. For some reason, the snake didn't notice my shouting to Dan, and, as I tried to walk slowly and quietly up to the beast, I thought I remembered reading once that the place to grab a snake is right behind its head.

With this vast knowledge of snakes, I reached down and grabbed the sleepy fellow behind the head. Why hadn't he tried to get away? Could he be sick? Maybe the noise of the car so near him had masked my words and approach. Or did he live near the lane and get used to car noises and voices?

However, one of the biggest shocks of my life came the second I grabbed him. He didn't stay hanging out straight and relaxed, but in a flash, wrapped his whole, long body around and around my arm and wrist! This was a extremely healthy snake. I did remember that snakes are cold-blooded, but this fellow felt warm around my arm, probably because he'd taken a long nap in the sun. He was also fat and very heavy to hold.

The snake remained completely wound up around my arm while I managed to get back in the car, being careful to keep his head, with his mouth open and his tongue darting in and out, pointed toward the windshield and away from my body. Deciding that "Snake" would be his name, he and I looked straight ahead out the windshield, with my right elbow resting on my knees as I held him. I hadn't considered how big a snake he was. I tried to give a synopsis of the previous "dead snake in the gutter" episode to Dan, but he told me later that it was a bunch of confusing gibberish.

I came home to our feverish boys with a special gift, all right, but what to do with this huge creature? How about taking the current resident guinea pig, out of his big cage? She could stay in the laundry tub on a bed of straw, and Snake could have Sweet-Sweet's home. Anyway, the kids would be made to turn Snake loose before long. All this was discussed while the increasingly heavy reptile was coiled tightly around my arm. His quick little tongue continued flicking in and out of his mouth, but he contributed not one useful comment about what he would like in a new home.

Another traumatic moment that I also hadn't anticipated came next. I unwound Snake with my left hand until he was long again, and while holding the tail of him with my left hand to keep him stretched out, I got my right arm and hand holding his head inside the cage and stuffed the rest of him in with my left hand. At that instant, horror and panic struck again—what will he do when I loosen my grip of him behind his head and try to withdraw my hand and arm? True, he's not a rattler, but will he turn and close those open jaws on my hand? Does he have teeth?

Seconds passed, and no brilliant alternative solutions came to mind. I finally pointed his head into the far corner and let go. None of the "What ifs?" came to pass. There was no snake attack, I shut the door, and the snake began to calmly "snake" around and explore his cage and then he curled up and snoozed on the bed of straw, seemingly resigned to a future in the presence of humans.

It then became a different kind of an attack for me. Immediately, I started shaking all over and had to grab the nearest chair and collapse in it. Yet, even with the shaking, I felt rather pleased that I'd brought the spotted kids such a special present. The shaking and weakness continued for most of an hour. Shock, perhaps.

This should have been the end of this story, but I've got to tell you that a mom's work is seldom done. So, one more less-traumatic part faced me, even as I firmly told myself I had done enough of this kind of thing for a long, long while—perhaps for a lifetime. The boys quickly phoned to tell their friends about the critter that was residing in their house. Next morning, they phoned their teacher in the two-room schoolhouse. Mrs. Bell insisted I bring the snake to school the next day, "to share." She suggested I could explain to the students what Snake eats, where it lives when not with its present family, and what kind of snake it is. There were no Britannicas unpacked at the time, and morning came early.

I went to school carrying Snake in the guinea pig cage to be part of Show and Tell. The students in grades four through six came in to stand at the back of the room, while those in grades one through three sat at their desks. Talking before even a room full of little children is "public speaking" to me, so it wasn't easy. In fact, I began shaking some again.

Only guessing about the previous life of Snake, I explained he lived in gopher holes and ate field mice, birds, lizards and gophers. It seemed reasonable. Kids must love snakes, for I was hardly through being the snake expert when all the children came up to get close to the cage. Several asked if I would take it out of the cage for petting.

"Oh my no!" I responded. "He might bite." I immediately wished I'd not said that, for I knew that many snakes were useful and didn't deserve a bad reputation or to be killed. I continued to ad-lib answers to their questions through recess before returning him to Oak Hills and setting him free in a pasture for the horses. One never knows just when an experience like this one really ends. King snake? I think so.

Chapter 29
The Merry Old Ladies Take Over

Dan and I wanted to take a trip to northern California, Oregon, and Washington in order to write about farms and ranches in those areas. Our work-conquers-all philosophy had us wiped-out and desperate to recharge body and mind. Several agricultural magazines had agreed to buy the articles. We had never left the kids with others for even one night. Now Nancy and Danny were much older, and even the younger boys were of school age. I decided to ask Ada and Margaret, who had been close family friends and a large part of my mother's life for almost as long as she lived, to come and stay while we were away. Ada and Margaret had no idea at all that sixteen days of caring for four children—or four children's caring for them—would change them for life and give them some of their best memories.

Ada McLouth had been a librarian in San Diego who had never married and, except for summers of seeing her nephew and me as children, probably only met youngsters when they came to the library. She was deathly afraid of all animals. Dan and I had visited her in Solano Beach many years earlier, and she had told vivid stories about dogs that were turned loose on the beach. Beach walking was the highlight of

her days, yet she was sure that some of the dogs she met had wanted to
attack her. None ever had, but some had probably approached her for
a pat or just to say hello.

My mother, father, and I had spent many long summer vacations in
San Diego, just so Ada and mom could enjoy each other's company. Ada
lived in a cottage perched on the side of a steep hill above the bay. Mom
and Ada prepared imaginative meals and served them on gaudy Mexican
plates, while our drinks were poured into her hand-blown blue glasses.
Many long hours passed while they talked of books, authors, plays in
town they might want to see, and dear friends they planned to phone.

Now Ada was retired and ready for new adventures. Ada had a great
sense of humor and the happiest chuckles and laughter I've ever heard.
I knew she would do her best to take good care of the kids. I figured
that Nancy and Ada would delight in talking about books with each
other—some of the best horse books I ever owned had been mailed to
me at Christmas by Aunt Ada when I was small.

Margaret Anson had also never married and had spent most of her
life as an elementary schoolteacher. She had a lot of experience working with children, though she had never experienced living with them.
Both of the retired ladies said they would love to come.

Dan went in the pickup to meet their train, while I dashed to town
for more last minute food supplies. Even with the garden and the full
deepfreeze, they would need other supplies. A busy neighbor would
come by to milk the cow for us, but he wouldn't have time to shop for
or transport Nancy or the ladies anywhere. Ada had never driven a car,
and Margaret no longer had a driver's license. Sixteen days would be a
long time without transportation.

Four or five horses whinnied, tossed their manes, and stretched their
heads over the fence bordering the long, dusty lane to the house as the
ladies arrived with Dan. This large field still had horses that were boarded
with us; they were usually fed hay from a wheelbarrow, and it was past
dinnertime for them. Boomerang and Lady Lu raced out to bark their
arrival, and the children spilled out the back door of the house.

Dan was explaining to the ladies that no one could remember when
the real front door to the house had ever been used, as there was no path

or parking area on that side of the house. Nothing wrong about entering the kitchen first, especially on a ranch, but we always thought about
how it must look to others who had never even gone to a back door to
call on any of their friends.

As Dan and I began lifting their bags out, I heard Ada whisper and
whisper to Margaret, "Look at them. The dogs are huge! I can't get out
here. What a terrible mistake. Oh my. Look. Now there's a cat coming
out. This is absolute chaos!" It was clear that beautiful, white-haired
Ada, at about age sixty-five, was still terrified at even the sight of animals. I hadn't seen her but twice in about twenty years and had by that
time forgotten that she was very afraid of animals.

Margaret just said, "Shhhh, I'll handle the dogs and cat."

Nancy told me much later that she, too, was surprised at Ada's extreme fear of the dogs, and she had decided that maybe the ladies could
do all the cooking and housework, and she and Danny could do all the
feeding and farm work. For Nancy, the worst part of our leaving was
not having a car to drive.

My flowering thespian wailed after the ladies were in the house,
"How will I see my friends? I can't stay here all the time with them. I just
can't!" Dan and I were taking the only car we owned. Why did Nancy
look at me as though I might never come home? Maybe she wondered if
she would be baby-sitting the ladies. Now I had not one but two lovely
ladies as sitters, and I was still feeling full of guilt.

I leashed the dogs in the garage to the car's bumper and showed Ada
and Margaret to their bedroom. Then it was time for the ranch tour.

"The kids will do most or all of the feeding, but you might like to
know how it's done," I suggested. "This is a flake of hay and is about
the right size to give each horse every morning and evening. Don't feed
them too close to each other, or the horses may fight, and the losers
won't get much to eat. This is the oat hay, and here is the alfalfa hay.
The wire cutter for breaking open the bales is hanging over here. The
children make a habit of looking over each horse when feeding to make
sure they're all right—no cuts or lameness.

"The faucets for the tubs of water are around the corner; all animals
need lots of water at all times. However there are floats in each tub and,

hopefully, no one will need to fill the tubs with a hose. However, Danny is good at repairing the floats.

"The livestock medicine is on this shelf, and Nancy should put several drops from this bottle in April's eye each morning. The chicken feed goes in this feeder, and the rabbit pellets are in this shed. Both the dry and canned food for the dogs is stored on the porch of the house, as is the cat's food."

The station wagon was loaded and ready to go. I had cooked a large dinner for Ada, Margaret, and the kids and packed a sack supper for Dan and me. This trip was hardly what I'd imagined for our first true vacation with just the two of us. I'd packed enough food as if we were going to a third-world country with no Safeways in the towns—stuff like crackers, canned soups and stews, raisins, cold cereals, and oranges, to name a few.

As the heavily loaded station wagon rolled down the lane, we crossed our fingers and grinned at each other. We would get as far as Salinas this evening. The first night would be easy, since a friend had invited us to park in his ranch yard after we had refused his guest room.

Dan began holding his interviews and getting photographs of rice, grain, dairy, and cattle ranches as well as various kinds of farms as we traveled up through the Northwest. It was a strange and happy time to sort of vacation, yet I worried about the zoo back home. Of course it was a "vacation" of sleeping almost every night in the long station wagon on an old double bed mattress, swimming in some lakes and rivers to bathe, and fixing some meals on a little camp stove balanced on the tailgate of the station wagon.

Many of the ranchers and farmers offered to have us stay in guest bedrooms, but we didn't want to lose too much time being sociable and only relented once or twice. As we traveled along, both of us thought up some good lead sentences and endings for the articles we were writing, and Dan even got several of them completely handwritten while I did some of the driving. Before it became too dark, I then typed the articles up in final form on the same old typewriter I'd used in Arizona. The stories paid for the work-holiday but not much more.

As soon as we returned home, Dan went out to take charge of the feeding and milking while I listened to some stories. This was the first story we heard of what happened one early night on the ranch—as close an account as I could glean or imagine from all concerned:

The two, small, elderly ladies had sat on the old green sofa facing the TV after supper. Surrounding them were the four children, all of them probably feeling that they had somehow made it through another long and confusing day. How could so many things need doing at the same time from dawn 'til dark on the Oak Hills Ranch?

As a program changed on the screen, Ada observed, "You know, Margaret, when I got home from eight hours at the library, I always felt the day was over, that only tea, dinner, and a good read lay ahead. But here I'm always tense, listening and thinking about what might happen next. The two loose horses last night didn't help. So many beasts!"

Margaret nodded, "I feel the same way. My regular school day with second-graders seemed long, but I never really gave much thought about the children's life before and after school. And, do you know, I've discovered something both funny and amazing—all the horses, cows, dogs, and other animals seem more and more like my students. Every one of these beasts knows more than they let on, don't you think?"

Suddenly Danny pointed to the hearth in front of the TV. A little brown timorous mouse was running part way across the hearth and then stopped to sit, totally perplexed and scared by the lights and embers in the fireplace and not able to see an exit. The mouse had completely forgotten the route he'd taken to get in the house.

Danny quickly left the room, and the two younger boys immediately suggested, "Let's catch it."

Their big sister, who daily was acting more and more like their mom, replied, "No way, but maybe we can get the cat."

Aunt Ada and Aunt Margaret said not a word, not even the "Oh my!" that Ada seemed to say at least a dozen or more times a day. All they could envision was a mouse running up their legs and maybe a cat, with sharp teeth and long claws, in wild pursuit.

At that point, Danny came back with his long-barreled BB gun. He had shot a large number of mice in the hay barn over the past several years.

Danny asked his sister, "Mom said no gun while she's away, but may I shoot it, Big Sis?"

Nancy barely nodded a yes. She had seen Danny's deadly aim in the barn; but she thought that killing mice, even when they were running through her horses' hay, was very much like murder.

Immediately, the shot sounded in the living room, and the mouse was dead. Edna and Mary still could not talk about it. Instead Edna said, "Come along, Jeff and Doug, I'll read you a bedtime story in your room."

Margaret then told Nancy and Danny," I think it's also time for me to retire and read. You both get to bed pretty soon and don't unlock the doors." One more day on a ranch had ended; they were all certainly checking the calendar and counting the time remaining several times a day.

However, the ranch and this family of critters and kids had actually gradually won the ladies over! Ada took pictures of Margaret feeding the horses from a wheelbarrow, and Margaret got snaps of Ada feeding the rabbits a dish of rabbit pellets and standing next to Boomerang. The dog had somehow actually made friends with her, and that was an incredible giant step in her losing a lifelong fear. How I wished I could have seen how Boom managed that. It was a miracle!

The whole cast cheered and clapped when we arrived unannounced and opened the kitchen door, not for deliverance, but as comrades in both mirth and happiness. Boomerang was in the kitchen, seemingly part of the family! I came home with the makings of a fish dinner and with lots of fresh tomatoes and a watermelon—things that weren't ripe yet in my garden that month.

While I took over making dinner, there were six voices, all wanting to report to me and later to Dan. Ada, with her melodious laughter and Margaret's fine reporting began, but the kids also tried to report on the daily rituals of work, play, and "special happenings." It was all reassuring. Ada and Margaret had made it more than just "baby-sitting." No wonder these two ladies had been close friends of my mom during most of her life. Not one of the kids was complaining; Nancy hadn't had to fix meals after all and had found time for some great horseback riding, and Danny had a school chum driven out by his mother a number of times to spend the day with him fixing a couple of engines.

The worst tale, besides the shooting of the mouse on the hearth, was a trip that Ada tried to make into town by walking. She loved to walk and had kept it up after she retired and moved to Solana Beach, but this was a distance of several miles each way. Beautiful Ada simply had to get her snowy-white hair washed and set.

When she became lost while walking home, there were no "safe" houses where she could ask her way to the ranch, for there "might be vicious ranch dogs" at the few houses she passed. Finally, a farmer stopped his pick-up truck and asked this small lady, wearing a go-to-town dress, her "better shoes," and a drooping set of new hair curls, if she would like a ride, and he brought her home. I never did find out who this knight-in-shining-armor farmer was. Ada couldn't even remember the color of the vehicle, much less what the man looked like, but, with her droll humor, she could already laugh about her awful trek to a beauty shop.

About dinnertime, Boom trotted into the kitchen, and again I was dumbfounded that Ada not only stayed seated but exuberantly said, "Hi there, Boom-friend!" I looked down at Boom with wonder at his part in somehow changing Ada's attitude about dogs. If only he could talk and tell me what psychology or spell he'd woven.

Even after the ladies returned home, they savored and remembered more little happenings to regale us with in their letters. With brightness and humor, they wrote about the abundance of cream for whipping and slathering it over most desserts, from red Jell-O to Apple Betty. They had never seen such a gigantic deep freeze or so much beef and chicken completely disappear at the dinner table. Our ranch-sized breakfasts were a feast compared to the ladies' usual toast, juice, and coffee. Most of all, they both wrote about every one of the animals and how easy it had been to become "friends" with them as well as with the children.

Both the kids and the merry old ladies had somehow found common ground and made it a time of the children protecting and taking care of the ladies and animals, and the ladies trying to do the same for the children and animals. Ada's lilting voice and wonderful laughter seemed to reach me, even in her written letters.

Sometime later, I also came to the conclusion that perhaps the clue to Ada's bonding with Boomerang was because this dog, like Treve before him, always came like a magnet to any sounds of laughter and fun. Laughter was contagious, and most of our dogs and cats learned that when we laughed, life was not just o.k., but very fine. Ada's laughter was spontaneous, merry, and melodious and made all those around her laugh with her. There is a saying, "Laugh and the world laughs with you; cry and you'll cry alone." Humor had made Boomerang's day. In fact, it made everyone's day. Since Ada found some kind of comedy almost continually on the ranch, Nancy reported to me that Treve often picked up one of the numerous tennis balls on the floor or yard, dropped it at Ada's feet, and then sat in front of her and smiled, clearly saying, "It's wonderful that you're so happy and laughing. So, how about a game of Fetch?"

Chapter 30
Bumping Along with a Travel Trailer and a Dolphin

Even sabbaticals with full pay had seemed too expensive for Dan to accept throughout his many years of teaching. If we took one, we would also lose the income of all our "extra jobs," and there would be the cost of traveling. And who would care for all the animals and the rentals in town? Still, it seemed the best of times to take a leave from teaching. Nancy was taking classes at UCLA, while Danny attended UC Davis. I no longer held even loose reins to their daily lives. Also, the younger two wouldn't want to go and leave their friends if we waited much longer and they reached high school age.

Mostly, it just felt wrong that we should be so busy and broke that we couldn't take one summer and fall sabbatical in all the years of Dan's college teaching, both at Arizona State and Cal Poly. He was head of the Agri-Business Management Department, which he had established in earlier years, but fellow teachers could take over his class work.

In addition to Dan taking a leave-with-pay for the fall term, I sold a small rental house for additional funds, and a married student couple with a good farming background agreed to live in our home, care for the animals, and follow a book-sized list of my warnings and directions. Most of my list was for nightmarish events that might go wrong, even though not one of them had ever occurred.

The car hadn't been cleaned inside since Dan and I'd taken the writing assignment through the northwest, and I was aware that the contents were a regular lost and found. In the trunk there was a coil of baling wire, a rug to lie on when I had to find an extra car key hidden under the car, screws, nails, two hammers, horse ropes, and the family's fishing poles and tackle box. Inside the car, under and around the seats, it was a similar "Lost and Found."

"Hey, mom, here's that library book and those gym shorts"—the car was the hiding place for pens, pencils, my lost set of keys, and a variety of candy wrappers, bottle caps, and rotted rubber bands. The stuff in the glove compartment was worse. Some reading glasses had turned yellow, and a lipstick had lost its top and covered the Owners' Manual for the car with messy kisses of coral lipstick. The big pair of unmatched garden or car-repair-gloves were there, stiff and stained almost black with oil and dirt. The biggest mystery solved in the cleanup was an important school theme that had created an uproar with Danny, his teacher, and me years ago.

With a small travel trailer that could sleep four hooked up behind the station wagon, we left as soon as the schools ended that spring for over six months of travel. Dad would visit a number of universities across the country and write a rather lengthy report at the end of the journey to justify the sabbatical.

Every traveling day I had to convince Doug and Jeff to keep up with their schoolwork—not only did they have to study for the classes they were missing, I forced them to begin filling large scrapbooks with a full page of writing each day. Other pages were filled with countless postcard pictures of national parks, rivers, mountains, valleys, towns and the photographs we took. They also pasted in the scrapbooks programs or leaflets from state fairs, historical sights, plays, and Broadway musicals. Each scrapbook weighed eight pounds upon our return. They took the books to their schoolrooms to try and assuage the feelings of teachers who hadn't been too sure about their playing hooky for a whole semester. It worked—the teachers were pleased and gave them fine, belated report cards.

While Dan was visiting universities, the boys and I scoured antique and second-hand shops in some of the towns, and each of us became an owner of an old clock. By the time we'd meandered up to the Bay of Fundy and on to Halifax, our collections of antiques filled the trailer shower to the top, and we could no longer bathe in it. In addition to the six old clocks, one for each member of the family, we acquired a mirrored hat-rack, another large mirror with a big, heavy frame about four feet by five feet, an umbrella stand, and small treasures like copper teakettles, a bed-warmer with a long handle, and heavy irons that had to be heated on a stove to use. With all this weight toward the front, I had to figure out how to put more heavy things in the back to balance this trailer on the long way home. I also began to read the heavy travel-trailer guidebook extra carefully, and we always stayed in trailer parks with three stars. At that time, three stars meant there would be clean tiled bathrooms with showers, a laundry room, and other facilities, such as sewer, water, and electric hookups. Warm swimming pools were also high on the boys' lists of "must haves."

After failing miserably in trying to teach the "new math" as we traveled, my salvation arrived on the scene with the appearance of a handsome, sun-bronzed, blond high-school student vacationing, as we were, beside the beach in Florida, an area that's now surely a solid chain of high-rise hotels.

Random acts of fate so often saved the day. This beach boy, John, who looked like he also never studied, actually knew all the right math. He was a genius compared to mom and dad. The boys thought he was great and were inspired to cover about fifteen pages of homework every day "for John" after his hour-long tutoring session. After a month there the boys learned their lessons so well that math, especially, seemed easy and mostly pain-free forevermore. Dan, meanwhile, wrote up his final report for this leave of absence, and I typed it up in the proper form. Doug was stung by a man-o-war jelly fish, but we all continued to swim each day in that warm and great Atlantic Ocean, which was only several dozen steps away from our trailer home.

Another encounter with new creatures was a happier time. We drove "out to sea" on one of the most spectacular and unusual roads anywhere in the United States, extending roughly a hundred miles out into the ocean from Key Largo to Key West. Part of the route, including the Seven-Mile Bridge, was just road, sea, sky, and us. However, the road went across or near hundreds of tiny specks of land, and at one spot, on a small slice of land beside a lagoon, we stopped to tour a dolphin water-park. The sky became more and more cloudy and the air quiet and heavy by the end of the tour of the many large fenced pools with dolphins. It finally began to rain lightly, but, rain or not, the guide asked, "Are there any in this group who would like to swim with a dolphin?"

"Oh yes! Please!" We were the only ones to jump at the chance. While the rest of the tourist group remained and sat under a small roofed bleacher to see our show, in a nearby small building we quickly changed into swimsuits.

The guide then pointed out a low pier that went out from shore into the large lagoon and instructed us, "Each of you will walk out to the end of the pier there, and no dilly-dallying—immediately jump in the water and swim a few strokes out. When the dolphin swims by in about a minute, you have to be ready to grab his fin with your right hand. He'll take you down to that other jetty or pier, and then he'll suddenly dive, leaving you to climb the steps there, then the next one of you must jump in. If the dolphin doesn't come within a minute or so, slap the water once and he'll come. Who wants to be first?"

I jumped in and waited, treading water. The dolphin swam by at a greater speed than I had expected, but I grabbed his fin. At that moment, and until we reached the other pier or jetty, I only felt sadness for this very intelligent animal. He swam strongly, like it was a job to be finished quickly, and my body kept bumping against his warm side as he swam. While this was one of several large fenced enclosures, maybe several acres or more in size and part of an inlet from the sea, still the dolphin was a captive slave, trained to do this brainless thing. Instead of swimming free in the vast ocean with other dolphin friends and family, or playing in the waves and diving for fish, he spent his life ferrying my family, and countless other humans, from one point to another, and probably was also having to learn dolphin tricks for other audiences.

The guide and owner mentioned that he had quit some of the movie work with these animals, because he discovered that he usually had to be there in person to be sure the dolphins were treated right and kept healthy at all times. The animals needed proper food and exercise while being kept in a clean saltwater world that was kept at the proper temperature at all times—an almost impossible job on many movie sets. Here they were in pens that were a healthier size, and I could see he cared for these animals and felt close to them, but, as with all wild intelligent animals, and those not so intelligent, captivity had cruel aspects—these wonderful creatures needed to be free in their natural habitat.

There were maybe about forty bridges spanning the many keys at that time, with the road finally ending at Key West. We quickly met a very elderly black man there who was fishing from some large rocks; he told us that he'd known Ernest Hemmingway very well, and pointed out the writer's nearby house while laughing about the many cats that had called the author's place home. The man then showed us a small stack of large abalone shells on a cloth nearby and offered to sell us several of them.

Some days later, we headed west to be home in time for Christmas. Before leaving, we received word that our longtime precious family friend, Grace, who had a tremendous ability to love and care, had died. She had been like family to us and was always Aunt Grace to the children. Since she was the owner of Oak Hills Ranch, it would probably be sold. I just hoped that her verbal will, stating that we'd have first chance to buy the ranch buildings and about twelve acres, would be honored.

Chapter 31
Many Tomorrows Ahead

The ranch had been in good hands, and all was fine upon our return. There was a love fest of multiple hugs and kisses for all the animals. Nancy and Danny came home from college for Christmas, but we were was so low on funds that I wrapped the antique clocks as our only Christmas gifts to each family member.

After marrying, Nancy had started her practice-teaching in a high school English class. While her supervising professor suggested that Nancy "stick entirely to what's in the text book," she silently rebelled. She followed the text, but also brought magazines, sheets of poetry, and short stories to class. The students enjoyed her and wrote acceptable paragraphs on many topics, and even enjoyed some poetry. However, for the next term, she decided to go on her own and chose a paying job to do a year of teaching English classes in lieu of finishing through the University system. Turning down a position at a more affluent high school in Glendale, she chose to take a job teaching at a junior high school in Watts, in Los Angeles.

Some of these students had never even seen a live cow, but she got them interested in writing about their own lives and feeling better about themselves by telling them a story about herself when she had milked April with her mom during a rain storm. This is about the way she told them a sample story:

"I lived on a ranch before I moved down this way. When my dad had to be away on business, mom and I had to go out to the corral, which was a fenced-in area near the barn, where we kept a milk cow named April. She was a beautiful, rich, chocolate colored cow, with big brown eyes and long eyelashes. Each year she gave birth to a cute little wiggly and happy calf who drank some of her milk.

"The trouble started when mom and I had to do the milking. It takes a lot of strength in your fingers and hands, and you have to kind of squeeze each finger in turn, like this, to get the milk out of her four teats. There was a rainstorm, just like there is here today. Mom and I got the bucket and put raincoats and hats on and went out to milk. April stared balefully at us as we opened the gate, but as soon as we gave her lots of hay, she settled down to eat and hardly noticed us for a while. Mom had found an extra wooden box to sit on to use as a milking stool, so we could sit on opposite sides of the cow and milk her at the same time.

"The ground was muddy, and the big fat sides of the cow were wet. We only had tennis shoes to wear on our feet, and they became muddy just getting to the cow and tying her to a fence post. Not all cows would like two inexperienced people milk them at the same time, but she was hungry and sort of knew us, even with our raincoats and hats on.

"Nevertheless, she shortly started to swish her long, wet, and dirty tail in our faces and moved her feet around in the mud more and more. Our hands became cold, tired, and hurt from squeezing the milk into the pail. We felt like crying, and, wet fur or not, we laid our heads against her warm flanks to face away from her waving tail. Cows have to have every bit of their milk taken out of their udders every morning and every night—even on Sundays, Christmas day, or when you don't feel like doing it.

"When it was getting almost dark, we finally finished, but by that time, April was through eating and getting very impatient with us— while trying to walk away, she raised a back hoof and put it right in the almost full pail of milk.

"Oh my! There was no keeping that milk—we poured it out on the ground and ran to the house. Twelve hours later, we had to go back out there to feed her more hay, and this time we took an extra pail to pour some of the milk into now and then as we milked. That worked, and we carried a full pail safely into the house.

"Mom then put a paper-like filter in a big milk strainer and poured the milk through the filter and into gallon jars to set in the refrigerator. Cream rises to the top of the milk as it gets colder, so later that day she skimmed off some of the thick cream to make butter and to use for whipping cream. My family drank lots of milk and also fed some of it in a bucket to several little calves.

"However, the milk you students drink is milked with clean, stainless steel machines inside nice barns—barns with cement floors that can be hosed until clean, and the milk is taken away in special trucks to be pasteurized. Pasteurized milk is milk that has been heated to kill any bad germs in it."

Nancy's students looked up to her a lot more after that story, and quite a few wrote short stories about their lives in the city and some of the things that had happened to them while growing up.

Nancy was pregnant that spring and wouldn't return to teach the coming fall, but she told her students over and over how much she would miss them, how well they were doing, and how they should try to explore the world around them, perhaps by walking, bicycling, or riding on city buses. "Get to the free libraries to check out a book every now and then, go to the nearby beaches, see the mountains, and most of all, stay in school, even if you have to work part-time."

Dan and I, meanwhile, waited impatiently to find out if we would be able to buy and keep the house and twelve acres. The answer came and it was: "Yes you can buy, but you'll have to raise money for an 'all cash' sale because of the inheritance taxes." The rest of the ranch would also be sold. After a frantic period, with endless paper work, time, and lots of fast-talking to refinance some of our rentals, we raised the money.

It was all for naught. At that juncture, the owner found a qualified buyer who insisted upon acquiring the whole ranch for development, and the buyer wouldn't take the property without getting our portion. We lost the purchase, and in a couple of months all of us and all our animals would have to leave.

"Let's vamoose, move completely out of here as quickly as we can: find a house in town, pack, and go," I pleaded. "There're no other small ranches nearby for sale right now, and waiting to find another country place would certainly take much more time than we have." All aspects of our ranch life, both big and small, quickly unraveled.

So many yesterdays had been spent in the country. Would all the family be able to lock in their minds the many, many years of rural living, the multitude of special and much loved animals, the farm kitchens, and the love and laughter? It was especially hard to leave Oak Hills, but there was actually too much to do to fret, reminisce, or even think about what couldn't be. Fortunately, we'd never been paralyzed by inaction when decisions had to be made.

"Dan, we've always tried to take the long view," I said, " but right now it's better to take a short view, find a way-station to regroup and resurrect some goals. Nevertheless, we've got to remember our belief that if one thing goes bad it often leads to something much better."

Dan rolled his eyes, then grinned and said, "Sure, just a short derailment."

How does one get rid of six people's lifetime paraphernalia? I decided to start with three storage garages we owned in San Luis Obispo where we'd taken "things to keep" on our many trips north. If we cleaned those garages out, they would be ready in case we needed the space for our current ranch belongings These garages were full of ancient throwaway paint, old furniture, books and pictures, and dozens and dozens of big boxes on shelves reaching to the ceiling. Many of the boxes held the memorabilia of almost thirty years of Dan's high school and university teaching materials—hundreds of books, government bulletins, pamphlets, and about thirty USDA Yearbooks, each one as heavy as a big city phone book.

Dr. Cline, at the University of Arizona, had been an exacting taskmaster during Dan's undergraduate and master's work. He believed that no vo-ag teaching day could be successful without about twelve hours spent preparing teaching "goals, ways, and means." Since an agriculture teacher in the Salt River Valley of Arizona dealt with a host of different crops, animals and businesses, there were thousands of pages of lesson plans. Then there were books and papers from his doctoral studies. We took it all to the dump in the pick-up truck.

While I had less stored, it was still a tremendous amount, with my university years in California, Arizona, and Pennsylvania. There were things I had saved for the children, like report cards, birthday cards, first books for piano lessons, and thousands of other things that I wished were organized in scrap books. The rest we tossed away.

Back at the ranch, the house already felt different and vulnerable: would it be saved or torn down? The wooden frame of the door to the laundry room held the record of all the kids' heights over the years, marked on their birthdays, with four vertical lines with their names, and then cross lines, giving dates and names, going up higher and higher. No way to move that record. Since these were ten years of the children's extra rapid growth, it was also a chronicle of how many times I must have bought bigger shoes and clothes. Even with lots of hand-me-down clothes, the shoe and clothing store clerks knew me by name, for it had seemed as though the kids changed size monthly.

How often had these gangly children suffered with taunts or remarks about their height? I remembered that I hadn't liked being called bean-pole and curtain-rod, or strangers asking, "How's the weather up there?"

I wished I'd saved the big wall calendars that had hung near the phone. I always used the kind that arrived free with ads, with big squares to cover with notes each day, and they would have been a humorous and revealing record. The calendars were always written on in the margins, top, bottom, and sides, as well as in the squares with the dates. There were all the appointments to orthodontists, clubs, meetings, tennis matches, and deadlines, written in all colors of ink and pencils: DON'T FORGET GYM SHORTS—GET ME AT FOUR OR ELSE!!—MOM, NEED THREE DOZEN COOKIES TUESDAY—DAD PHONED, NEEDS RIDE AT FOUR NOT FIVE! All in six different writing styles that somewhat corresponded to the age of the child or parent, and embellished with circles, underlining, and lots of exclamation points of life-or-death demands and reminders.

Doug and I had made the page even harder to read properly because we both doodled on it as we talked on the phone—he with nice art work of fanciful animals, trees, and complicated modern pieces, and I penciling simple squares, circles and triangles that had a way of growing bigger with daily additions. By the end of the month, the whole page was also overlaid with fingerprints of jelly, peanut butter, grease, and other grime.

I'd miss the kitchen, how it used to have all the family around the table, the warmth and fragrance of bacon and eggs frying, toast and cereal cooking, and disappearing big pitchers of milk and orange juice. Up to the last minute, schedule changes had to be discussed and lunches made. Finally, there was the sudden stillness each day after the dash of Dan and the kids to their various schools, a stillness that always seemed to catch me by surprise.

Now there was a house in town waiting for us. The kitchen table would fit in the new kitchen, and I silently vowed to continue big breakfasts, though word was getting out that I had been serving deadly foods all my life, foods like steaks, bacon, cream, pies, and butter spread thick wherever it was spread.

Only as we prepared to leave did I suddenly wish the Oak Hill Ranch kitchen could have been twice as large while the four kids were still growing up—a sort of family room, a kitchen that could have included a fireplace in one corner, a sofa and more chairs, a bookcase for school and currently-being-read books, reading lights, a small table and chair beside the phone. The dining table itself needed to be much larger, large enough so even friends of friends could find a seat and so that there would be room to fold wash, do bookkeeping, and write letters. More counter space for making meals, snacks, and drinks. More shelves just for collections of rocks, shells, tadpoles, and jars of flowers. Several rugs for the dogs on the floor, and large picture windows on two sides, facing the barn, lake, valley, and mountains in the distance. The refrigerator should have been almost commercial size, and most of all, the stove should have been a huge, old-fashioned one, with the stove's ovens built above the burners. In other words, almost a home in one big room, cozy and warm, a bit ranch-like but also practical.

Later, I stood outside and also wished I had had more time to ride out over the hills under a warm sun or a full moon, or even more time to have walked around the farm and talked with the animals. They, too, had always felt the mystery of moonlight—the cats begged to go outside, and the dogs provided a lot more barking, perhaps spooked by shadows that moved in any light breeze. Often the owl hooted or mocking birds sang. Horses thought they saw ghosts in the shadows and snorted and blew out big gulps of air. They danced about and nipped each other, but weren't often willing to run far into the fields. Even before leaving, with these thoughts I found myself voicing a little eulogy for our animal family, soon to be scattered to new places and, perhaps, new owners.

Fortunately, I was able to promote a very special ride at the last minute before the horses left in trailers for new pastures. With Doug and Jeff on Blue, Dan on Pepper, me astride Shorty, and the dogs following, we rode out slowly on that most worn and easy trail to the west just before twilight. The hills were dappled with deep blue shadows, and a half-moon eventually made our way magical with a soft yellow light out over the valley and on the trail ahead. As we all rode to the far western boundary of the ranch, I hoped we were trying to quietly store up the memories of our ten years on this beautiful ranch and trying not to forget what we were seeing, feeling, and remembering right then. The ride seemed to wrap it all up: this part of lives was over, and yet there seemed to be few loose ends. Maybe it was time to go. In ways, I was glad that Nancy and Danny had already said their goodbyes and were off on their own new trails. No one could take away any of the thousands of special events or even just the moments, sounds, smells, and pictures held in our memories. And, please, dear God, always fill each of us with hope, dreams, and laughter, and keep our animals safe and content.

I trailered Blue, who had become a very white horse in her mature years, to a farm pasture south of town. However, the field had such lush green grass that she soon foundered and quickly had to be trailered back to a great farm in the Los Osos Valley. We moved the remaining bales of hay to a garage we owned in town. Then someone reported the hay, and I learned there was a law against hay storage inside the city limits, so it too had to be moved a second time.

Nancy never outgrew her love of horses, even when she fell in love and married. Soon after her baby Laura was born, Nancy took a job exercising some thoroughbred horses near Westwood before coming back to San Luis Obispo and starting to teach again.

Pepper went to the Fresno area, where a classmate of Nancy's lived on a farm when not attending Cal Poly. That girl's little sister, Mardy, made me feel secure and content that this wonderful old horse had one more fine home when the story came back to me that, during a rain, Mardy had gone out with a slicker and umbrella to ride Pepper around in a large arena. She bridled him, got on bareback, and opened her umbrella.

This giant horse either was truly petrified of a big black umbrella opening above his back or decided he needed a bit of exercise and it would be fun to act frightened—Pepper took off at a run, while Mardy hung on to both his mane and the umbrella. The umbrella turned inside out, and around and around the large corral they flew.

Mardy's daddy rushed out and shouted to her to drop the umbrella. That quieted down Pepper, and Mardy slipped off the horse safely. Only good ranch parents would have let their daughter go out to ride in a storm, and only a little girl who truly loved horses would have wanted to go out to ride. Pepper would end his days happily.

Shorty was trailered to a large arena beside a red barn that was almost in town and not far from our new house. He would be boarded until a good home could be found for him.

Although I had had a limited number of domesticated and wild birds and animals to observe, it was increasingly clear to me that all humans and beasts were part of a global scheme of life. I worried about all the wild creatures, their fragile and vulnerable lives in jeopardy as their homes, food, and water supplies on Oak Hills and all over the world grew ever smaller. Many water supplies were becoming more limited and polluted, food supplies scarce, and forests and other natural habitats destroyed while cities and towns spread increasingly over farmlands, deserts, forests, and valleys. Ever so soon there would be huge bulldozers on Oak Hills Ranch, pushing the dirt around over all the low rolling hills, and there would be other machines digging ditches for sewer, gas, water, and electricity for a forest of a different sort: cement sidewalks, asphalt roads, and a new large crop of houses on lots too small.

Both the land and its wild creatures, tiny and large, will be gone, either slowly or like a flood, with land no longer available. There won't be a place for even the grass and brush lands or massive oak, willow, and sycamore trees. I remembered the poignant scene of the vulnerability, yet the majestic dignity, of a big buck I saw one evening along Prefumo Canyon Road. He was poised for flight, yet petrified and unable to decide which way to go to find a safe haven. Finally, he bounded away down the embankment near the meadow. There were the quails and doves that came to glean seed from the lane and the horse-feeding areas, and that old owl down in the barn. All would go, although I hadn't seen the owl for some time. With fewer and fewer sanctuaries providing safety, wild and fast rabbits and squirrels that the dogs had never caught would find little food up on the steep mountainsides, even if they managed to evade the giant land-grading machines.

The ancient, slumbering barn that had been nesting there at the bottom of the hill for way over a hundred years had continued to be my retreat. Was it really only ten years? Even as time became short it drew me down the hill to say goodbye. "I'm so sorry, beautiful, weathered friend—You won't last long after the developers arrive; but what memories you must hold of countless horses, humans, cows, calves, horses, and other animals. Certainly, there have been many wonderful owls, and swallows who put on air shows and built their mud nests each year, as well as countless other birds who nested inside or under your eaves. I'll remember you, ancient barn."

I never felt a natural aptitude as a mom, but maybe just being there had made some difference. I hoped that the children had lived on this ranch and the other rural settings long enough to soak up the feeling that life can be simple yet full of love and countless attainable goals. I wanted them to remember the fragile souls and the beauty of all the players here—horses, cows, calves, dogs, cats, and all the other critters—and keep a respect, caring, and concern for all living things.

I tried to encourage and comfort the younger two: "Happiness comes from your attitude, and you can decide what that will be, so go for hope, optimism, and a can-do spirit. I assure you, Jeff and Doug, we'll all build various kinds of new lives that will open up and grow. Maybe things have become too easy and comfortable here and it's really a good time to leave for increasingly different dreams and visions of the future. Anyway, we're being separated from land that was never ours. Dad and I now own our own home for you and several other new properties that are not far away.

"One more suggestion: don't see a curtain coming down, just look at it as a curtain rising on a whole new show. Any change, even supposedly bad ones, may well produce surprising windfalls for good outcomes and happiness. What's that saying, 'When life hands you lemons, make lemonade?' You can do a lot better than that, and your challenges may be smaller and easier than you think.

"Don't look so darn solemn! Many of your friends will be the same, with your scout groups, church, sports, and the friends you made when first coming to town. These country school kids you like will join you soon in junior or senior high school. Plus, you're not homeless. The new home is just a block from your school awaiting you, and Boom and Smoochie are coming with us. Nomadically, this is hardly a change; we're only going about five or six miles— a minor detour." At least on this ranch, the kids had had lots of experience avoiding potholes of various kinds, including the ones in that long lane that forever needed leveling and loads of red rock.

Had they learned the value of hard work that is rewarding in what it brings forth; that opportunities are everywhere and endless, and that one can't just stand still but go forward, fix it, figure it out, take chances, and try? In their spare time, will they plant gardens and fruit trees around their homes, build up the earth, and, in time, teach their children to treasure, care for, and laugh with animals?

Then I suddenly remembered there was one more very good reason it might be just as well we couldn't buy the homestead acres. The town was currently engulfing the whole area so rapidly, the scenario for a time bomb of development was probably already set for all of the 760 acres of Oak Hill Ranch. We would have been living on borrowed time if we had stayed. The hills would not hold waves of oats swaying in the wind much longer. It wouldn't have worked to acquire a dozen acres with the house and barns if there were a maze of houses being built and blanketing much of the ranch on three sides of the property, and a golf course was already in place on the fourth side at the bottom of the lane. We would still have had to sell to the developer and move. There's a time to hang on and a time to let go.

These thoughts made me recall, with increasing amazement, how many times in our lives when things had gone wrong, and the twisting trail we tried to follow sort of faded out before us, the setbacks usually turned out to be the best thing that could have happened to us. Good outcomes often came and grew with coincidences that were hard to believe. Not only that, the journeys had been good, as well as the early destinations, with events coming and going in mysterious ways. We'd experienced a heap of living and fun on Oak Hills, but it didn't mean that more fun times wouldn't lie ahead.

Would we have even led such a wonderful existence in the beginning if Dan's health had been robust and he had followed a music career? I think not.

If we had been more affluent and less hungry, would we have been spurred to stay the course so well, with advanced degrees and interesting careers? Maybe not.

It also entered my mind, what if we had used the large sum of money, that had been almost impossible for us to borrow, to pay cash for a piece of this ranch? Would we ever have acquired the fine investments of three new houses during these last several months, plus purchases of property in Santa Maria and Grover Beach for branch real estate classes?

And, when we made the decision to not move into one of two large houses we had quickly bought, I had found a better third house on the hill almost next door to the younger boys' schools, and we moved there. Never feel like a victim. Stay flexible, look forward, and work like crazy toward a bunch of new tomorrows. There's a saying that "it's always darkest before the dawn." Days may become bright and sunny, even if we're metamorphosing into town people again.

Chapter 32
A Taste of Town

You'd think that two kids leaving for college, getting married, and setting up homes of their own would have mostly emptied the closets and garage and left only with bare-bone furnishings. Our pick-up, loaded full, had delivered to Nancy and Danny many a load of college books, blankets, furniture, clothes, pots and pans, and just junk that they valued dearly. Still, the Oak Hills Ranch house had become just as cluttered and full as always.

There was also the fact that I never throw anything away if I can help it, and constantly acquire more and more. This time, however, it wasn't completely my fault. When we bought the house in town on Fixlini, the sellers were buying a boat and wanted the sale of their house to include our keeping a lot of their furniture. The man had been a ship captain, and sometime in their lives they had acquired a lot of nice cane furniture, perhaps in the Philippines, and had brought back dressers, night stands, a table with six chairs, small end tables, and several chaise lounge chairs. To buy the property, we acquired the furniture. I could hardly believe that I, who had never lounged away even one afternoon as far as I could remember, now owned two heavy and beautifully made cane lounge chairs, at least six feet long, and covered with thick pads. I flopped down into one of them and sighed, "If I lie in this too long, I just might unravel into a pool of bliss on this patio and never get up."

There was, however, a different outcome for the sellers—soon after we moved to the house in town, I heard that the beautiful boat the captain and his wife had bought and carefully refurbished had sunk on its maiden voyage up the coast from San Diego to Morro Bay. The wife had once been an "Olympic tryout swimmer," they said, and the captain also swam well. In the dark of night, as their boat crashed on the rocks, they and their dog swam through huge waves of a big winter storm to the beach along the far-reaching, military-restricted lands of Vandenberg Air Force Base.

Wet and cold, the dog and his owners wandered the countryside for two days and nights before being found. When they were finally found, the captain's fury was not as much over losing his new boat, as it was over the lack of security. "The whole Russian army could have landed," he reportedly declaimed, " and the base never would have known! " He was a true patriotic American, and this was during the Cold War. The couple never asked for their furniture back, and I don't know if they bought another boat or decided to take up something like farming.

By converting the garage into an extra sleeping and family playroom and making the "mother-in-law" wing of the house over the garage a rental for a couple, I was able to find a place for more or less all the extra furniture, but the variety of different styles made our house look rather like a furniture store. The lounge chairs and a couple of end tables we moved up the hill in our back yard to a cabana and sitting area beside a small swimming pool.

Relocation also came with some "firsts." There sat my first clothes-dryer, but it wouldn't be used—old habits die hard, and I used the sun-powered clothesline up the hill in the back yard except on rainy days when the wash hung in the house. The house also had my first dishwasher, but I was still in the dark ages and continued washing the dishes by hand. And, lastly, the house had central heating, though I seldom used it.

Living in the Spartan houses we'd had in the past, I never had the chance to develop any artistic or decorating talent, so with this one I made some poor decisions in minutes—I bought green carpeting to go with our green sofa and two upholstered chairs. Green goes with green, doesn't it? After the sunny rooms of the ranch, the whole house had seemed dark, and now my hasty decisions made it even more so.

Brown also matches brown. The garage that I turned into a sleeping and rumpus room for the younger two boys and their friends had only one half-glass wooden door and one very small window on the side. The room begged for light, cheery tones; instead, I had chosen walnut wood paneling for the walls and tannish-brown carpeting for the cement floor. Obviously, this would require lots of fluorescent lighting installed over the pool table. No wonder the boys began to do their homework upstairs on our old kitchen table.

And oh, how pink can go with pink! The main bathroom was entirely pink when we bought the house, including the walls, ceiling, countertops, floors, shower and window curtains. We all hated it, but since most of the room was tiled and "like new," it remained. Even Smoochie and, later, Truffles hated to be given baths there. So what did I do with my non-functioning brain cells, but order six sets of new pink towels— towels bought back when they were created to last for generations. Some years ago Nancy finally sneaked these towels out to the trunk of her car to take home and burn or put in the garbage, but I discovered them and saved them before she left. Why didn't I buy white towels or other colors? None of us was ever fond of that home, and I was partly to blame. If color is used as therapy, we'd all have become basket cases.

Moving to town was horrible for Boom and Lady Lu. Boom's loss of the ranch life was especially difficult because there he had hundreds of acres to roam free on, and kids still living at home to love, protect, and be loved by in return. Lady Lu's feelings and thoughts were probably more diffused and vague. Boom hated the small and lonely back yard, with its high fencing and the wall of the house conspiring to block all view of the outside world. To stay near us, both dogs insisted on hovering constantly on the shady, cold, and often damp cement patio next to the back door instead of spending some time up the hill where there were the pool, a cabana, a small lawn, and some sunshine. Smoochie fared somewhat better by living in the house more and more, or going outside and catching the warm rays of the morning sun while sleeping atop a low redwood shed that had been built across the far side of the patio and held our giant deepfreeze.

The dogs' frustrations erupted in a huge dogfight one evening. We all remember it well because Smoochie jumped on the back of Lady Lu while the fight raged, and the cat yowled along with the dogs' fierce growling and snapping. In retrospect, I felt horrible for not taking Boom and Lady Lu on more walks and rides in the car. I finally decided we had all probably become a bit off-balance after the loss of the expansive views and lands of Oak Hills Ranch.

After the dogfight, Dan and I tried harder to begin taking the dogs to beaches where we could turn them loose. This meant going out north of Morro Bay to the strand, or down to the sand dune area below Pismo Beach. In addition, the boys also took the animals up on the hillside behind our house, and that also helped. Still, there wasn't the daily freedom that Boomerang missed so much.

Even I had to be more locked-up: times had gradually changed over the years regarding security, and we could no longer leave "the latchstring out." We now kept the house locked at night or whenever we were away.

There were a few pluses, however. Since the junior high school was less than a block up the hill, and the senior high was not far beyond at the bottom of the hill on the far side, for the first time in a century, it seemed, I didn't have to run a taxi service for multiple children every day. Instead, I filled hundred hour workweeks with other stuff. In addition to taking hours of phone calls and doing the business end of the ever growing Lumbleau Real Estate School, I managed all the rentals, and Doug, Jeff and I still spent summers cleaning and painting the houses.

These younger boys, however, had grown older, gotten smarter, and fomented a rebellion. "We want to be paid for painting this year,"

Doug informed me. "I want a good camera, like dad's, and a pool table for downstairs. Jeff wants a portable electric organ—not a cheap one." The younger two of my troupe of workers were suddenly big guys, taller than I was, and wanting money or loot for their labor. They had been underpaid farm hands and painters since becoming old enough to hold a shovel or brush—they got the loot.

And I got a broker's license. Since I tried to get it after only about six weeks of study, and since I thought there was a fifty-fifty chance I'd embarrass Dan by failing the exam, I made him drive me all the way to Sacramento to take the state test, where there should be no students of his taking the exam and asking him later if his wife had passed. Well, there was a student of his up there taking the test that very day. Fortunately, I got through the tests all right, but just by a point or two, I bet. I hadn't gotten a sales license, but in those days if you had a college degree the state allowed you to go directly for a broker's license.

I then bought a large ranch-style house on a busy street in town to convert to my real estate company, Chase Pacific Properties, Inc. After re-roofing, painting, carpeting, and putting in a large asphalt parking area for that house-turned-office-space, my business grew quickly from that location to three branch offices in the county and to about thirty sales people.

Dan soon complained, "Maybe we're more like ants than the crows who hoarded goodies on the ranch. I don't know how much ants work at night, but we're taking moonlighting to a ridiculous high."

Dan and I were still in love with pick-up trucks, and he had recently bought a new one, while I was still driving one of the "Sherman tanks," or "whales," as the children still called my fine old station wagons. Now, the salesmen working in real estate with me decided their broker needed classier wheels sitting out there in the parking lot. With my large sales staff, the growing number of rentals, and the Lumbleau Real Estate School work, I was too busy to do any sales or listing work, but, finally, I gave in to my staff and parked a new white Seville beside the house. To everyone who asked I politely admitted the car was "pretty," but in my heart I longed for the old station wagons.

A tall, working windmill sat beside this ranch-house-turned-real-estate-office on Santa Rosa Avenue. A windmill was something I'd always wanted to have when living in the country. Now I got my first and last one when it was no longer even on agricultural land. Nevertheless, I treasured it and used a windmill design for my company logo (the windmill is still on the property, though it was moved to a new location after new owners added another building).

"Let them eat cereal!" Workweeks remained over a hundred hours for us. I still believed in the saying, "Do all you can and results multiply," but I never had time to figure out just what the "results" would be or when they might show up or multiply.

No longer were there berry or cherry pies drooling all over the oven and sending out the delicious hot smell of desserts for those who "ate their chard." Before Jeff left for USC that year, out of frustration and hunger, he had begun to cook for himself and fleshed out my fast-food dinners with chocolate cakes made from mixes, and with anything he could fry, such as hamburgers, wieners, and potatoes. At bedtime, I often found him eating a large bowl of cold cereal, with dad shaking more cereal and milk into a bowl across the table from him. This was not the "simplifying" that I had planned.

Chapter 33
Anyone Want a Cat?

S tray cats in town usually had an easier time finding us than they had out in the countryside. Since the dogs were confined to the back yard, except for walks and excursions to the beach, a homeless cat could be relatively safe on the small covered front porch on Fixlini Street—and soon a kitten began to greet me daily on the porch to tell me her story of being lost and hungry. She often went first into an act of rubbing my legs and purring loudly, following that with a sudden dash to try and get in the door.

She wore a thick, rich, chocolate-colored coat, and her large round greenish-yellow eyes never lost contact with mine. I guessed she might be about three months old. Her tentative, soft and faint meows were not a Siamese voice, so I wondered what breed she might be. I had seen her in the neighborhood for a number of days and could easily believe her tale of being lost. By talking with her and sizing-up her condition, I noticed that she had a very bad pendulous tummy. Here was a precious cat, probably needing expensive surgery; it was probably why she had been dropped off to find a new home on this street with two nearby schools and students walking by.

Smoochie was now extremely old and getting more and more ill and thin each day, even with Dan's ever more creative gourmet meals to tempt him. I didn't want to upset this dear puss during his final year or months of life by bringing another cat into the house. This wonderful old cat had owned and trained grown-ups, dogs, and children all his days and had reigned over the house with joy, close attention, and loyalty. It had been a full-time job, and he had earned a peaceful end to his long life. Moreover, Smoochie was always very curious, but didn't like surprises. I assumed another cat in the house would upset him greatly. Honestly, who would like a stranger suddenly appearing to live in one's home, especially when one was ill and hadn't been consulted or forewarned?

"Does anyone want this darling kitten?" I walked up and down the street trying to find her a home. What I learned was that this puss had already, systematically and intelligently, gone to every door on both sides of the long block. She had even jumped up and draped herself around the neck of a man sitting down to refinish a chair in his back yard, and purred up a storm. Kitty and I did a masterful sales job, but even joint begging failed in this neighborhood. No one wanted her, even if I paid for the surgery she needed.

Maybe I was being punished for refusing to adopt the many kittens and cats offered to me by friends through the years. Once again, Dan wrote a plea on a schoolroom blackboard, "Free Kitten to Good Home." He had no takers; the whole world seemed to be fully supplied with cats.

Many warned that if I fed the kitten I wouldn't be able to get rid of her. They made it sound like absolute law: feed a cat once and he's yours for life. I agreed, but I was already feeding her on our porch every morning and night, and sometimes at noon, and I had provided her a baby-blanket in the corner of the porch to sleep on.

My refrain grew to include everyone—from friends on the phone to grocery clerks: "Know anyone who would like a beautiful, young cat?" One can become quite unpopular with that question, asked over and over again. It's good that dog and cat pounds charge for their animals. People don't always value free gifts. Maybe I should have said that I'd paid a fortune for her.

In the end there was no choice—with costly pendulous-tummy surgery in her future, she would be put down at the pound. There were always too many healthy and nice kitties out there for anyone to have to choose one needing a major operation.

Finally, I gave up. Actually, the cat didn't seem to like any of the humans I showed her to any more than I did. We shared the same belief that those people must not be friends of cats. Sharing such prejudices as we did, it became evident that we were meant for each other, and I had a long talk with Smoochie. "There's this kitten out on the porch who came to this house, scared, lonesome, and very hungry. She needs a home. All of us love you so much, but would you really care if a very considerate little cat came to stay here?" Smoochie was more into dreams than active life and slept most of the time I talked. He really didn't seem to care what happened. Somehow, I felt it might be all right, even though I hated to bring the kitten into the house.

The velvety brown kitten could admire her own chutzpa; she'd stayed the course by pretty much living on the porch and had finally won a home and family. As I officially opened the front door wide, she definitely let me know, with a different meow and complacent manner, "By Golly, I was certain all along you'd see it my way." With tail held high, she stepped daintily but confidently past me into the living room. She then waited at the edge of the carpet, as though wondering what the house rules were or how quickly she might dare explore and, with luck, discover a well-stocked kitchen. This polite puss was obviously from an affectionate and caring home. She had been pampered and certainly would not have had the skills to capture enough mice and birds to stay alive outdoors.

I sat down and watched while she became brave enough to circle the room. She went up to Smoochie, lying on his blanket, and they looked at each other and sniffed noses. He didn't bother to get up. She seemed to sense that he was ill. This kitten never did try to get him to play games, but now and then they touched noses, and one day I saw Smoochie carefully lick her face. Cats don't become close buddies to each other right away, but the new kitten respected old Smoochie and both cats were polite and gentle souls. Animal psychology is complicated and mysterious. I hadn't needed to worry at all about Smoochie and the kitten.

After dinner, Jeff, dad, and I sat in the living room and, while puss met and explored us by jumping up to our laps and beginning the habit she never lost of then jumping up to our shoulders and draping herself around our necks, we tried listing possible cat names for her. Her soft Hershey-colored fur had us coming up with names of things brown. Several friends had wondered if she were Siamese, but a friend with two Siamese told me she thought the cat was Burmese. She pointed out that my kitten's coat was a much darker brown. Her eyes more round and a rather golden color, instead of blue, and even her head was more round than her Siamese cats; in addition to that, our little cat had a beautiful voice compared to those Siamese. I looked Burmese up in a book and learned these cats were originally from Burma, and they mentioned Brown Burmese and Chocolate Burmese. Though we never could quite be certain of her breed, we decided she was likely Burmese.

For once the family agreed to a name that I had chosen—I settled on the name "Truffles" because the cat's coloring reminded me of the rich chocolate candies. Truffles learned her name because she was mostly an inside cat (even if, with the true behavior of most cats, she only came when she wanted!). Still, dinnertime calls, along with the fragrance of meat cooking, usually brought her running.

"Think kindness and other good thoughts, Boom and Lady Lu. Come in and meet the new cat." The dogs were a pushover for this kitten to manage. All their lives they had lived with cats, and Smoochie, O.J., and others had trained the dogs well. But if non-family strays or frightened cats ran from them, the dogs always felt free to race after them. This little one froze where she stood and made no attempt to run as I lectured the dogs long and severely. "This is your cat and this is my cat. She is going to live here, so you be nice." Then I set Truffles down on the carpet in front of them, and they sniffed her all over. The kitten was clearly spooked by the big brutes, but she didn't run. Her hair rose, her tail went up in the air, and she hissed and tried to swat them as best she could. Boomerang knew what I had said, but I couldn't be sure Lady Lu understood; fortunately, she usually just went along with whatever Boomerang did. Both dogs were very old when we moved to town, and after a few years both had to be put down.

Truffles found everything fine in the back yard, and on some sunny days, Smoochie still walked out with him. There was a high stack of firewood by the back fence and a cabana-like room without a door by the pool, as well as a several trees for climbing if Truffles decided she wanted some private places to sleep or explore. Cats like change only on their terms and feel better with order and routine. During the day it was a quiet, regular routine, and both cats appreciated those predictable times.

Smoochie had given up sleeping on our bed at night since it was hard for him to jump up on it. Instead, he stayed much of the time on a blanket near the wall heater. That helped the cats' relationship, because Truffles began a long life of sleeping on our bed. Placid and softly purring, she exuded a deep satisfaction with life.

It also helped that, unlike Smoochie, who had prattled on and on about anything or nothing, Truffles was a cat of fewer words. Only at mealtime did Truffles talk, mainly asking for dinner. Sometimes, Smoochie and Truffles joined together with their "feed me" voices, but both were usually soft-voiced cats when talking about other small concerns or wishes.

Even with all my jobs, I found time to plant a vegetable garden up in front of the wood stack by the back fence on Fixlini Street, and Truffles tried to become a farm hand. The cat dug around in the soil, perhaps because she'd found some bugs and earthworms there, and always went with me when I brought in the harvest. With tail high, she paraded ahead of me through the back door, as though to tell anyone in the kitchen, "See what we have dug up and picked for you!"

I didn't have to do much detective work to decide in more detail what sort of home Truffles had been in before coming to us. Animals, as well as children, seldom enjoy being alone for long, and she followed me around the house from room to room. When I sat down at the dining table to do office work, she sat among my papers and tried to bat the pen away from me or wrapped both paws around the pen and drew it to her mouth to chew or held it to her chest while she lay on her back and kicked at it with her back feet. Since these games with pens and papers flying to the floor had been perfected, it was surely a student or writer who had owned her. A student seemed most likely because the junior and senior high schools were both so near, and a student whose parents couldn't afford the necessary veterinarian bills may have been told she would have to get rid of the cat.

Kittens, if left long enough with their mommas, get plenty of lessons in things like hunting, fighting, climbing, hiding, playing, and managing adults. However, this waif had also learned to sharpen her claws on almost everything within reach, shredding furniture, curtains, bedspreads, groceries, and even the daily mail. Dan tacked scraps of carpeting to a 4" x 4" post and nailed it to a large wooden base, also covered with carpeting, to make a claw-sharpening alternative. By keeping Truffles in the kitchen or bathroom for hours at a time, she actually began to use the post as intended, but I still had to switch ends of bedspreads and drapes to hide sections that she had changed into long ribbons or string-like fringes. Even some of the upholstered furniture had to be rearranged or kept covered. Before long, several of the kids, who had homes of their own and had acquired kittens, were asking for more pieces of the green shag carpeting to make scratching posts for their pets.

I also acquired a new helper in making the beds. In fact, it was a highlight of Truffle's mornings. As soon as I shook a sheet up and down, Truffles, with round, intense eyes and twisting body, dived under the sheet and scurried around from one side of the bed to the other, ending up suddenly very quiet down at the foot of the bed under all the bedding. I had to either pull her out at that point or make the bed up and hope she wouldn't suffocate under the blankets and spread. Changing-the-sheets day was still more fun, for there were two sheets on each bed that I shook out to billow above her. It seemed more likely that in her previous home a girl student, rather than a boy, would have let her play this way, shaking the sheets up in the air longer than necessary just for her pleasure.

As with all our cats, she spent a great deal of thought on food, and kitchens were always a place for her to hang out. Again, she was spoiled like Smoochie and successfully begged for snacks. The dogs wolfed down a whole meal in seconds, while our cats, including Truffles, ate slowly, taking tiny bites to see if the food was really edible. It had to be just right: the right flavor, the right texture, and the right temperature for that particular day. Cats may insist on some completely different menu the next day.

After learning a bit about this dear puss and giving her a new name, it was time to take her for the first of what turned out to be three necessary operations to correct the tummy that hung down. On the third operation the vet was able to add some mesh webbing inside, which held for the rest of her long life. On top of the stomach surgeries there were all the usual shots and then spaying. Truffles handled the surgeries well, but I hurt for her. Yet in spite of those frightening surgeries and her meows of apprehension when I put her in the car for trips to the vet hospital, our little stray remained loyal and kept us as family. We spent a fortune, but Truffles gave us back—for a little over an amazingly long twenty-three years—a great wealth of laughter, love, and companionship. In addition to the dogs' exuberant greetings, it was also lovely to come home to a cat member of the family waiting there with a soft purring welcome.

However, I had completely forgotten the problem I had run into decades ago of having guests in a house with a cat who might want to help me with some cat-hospitality… or inhospitality. Once again, I had a large group of ladies in for a meeting. I'd carefully vacuumed, dusted, mopped, and spent a lot of time brushing and getting the brown cat hair off the furniture, so that nice wool suits and other clothing wouldn't leave the house with a coating of hair on their back sides. Refreshments had been made after much thought and sleepless nights, since I still didn't prepare anything decorative and tasty with confidence or ease. Finally all was ready.

Two ladies sat where the cat slept much of the time, one on the upholstered chair and the other on the sofa. Immediately, they began to cough, sneeze, and search for hankies. At least I was a quick learner this time. I asked if they were allergic to cats. Of course the answer was yes, so I explained that once in awhile our cat sneaked into the living room and got on the furniture. I made it sound as if the cat came in the house once or twice a year, not every night and part of every day. Some of the all-wood dining room chairs had been placed in the living room, so I suggested, "Maybe you should move to one of the wooden chairs and I'll open the window."

Before the second lady had time to move to the wooden chair, it got worse. The younger boys came home from school, and, considerately, quietly came in the back kitchen door. Truffles came in with them. She immediately trotted into the living room, and it became a rerun of the scene on the ranch with Smoochie and another group of ladies. Before I recalled that other cat scene and could stop her, the cat walked casually around the room and stopped in front of the one lady still sitting on the couch who was not a "cat-person." In fact, she loathed cats. She was holding a plate with a small sandwich and a couple of strawberries that she'd dunked in powdered sugar, and had set a cup of coffee on the coffee table in front of her, preparing to move to the wooden chair.

Truffles sprang up between her and another lady. The strawberries and sandwich landed on the carpet just as the lady tried to place the plate on the table. She jumped up as though she had been attacked by a tiger. Her coffee cup clattered over on the table, as the coffee spread out and dripped onto the carpet. The fruit and sandwich were also now on the carpet. Truffles seemed frightened and fled the room in a blur of brown fur. One cat-lover made it worse by saying, "Oh, poor kitty! She's frightened and maybe the coffee burned her." She got up and ran in search of the cat down the hall to the back bedroom.

This was too much coincidence. I firmly believe cats and dogs, and other animals as well, often know, in some way, the feelings of people toward them as well as people's attitudes or moods about many things. There were now two meetings of groups of ladies at my homes over the years during which this sort of thing had happened. Each time the room had been full of welcoming laps but for the lap of the one cat-hater whom the cats chose to approach. I think Truffles knew darn well what she had done, and I bet she had an excited grin on her face as she ran from the scene. Years earlier there had also been Sage, in Arizona, who had spent weeks winning Dan over to her side when we first gave her a home and Dan's immediate inclination had been to kick her out and make her an outside cat. Animals' sense of human feelings and the feelings of other animals they come in contact with have been told in countless books and true short stories throughout history. That lady must have given off some kind of scent or signal that triggered the response, and cats definitely have a sense of humor and a desire for fun.

In fact, both cats and dogs seem sometimes to understand people better than people understand them. If I'd understood Truffles better, I would have known that she wouldn't like to suddenly come across a whole room of strange people in "her house." It was what any cat might try when suddenly coming in to find a dozen intruders sitting and chattering in her "cave". And she certainly seemed to recognize the one person who disliked her as she padded around the room.

There had also been a lot of stress in this pussy's life. She not only lost her first home when not much older than a kitten, but had to adapt to a home of big dogs, an ailing old cat, and new people coming and going. There had been the multiple trips to the Animal Hospital for the three surgeries, plus needed follow-up visits. No wonder she was disturbed and up to a little mischief.

I decided that in the future I would somehow research the cat allergies, both physical and psychological, of all who came to the house, and I'd shampoo the two chairs and couch, if need be. Some of these women I seldom saw except at these occasional meetings. In the future, this calculating cat would have to go out and stay in the car with a litter box, food, and water for an afternoon. I did this several times, but once forgot and left Truffles in the car all night. She clearly showed her displeasure over being in that jail cell when I finally remembered her the next morning. Giving me a look of disgust, she held her tail high and swished it back and forth as she stalked seriously and purposefully back into the house to groom herself free of all that car odor. Dogs wag their tails when happy, while cats sometimes do it when extremely irritated.

The non-cat person was spunky and did come back to my home a time or two, but, even knowing the cat was in the car or the boys' room downstairs, she seemed to peer about the room more than was necessary.

Chapter 34
Wendy with the Laughing Face

J an was a great lover of dogs, especially big dogs—most of those she had owned were Great Danes. Since she was my key helper in managing the real estate offices, her reception desk in my main office was next to the front door and faced a large picture window that looked out on a busy street and nearby intersection. Since I used a desk at the back side of the room, we often talked about our current pets and love of animals.

This day, suddenly she spoke sharply, "Judy, come help me! We've got a momma dog and three large puppies right out in the middle of the street. Cars are just missing them."

Jan and I ran out and, while waving our hands at the cars to stop, waded into the lanes of traffic, and called to the momma dog. The dog had no collar or tag, but was immediately friendly and relieved to see two ladies on foot out among the cars going by, and when we called to her, she came happily to us and safety. Three large pups, about three months old, gamboled along beside, behind, and ahead of their mom, with no idea that this wasn't just a fun outing.

We all fled into the building. Both the dog and her puppies looked like Dobermans. This Dobie was a black dog with some fawn-colored fur on her lower legs and face. She had a long tail, instead of the usual docked one, and her ears turned down, rather than having had them cut smaller and trained to stand up. Mom was still letting her big pups nurse, and she was very thin, with large pendulous teats, making her anything but good-looking. The foursome still didn't know they were lost or abandoned, and tried to play with each other.

With a friendly and laughing voice, Jan called to them, "Hey, mom and kids, want some water?" Jan decided they looked quite warm and thirsty. The Dobies promptly followed her to the staff snack-room where I had installed a small sink, refrigerator, table, and chairs. They drank out of a cottage cheese carton Jan stole and emptied from some hapless salesman's lunch to create a watering dish.

"Jan, you'll have to phone the pound to come get them as soon as possible. Hopefully, the owners will come for them at the pound right away." Such happy dogs surely had been loved and treated well. Dogs usually behave with just a bit of praise, some tidbits of food, or a stern "No." This dog didn't seem to have ever been hit, slapped, yanked, or pushed around. She trusted us and seemed to love hearing our laughter.

Mother dog continued to feel her aim in life was to have as much fun as possible. She ran upstairs and stole a sock from a box, and soon a stampede of paws was running up and down the stairs as the pups kept trying to take the sock away from her as she ran through the rooms. Because I was laughing so much at their game, she came over to me, dropped the sock at my feet, and panted and grinned from ear to ear while wagging her whole body with her tail. That wonderful, youthful, and ugly mother could actually laugh, or at least give a big wide grin—a toothy, wide grin on a Doberman!

Dan came into the office from school before the dogs were picked up by the pound, and Jan immediately said, "Judy has just this minute decided you are going to adopt a new family of four. What do you think of them?"

All he could come up with was to shake his head back and forth and sort of sputter, "You gotta be kidding. They're ugly, super ugly!"

The man from the pound informed Jan and me that the dogs would be kept until Friday morning. All week Dan and I debated what we would do if they weren't claimed. I kept telling him about the dog's love of life and her laughing face. "I'm not sure if her lineage is all Doberman, but I swear she will always be bright, full of gentle love and the joy of life: a free spirit expecting the best. Also, she would make an excellent watchdog because of her looks. She'll get her girlish figure back when she no longer has the big pups."

Jan tried not to phone the pound about a dozen times every day that week, but I know she phoned often. Friday the final word was, "No, the dogs have not been claimed. You have 'til about ten this morning to come and take 'em." I phoned Dan at school, and he agreed we could keep the mom, and I would take the pups to a different animal shelter to get adopted. If we were the actual owners of the pups, this other animal rescue place would take them. They didn't take strays.

It wasn't just Wendy's puppies and finding a second horse that Dan talked about with his students that day. His Ag-Business and Farm Management majors always got a bit of his philosophy about picking the right spouse who'd work as a team-partner for life, share the same goals, care about all living things, plus choose a degree and line of work that would be enjoyable. He also believed these young students should learn a lot about all phases of agriculture, no matter what their major. When he discovered that many students had never eaten one bite of an artichoke, he had me cook six or seven of the vegetables, and passed them around the room the next day along with some salted and peppered mayonnaise, showing them how to eat "the good parts." I had cut the artichokes in fourths so that all students could eat some. One young man observed, "There's no way to clean our plates—with all these leaves, there's more left on our plates than before we ate."

Another student in that class happened to have a dad who raised artichokes near Watsonville, and for a number of years he had his son bring his teacher a full box of extra large, fresh artichokes at harvest time. They were always my all-time favorite vegetable—usually steamed and served with salted and melted butter or a little mayonnaise.

While Dan's students were eating artichokes in class that day, Jan and I drove out to the pound, and I paid to become the owner of the four dogs. After just five days in that jail, they all looked sick, with runny, dull eyes and shivering, thin bodies. The building they had been kept in was plumb awful. The floors in their small pens were icy cold, wet cement, with nothing dry for them to lie on, and the dimly lit, almost windowless room somehow had a freezing wind blowing through it. The vulnerability of animals from uncaring humans is so great and so often cruel. How could any pound be so totally unfit for animals? I had the strong suspicion that the dog knew she was on death row in that small, uncomfortable, and unclean cage. With her keen sense of smell and the sounds she had heard, it might not have been hard for her to foretell animals' dying there. Why had a dog who had obviously had a happy home been turned out at a busy street intersection? If lost, why weren't the dogs claimed at the pound or advertised for in the paper under Lost Pets?

I dropped Jan off at my office and delivered the dogs to the veterinarian a few blocks away. The doctor shook his head, saying, "Don't tell me these Dobies were handpicked! How'd this hard-knock family fall in your lap?"

He only wanted to keep the mother dog to work on and suggested I drive out to the animal shelter south of town with her pups right away. The vet assured me the shelter would be able to give the pups their shots, take care of them, and probably find homes for them. I could pick momma dog up on the way back after he'd given her some shots and a physical. Spaying would have to be done when she was in better health.

At school, Dan wrote a message on his blackboard—Ranch Pups Free to Good Homes—and also mentioned the dogs to his classes. Two students were immediately interested, and each took a puppy for their home farms.

Momma Doberman came home from the vet's animal clinic with me that night. She was obviously a bright dog, yet she didn't seem to worry about her missing children. Maybe just too much had happened to her that awful week at the pound. Maybe she had also wanted to wean those large puppies. She was still shivering and seemed ill. She must have been deeply relieved to get out alive from that terrifying Animal Shelter. Much has changed at many animal-control shelters since then, and not all pounds are the cruel, unhealthy places many were back then, but some pounds still need improving.

At home, Jeff had a hard time absorbing the fact that mom and dad, and probably mostly mom, had given a home to this unattractive, angular, bone-skinny dog with swinging milk bags underneath. As I fixed dinner I put Jeff and Dan to work thinking up a name. But their choices were slow in coming, so as with Sage and Truffles, I once again got to name this lovely wandering dog. She would be "Wendy." It was a name I had sort of wanted for Nancy; yet, at the time, "Wendy Chase" had not seemed to sound quite right. However, a dog seldom needs a last name, and she had completely wended her way into my heart.

I somehow knew that this sensitive dog would be kind to Truffles and Smoochie. If not, the cats would let her know what was acceptable behavior. Smoochie had easily trained Boom and Lady Lu years ago. Right away, Wendy knew instinctively that the cats were part of this new family and was willing to accept not only us but also the cats with all her heart. Pets have a way of telling the truth, and you can tell a lot by their eyes, tails, sounds, ears, bodies, and actions—all things that help make up their conversations. Both cats and dogs had always seemed to read us like a book. Indeed, they always seemed to understand me far better than I them, much as I tried. However, they understood that I loved them, with my endless hugs, pats, bits of food, and talk. Soaking up the attention and hugs was probably enough to make them happy and well-adjusted. In turn, they tried to return similar feelings.

Unlike some of the cats, Truffles hadn't batted the dogs away to make them leave her alone. She actually had liked the dogs, especially Boomerang, and often sat and purred near him by the back door. Now, with Wendy and some of us hiking up the hill behind the house, Truffles tagged along if she sensed where we were going and got out the door fast enough to go with us.

As the only dog in the family, Wendy fortunately came with many of the human-like traits of Treve and Boom. She could become fearful, embarrassed, angry, joyful, loving, aggressive, gentle, full of dignity—you name it.

Cats are the same way. Truffles was so embarrassed when she had to be bathed after coming home wet and muddy that she just wanted to hide. Eventually, the baths made her feel nice, especially since I told her over and over again how beautiful she would be, all the while toweling her dry or using my hair dryer. Best of all, she learned to like the brushing with an extra soft brush.

Now Wendy was another super special dog, and I loved the bony, leggy, short-haired Doberman from the day she came. I told her over and over that she was "wonderful." She beamed and grinned with the praise, and, without her pups and with lots of food, her black coat became sleek and shiny, and her body shapely again.

Since she was our only dog for several years, it was easier to take Wendy in the car with us, both on long trips and just to town. When I wasn't driving, she insisted on sitting on my lap in the front seat. I was certain that she'd learned to be a lap dog in her earlier life, but someone recently told me about two other Dobermans pinschers who did the same thing. Certainly she had a great desire to see everything possible from the car windows and needed to be near us, but her bony frame was hard on my lap. This dog tried to see absolutely everything outside the car, and it was a special day for her if she saw one of the three kinds of vehicles I think she would have loved to chase. She spotted them blocks ahead or when the vehicles passed in the opposite direction; postal trucks of all sizes, UPS trucks, and garbage trucks all remained exciting and seemed to be more fun than chasing sea birds on a beach. Had she been threatened by such trucks before she lived with us? We would never know.

Back inside the house, it wasn't always the cat in the window. Wendy did her darndest to arrange her bony body along the back of the green sofa next to the large window facing the street, and I never had the heart to keep this dog on the floor.

On the beach, Wendy always chased sea birds until she was exhausted. The birds appeared to egg her on in a game by flying parallel to the beach and then landing on the sand a bit ahead of her, or now and then gliding around and landing behind her. As she raced through the shallow water, she was a beautiful animal in motion, stretched out with head high and alert, and eyes riveted on the birds in flight.

I wished so much to understand the language of this dog—her thoughts, hopes, fears, joys, memories, and perhaps some of the eccentric or special beliefs she held. Like so many of our animals, she needed and appreciated a happy, upbeat outlook from all those around her. She could also poke fun at herself and thus gain attention—as long as we laughed with her and not at her.

Chapter 35
River Ranch

After not coming home even once for lunch in a year's time because of his responsibilities as President of the Faculty Club and other time-stealers, late in his career Dan began arriving at my real estate office daily to take me out to lunch. The office was about four minutes from the university, and home was maybe ten minutes away. That should have made a difference—we could now eat six minutes more food.

Yet, as soon as the car doors slammed, he always asked, "Where do you want to go?" And I always answered, "I don't care. Where do you want to go?" "I asked you first, so you decide. I don't care either." Such indecision could continue for more than six minutes, so he was sometimes late getting back to the college and probably got the reputation for eating a five course meal or maybe enjoying half a round of golf on a long lunch-break. This nonsense was increasingly noticed by Jan who asked, "Your staff and I are increasingly curious—why do you always, always sit out there in the car so long each day before you leave?" To this day we carry on that same inane conversation.

One day there was a new situation when Dan arrived at my building. He walked in and asked Jan where I was. She replied, "Judy told me to tell you she's gone to Atascadero to buy a ranch."

Later that afternoon, Jan laughed and related, "That really set him back on his heels. He asked me, 'How's she going to pay for it?' And I told him what you suggested that I say: 'Judy said to tell you she'd figure that out later.'"

It was true that we had both begun to think about a part-time ranch where Blue and Shorty could live and where we could enjoy weekends— the horse trailer still sat in the driveway of our Fixlini house. Getting another farm or small ranch might also be called an investment.

On a number of weekends, we left Jeff at home studying for classes at the junior college while we traveled the byways of the county, looking for "For Sale" signs or trying to figure out where the properties listed for sale in the newspaper were located. The past weekend, we had finally let a real-estate salesman drive us around on the northern side of Cuesta Grade.

"Only show us the very smallest farms you know about," I warned, "maybe three to ten acres and near an area where we can ride horses." I usually confused real-estate salesmen because they typically showed properties with the largest, nicest homes, while I was worrying about fences, water wells, soil types, barns, views, and basement prices.

At the end of a long afternoon, we still hadn't seen anything we liked, but the salesman happened to mention that the white-fenced thirty-one acres we were passing, with a big white barn and small western-style home, was for sale. The price seemed very good, but we said it was beyond what we could pay. We both agreed with the salesman that it was a lovely place, and right across the street from the Salinas River, which began its life back near Santa Margarita Lake and traveled up the state to empty in the sea beyond Salinas. Some months this riverbed appeared dry, but there was water flowing beneath the surface.

The day I went alone to Atascadero, the salesman had called my office in the morning to report that he had been able to get more information about that white-fenced ranch. "The price is very favorable, and the financing terms will be made easy to a qualified buyer," he told me. "There's a good well, and the Bakers really want to sell." Mrs. Baker was a TV star, but since I never watched TV that meant little to me. I mentioned to the broker that we might rent the house to tenants who would feed our horses, and place our travel trailer up there so we could occasionally stay overnight to ride the horses on both Saturday and Sunday.

We bought the ranch. River Ranch was a composite of lifelong dreams—it gave us not only sturdy, well-made, white fences, a big white barn, and a long, low ranch house nestled under oak trees, but also, right across the street, endless riding trails beside the tree-lined sandy riverbed. The house trailer was soon up on the property, along with Blue's single horse trailer. What a long, long trail we had taken to reach this goal. I found tenants for the house who agreed to take care of Blue and Shorty.

Jeff was lying on the couch at home one day soon after the purchase, feeling the full effects of a bad case of the flu, which gave him a lot of time to reflect. He soon came out with the wish, "It sure would be nice if there were another good horse we could ride with Blue. Shorty is just not fun for anyone to ride...even you complain." The pony could still carry our weight, because we all remained skinny and he was very strong. Yet it was hard for us to keep from walking as we rode, since we always used Shorty without a saddle and there were no stirrups there to hold our feet off the ground. Still, he was family, and we'd keep him as long as possible.

I had already been scanning the paper for a horse to buy but was surprised to learn that our youngest was missing Oak Hills and wanted to ride, too. Well, people can change their minds. I would ride Shorty if need be, but with a new horse, three of us could enjoy rides along the riverbed.

The mare I bought was a young, sensitive, sorrel beauty named Misty. I've forgotten her breeding, but she was purebred and came with papers. This time I had a veterinarian check her out, and she got a clean bill of health. She was easy to bridle, seemed to have a soft mouth, and reined nicely. The young horse let me pick up her feet and seemed to like people. We decided to give Jeff the horse and had him registered as owner, even though he would soon transfer to a university.

Misty was very intrigued by the sandy river trail, with water flowing underneath on its way north to the sea. She constantly tried to pull the reins so as to lower her head and sniff the sand. That's a no-no: horses might then step on the reins, perhaps lie down and roll, or even buck more easily, if so inclined. I continued to wonder if she sensed water below the surface, or was she thinking, perhaps, about a good roll in the sand?

River Ranch should have been a place for great celebration, the fruit of all our dreams and work. But our needs and goals had changed without our even realizing it. Perhaps that's as it has to be—things come to an end at some point. Suddenly it seemed time for us to let go of a rural farm life and move on.

This lovely ranch just didn't work out like a goal or dream should. Dan and I were so busy with multiple jobs and school activities that we didn't even drive up to the ranch very often. Nancy, with her fast-growing little daughter Laura, was now teaching college English classes in San Luis Obispo. She and I also kept wondering if the horses were being ridden by others on River Ranch, especially when Blue was sweaty when we arrived one day. Doug and Danny now lived in other parts of the state and were married and starting careers. Even Dan and I might be leaving the central coast if he retired and we happened to find a retirement home beside the ocean rather than on a farm. And Jeff, our youngest, would be getting married and planned to transfer to USC in the fall.

I put River Ranch back on the market and sold it for the same amount we had paid. Blue and Shorty came back to San Luis Obispo, and this time Nancy found a fine home for both of them back in Los Osos Valley. She kept legal ownership, but gave them to a kindly family that was knowledgeable about horses and had young children who wished to ride both horses and would properly care for them.

Poor Misty was sold to a lady who drove a large truck over from the Fresno area to pick her up. I thought of Misty so often after the sale and hoped the ranching family didn't believe in heavy-handed discipline or usage. There was no way to know, and no other buyers had come along. There was Misty's one habit of wanting to sniff the trail, which hadn't been totally corrected. How would they train her not to do that? With no command of the English language, the total dependence of domesticated animals upon their many kinds of owners is sometimes a frightening thought.

There were several other reasons for selling besides family members' scattering off to different areas. During those last few years, saddles had gradually become harder and harder for me to hoist and swing across a horse's back, and the stirrups on the saddles had seemed to keep growing higher and higher to reach when mounting. There was also the endless physical work if we continued a ranch life. Even more difficult, there seemed no way to acquire a small rural acreage adjacent to a warm stretch of the coast. For what just might be our final home, we began to search the central to southern California coastline for property, this time looking for just a home or a large vacant lot beside the ocean.

"There are so many reasons for us to change directions," I mused. "Can we finally search for some place that's truly special and not go for what's merely practical?" For instance, try to recapture and let grow our great love of the Pacific Ocean and still acquire a house or a small plot of land to plant and treasure."

Time passed, lots of time, and the children all began to worry among themselves that perhaps mom and dad would never find that special place beside the sea. More and more often, from San Diego to San Luis Obispo, Dan and I drove up and down the coastal roads without finding the right piece of land to live on. There's a saying that suggests it's the journey that counts, not the destination, but more and more we craved that destination.

Chapter 36
Do Workaholics Ever Retire?

Coming home from Los Angeles one afternoon, Dan suddenly turned off the freeway south of Santa Barbara to again search a stretch of oceanfront properties. Almost immediately, we saw a sign tacked on a palm tree in front of a vacant lot. It was just a home-made sign, saying "Lot For Sale" and giving a phone number. I jotted the number down on an envelope, and we drove home to a thousand things to do. Still, this time I pulled the envelope out of my purse and made the phone call that same evening.

An elderly sounding man was home. "Yes, the property is still for sale. It actually consists of two lots—the buildable one on the land side and a second small parcel between the road and the mean-high tide line. The parcel of land on the ocean side's main value is guaranteeing your view.

"Yes, it's a great piece of property," the owner continued, "but it can't be built on right away. There's a water moratorium in Montecito, mainly to restrict the growth of population, I'm sure. I've checked, and there's no lack of water. Two others before me have bought the lot and weren't allowed to build. I'm sure this property and loads of others will get houses built eventually. I've had both a judge and an attorney tell me it's a taking away of property rights; but I'm not doing very well health-wise, and my wife and I've got to buy or build and move this year.

"Yeah, well, you can have the lot for the price I paid for it. I can't wait, that's all."

The price seemed very reasonable. Even when buying and selling real estate I'd never tried to drive a really hard bargain and certainly didn't want to with this seller, so I merely mentioned a couple of conditions. "Would you take terms? We're perfect buyers for it because we don't want to develop it right away. Maybe build about 1980, or a bit sooner." A payout over six years also sounded fine to the seller.

"For a final favor, would you give us time to make a quick call to a real estate friend of ours down there to ask him about the moratorium and the lot? We'll call you right back." He thought that was also reasonable.

Our friend had a much higher price for it in his files and thought the place could probably be developed in a few years in spite of the current building ban. "There are houses next door, as well as some along the street behind," he told us, "and the water main, sewer, gas, and electricity are in for those neighboring houses. Sure, it seems like a reasonable risk to take."

We then called the seller back and agreed to buy the lot after just briefly driving by that afternoon. Property, as I'd taught my salespeople, is all about location, location, location. We opened an escrow the next morning.

Yet, I had to laugh, "Impulsive one more time, aren't we? I can't even visualize what was there! What were the other houses like? We could have at least circled around the block. How far, exactly, is it from town and the freeway? Do you think we'll hear the freeway noise? We have no comps from sales in the area, no knowledge of restrictions, except the water one, or anything else. We're not even sleeping on the idea overnight before saying we'll buy it. Yet, as we age, the town and area will surely have good doctors, hospitals, and easy shopping nearby, plus an almost tropical setting of year-round flowers, green trees, high mountains, and the chance for a close-up bonding with the land, sea, and sky in all their seasons."

It became a rite of passage long in the making—it was more than six years before we were able to get a permit to build, and then it was only because we got a permit to drill a well on the lot and actually found fresh water instead of salt water on the back portion of the property. Finding it hard to believe, we had finally put in enough "active duty" to retire, and the big boss, Financial Necessity, hadn't kept us enslaved to the end of our days.

Sometimes we drove south just to stand on the property, listen to the sound of the surf, smell the sea air, and on clear days look out to Santa Cruz Island, with its vertical cliffs and mountainous terrain growing up from the sea.

Only about eight feet above sea level on the front ocean side, the buildable lot was 87 feet wide and 200 feet deep on the land side. With thick hedges on three sides and cars in front usually disappearing by mid-afternoon, our two parcels became isolated and "my" special place, even though it was far from being untamed virgin land. With the vast ocean and sky, there would always be countless sea creatures both above and below the water, and in the evenings, beyond beautiful crumbling cliffs to the west, we could see a curve of city, harbor, and the long Stearn's Wharf.

Santa Barbara was a rather lighthearted town, but had a long and colorful history. The town and most of the residential areas are built on a long coastal shelf. Many homes and buildings have red tile roofs, white walls, and plantings of bougainvillea, geraniums, palm, oak, and countless other vegetation. From our place we could walk west to the zoo, a small lake called the Andrew Clark Bird Refuge, and to the Coast Village shopping center just inland.

Inland, which is actually north of this south-facing lot and beach, the Santa Ynez string of mountains make a wonderful gray-green backdrop. Since we often arrived to visit in late afternoon, we stayed on our property to see the tall mountains turn various hues of pink, orange, and yellow, and then purple or dark green as the sun went down, finally becoming black outlines against the night sky. These mountains speak of another ecosystem, one wild and covered with chaparral and inhabited by many wild animals, both large and small.

Offshore, sometimes small fishing boats quietly glided by, returning to the harbor with a convoy of seagulls flying about the boat. The gulls, with their strident, loud and intermittent cries, waited for a crew that would often clean some of their catch or toss out unwanted fish. We then returned to the West Beach Motor Lodge, with an increasing belief that life would be good in retirement on just a small plot of land. It's not the past but what's now and ahead that counts.

Ranch life hadn't prepared me for one aspect of town life, and the situation would be more prevalent around our new lot. Security and privacy had become more important to people, while through most of my life we had rarely locked a door with even a skeleton key or latched a window closed. Finally, I had locked the front and back door in the house in the town of San Luis Obispo, but the screen door on the back porch on Oak Hills had just a broken hook latch; the other doors into the house had never been locked while we lived there, and probably few windows had working latches. This new home would probably have to have some of these unfortunate features.

The barbwire, woven wire, and wooden fences I'd lived with had been primarily to keep animals inside the fields and yards. Now, mostly in affluent neighborhoods, fencing had a different purpose and look. High brick or plastered walls and tall chain-link or wooden fences were built to keep people out. These sometimes prevented the magnificent sight of far-off mountains or the ocean from a road or house. Until there were codes restricting properties to the maximum height of walls and hedges, many hedges grew as high as trees, blocking views for others as well as for the owners.

We would try to get back to small everyday hellos, kindnesses and cooperation. Neighbors still need neighbors, like they did in the country's early history, to help in times of trouble, visit when ill, and celebrate good times. It made for greater happiness and better human beings. Notice the animals and children; pick up stray cats and dogs and take them to the animal shelter or phone the shelter to come and take them; read to children at a library; or help in a school room; pick up litter and fight with donations or work to preserve the plant life and wild animals of the land and ocean.

In spite of some delays in the road, we were finally ready to move and snag as much time as possible to celebrate living where wonderful

Pacific-Ocean waves would roll up to our own speck of beach and land. Somehow, we were becoming partial to both land and sea—as we had been in our earlier years—and ready to take in the invigorating sea air. A new gardener would help me plant every veggie, flower, and fruit tree we could crowd in on the lot as soon as the water moratorium was lifted and we had the blue prints. However, those building moratorium bumps on our trail had postponed the new life for over half a dozen years.

Chapter 37
Living in an Office

In spite of the purchase of the land down south, I decided it was time to make some changes. "Dan, does it make sense to sell this Fixlini house while we wait for a permit to build the new house?" I asked him one night. "With the last of the kids out of the nest and a retirement parcel of land finally figured out for some years down the road, let's begin to do things in stages. You and I could take our once-in-a-lifetime tax credit from the sale of this house, since we meet the age requirement. What about that?"

Dan nodded. "Sure. I've wondered about selling, but I should teach until we leave and also keep the real estate classes going at night. Go ahead and list it." In spite of the retirement site, neither of us could talk enthusiastically about the thought of our next home, because it was not a ranch in the country.

And where might we move temporarily if the house were to sell as quickly as past ones have? "Maybe I should also close down Chase Pacific Properties. We would then be able to move into my office building to live for several years, and then sell it and transfer the gain toward the new home down south—that is, if the city will let us change the office building back to a residence. Basically, it still looks like a big country home, with its garage and the old windmill." The city official I spoke with actually let us move back into the Santa Rosa real estate building to live. City staff members weren't always as reasonable, especially when there had been an asphalt parking area installed beside the house for about twelve cars for my staff and visitors.

Both Wendy and Truffles, as well as Dan and I, soon hated the new living quarters. Although we owned the big field out back, nothing was fenced, and the very busy intersection of the road to Morro Bay and the one to the University was just a stone's throw away. Wendy and kitty would have to remain inside the large, carpeted, two-story house except for walks on leashes or, for the dog, trips to the beach.

My staff of sales people and wonderful secretary, Jan, were told I would no longer keep Chase Pacific Properties, Inc. active. It had been a fun business, yet it had been years of juggling many jobs and hundred-hour workweeks for both Dan and me. I advertised desk, chair, and filing cabinet sales at each of my offices. Fortunately, some of the staff, along with loyal clients who would follow them, joined other offices. Others retired in those hard years of terribly high interest rates and big drops in real estate sales all across the country. With real estate in the doldrums, the timing was fine to quit. I sold the branch office properties in Atascadero, and Grover City, and closed the small downtown sales office in our Lumbleau School building.

In my office-building-now-home, it was easy to create a small kitchen in the "coffee-break room" in the back by installing a double-sink and cabinet unit, buying a small stove, and making room for our large refrigerator. The huge deep-freeze and small office refrigerator went in the garage along with the five big trunks and gardening tools. In one room, dining room furniture took the place of four office desks and chairs, and the living room furniture went where I had worked at my desk and Jan had met staff and clients at her desk next to the front door. I took one of the other downstairs office rooms for our bedroom, and put guest bedroom furniture in several other rooms that had had desks. The upstairs became a storage area for our patio furniture, pool equipment, clothes we seldom used, filing cabinets, and several desks I couldn't sell.

Jan gave me an acutely embarrassing number of hours as she helped me move the huge hodgepodge of my dismal housekeeping collections from the Fixlini house. For ten years, things had hidden and multiplied with mold, fungus, and ice—in both the big freezer and fridge. Other foods had shriveled and dried. Jars held sliced peaches and berries I had probably frozen a decade before. Moving time or freezer and refrigerator replacement times were the only occasions much of the stuff inside them saw the light of day. If freezer and fridge were that bad, no wonder gym clothes, socks, new pens, scissors, keys, and even my purse had disappeared now and then—they had had the whole Fixlini house to hide in.

Wonderful Jan, who had managed to keep all of the office staff and me organized and the records straight for so long, often let out her hearty laugh while helping me prepare to move—she found twelve full boxes of Morton's salt down behind about fifteen boxes of hot and cold cereal, the contents of which had in some cases caramelized to hard, sticky blocks. There were five bags of sugar and about an equal number of flour. A few canned foods had leaked through rusty bottoms or had swollen sides. It was a wonder my family and I were still alive.

In lame self-defense, I muttered, "Those cupboards under the counters start at floor level and go back half a mile in darkness. Crawling in on hands and knees to see what got pushed to the back has just not been a high priority in my hundred-hour workweeks."

She shrieked all the louder with laughter while pulling out another box of salt, and observed, "Well, you may work sixteen-hour days, but it's not spent keeping house."

Clothes had actually become a nostalgic diary of a time long past. When the Great Depression years were barely over and had scarred me so, I'd felt a need to hang on to everything I owned. In my closet were shirts, dresses, coats, and suits that dated back to my college days in 1939.

There was the long, black velvet formal from UC Berkeley years, the one white tennis dress I'd worn for "important" matches, the leather riding skirt, with fringes, that once had been my dream outfit in high school, yet had never been worn. Jan pulled out thick plaid skirts, sweaters, and long wool coats that had also never been outside any closets in the Arizona homes, or even those in this central California valley, where it had been more time-saving to just take an umbrella than to dig way back in closets for coats during rains. An old all-wool bathing suit was still "holding its shape." It was too good to throw out, but had long ago been replaced by modern suits that stretched out-of-shape in one season. All the closets had numerous boxes full of empty hangers, obviously waiting for more old, out-of-style clothing. Since our trash bins had always been extremely full each week, they had made me believe I threw out more than I carried into the house. Clearly it was not so.

She did convince me to take about ten boxes of the coat hangers out to the curb, and they were picked up in a day by eager college kids who were just then coming back for the next term.

Trying her best, she continued to make suggestions, "I've never seen you wear this skirt or this dress. May I toss them out on the curb, or at least take them to Good Will?" I would try them on and decide, "No. See, it fits just fine. I'll keep it a while longer." Why was it that I could weed a garden but could weed nothing from my closet? It was ever so.

She also caught Dan with a hoard of worthless items, which led to more laughter, even if the collection was much smaller than mine—it was keys, keys, and more keys, found in more places than one could imagine. First of all, Jan herself had kept in the office a neat and well labeled set of all of our current property keys, including those for our own rentals and office buildings. Another key cabinet held keys for all the office listings of properties currently for sale. Other keys were a thousand times more confusing, because I had new keys made whenever new tenants moved into a rental. Now in the garage, Dan's desk, a dresser, a nightstand, a filing cabinet, a toolbox, and even hanging on a pegboard, were countless duplicates, most no longer identifiable. Some fitted the doors of rentals and cars we didn't even own any more, or houses we no longer lived in. Like the other collections, maybe they contain a mysteriousyeast; keys continue to grow to this day.

Now, many years later, Jan still roars with laughter about my collections. Somehow the twelve boxes of salt and fifteen boxes of cereal are what she remembers most. Which reminds me, she's coming to visit next week—I'd better clean out the fridge. And since the now sixty-year-old clothes remaining in the guestroom closet will blow her mind away, I'd better bag the humongous mess and hide it in the garage while she's here. It won't wash to excuse this still growing clutter with hundred-hour-plus workweeks any more.

Chapter 38
Seagulls Are Calling

A home with both land and sea? Could there be a double love affair with our next destination on the trail? The lot, roughly one hundred miles north of the Los Angeles area and a little over a hundred miles south of San Luis Obispo, finally had a source of water with a new well out back, and we could begin to work toward acquiring house plans and a building permit.

With conflicting emotions, I realized that this move would probably be our final one—so many memories started shooting off in all directions: the long years of bare survival and endless work on farm and ranch lands, yet always with the love, laughter, and closeness of children, Dan, and animals—horses, cows, goats, sheep, cats, dogs, a guinea pig, a rat, a hamster, and even a snake for a few days.

I sketched and sketched more detailed house plans for a future building contractor and drove to furniture stores to measure future furniture purchases to help determine room sizes. My drawings were meant to fit the house's purpose: informal and easily maintained, with such things as tile floors (for a route from the ocean, spa, or pool to a bathroom for dripping wet, sandy feet). And there must be expansive views of the ocean from the key rooms. Additionally, there must be wood burning fire places for cold winter days.

We then hired a Santa Barbara architect and found a builder. Dan continued teaching at Cal Poly, which had become a California State

University some years before, and also continued teaching the nighttime real estate classes. I managed our rentals and painted them, sometimes by myself. It was a good time to pay off mortgages and not buy more property since interest rates continued to be extremely high. Farmers, with all their needs to borrow, were hurting like the real estate people, yet it was our endless on-the-side jobs that were finally making up for the low university salaries.

Continuing to live in the office building on the commercial street, where Wendy and her pups had been saved when Jan and I saved them from being hit in heavy traffic, began to test my endurance—as well as Wendy's and Truffles'—after quiet country living for most of a lifetime. Motorcycles revving up at dawn and garbage trucks with squeaky brakes and clanking equipment lifting cans in this business area at 4:00 A.M. were hard on an insomniac. I even noticed street grime on the windows more than when it had just been an office building.

Bright and frisky Wendy had never had a ranch life, except for a few runs when we owned River Ranch, but I knew both she and Truffles longed to be out exercising in the sunshine. When it wasn't too warm for her to be in the car, I tried to take her with me on trips to town, but she greatly needed space to run and explore.

Do people snack and binge more on food when they suddenly have too much leisure or when life might be easier? It was during those two years living in the office building that I bought candy, lots of candy. Dan and I discovered one-pound boxes of See's Candies and found we could each polish off a box in two or three days. With less need to stick to the bare necessities, I became a chocoholic; I should have given the stressed animals an equivalent variety of chewy, animal treats. The kids were off at college or married with careers, so no one could tattle on us.

And even without the cravings of pregnancy, I resumed my love affair with whole packages of carnival-type wieners, mustard, and buns for just the two of us. I hadn't eaten a hot dog since our last child left home, and, like the candy, it seemed a strange reward for our odd temporary living quarters.

Wendy was as excited as I was when our kids came for holidays, and more and more I realized how great Wendy's charisma was and how often she managed to figure things out, seemingly on her own. Maybe the children came home to see Truffles and Wendy as much as to see mom and dad, for they, too, deeply loved these critters, but it certainly wasn't the old homey ranch house they returned to. The building on Santa Rosa Street continued to feel like the office building that it really had become, and, even with everyone home, plus a couple of the children's dogs, we all rattled around in it and talked extra loud when the traffic outside was thick.

Each spring and into the summer, heavy jobs also awaited Dan and me on our acreage behind the garage and office building. Even on property in town, seeds, especially wild oats, foxtails, and mustard, grew thick and tall, then tough and dry. With two small gas-powered mowers, Dan started circling in one direction and I in the other until we'd mowed the whole large field; this we did several times each year. We came across rocks, clods, tough grass, old wood, bottles, cans, and paper. I joked, "Now I know we can 'cut the mustard,' and with only the help of our two Toro lawnmowers." They don't seem to make tough, almost indestructible mowers like these any longer. Of course, we, too, are not that tough any more.

Finally, there came a time, a turning point called "Retirement." At first, with a new home going up on our lot in Santa Barbara, we played hooky on weekends to look it over and often found things that were in need of modification or were not like the blueprints. The wrong insulation was up on one wall, and a wall that was to be brick was plastered. But in the meantime I found a buyer for the real estate school and its building across from the post office, and on weekends we began to take sleeping bags south to the unfinished house. Setting up camp meant rolling out our two sleeping bags on a cold cement floor and crawling in them fully dressed, usually in tennis warm-ups. In an unfinished and empty room, I listened to the murmuring, constant rhythm of the waves and felt a new sense of involvement, security, and closeness with the vast and ancient sea, as well as with this bit of land we owned. Even nearby street names were pleasing and evoked nice thoughts

In the morning, as Dan struggled to get out of his bag, I wondered, "I guess it goes without saying, we both feel positive this new life will be right? At least we made the move with both eyes open."

Dan nodded and added, "Yeah, it's the right move. My only reservation is that maybe I should teach another year. Neither of us are good at just killing time."

"You're right, but we've agreed some things turn out better when we pay attention to the construction going on here. It also might be later than we think. Why not retire this fall and go for it?"

"Maybe. Let's walk Wendy," he replied. In the early morning there was still the sound of the waves and the company of the seagulls, who often followed pelicans around as they dived for fish. Other pelicans, with their long wings spread wide, skimmed along, barely above the ocean's surface. Sometimes there were seals or sea lions, lazing along in the ocean swells, or gregarious dolphins gliding in and out of the water in a regular ocean chorus line on their way up or down the coast, or circled around in front of us to play and eat. As we came home, other walkers, often with their dogs, began to arrive from nearby homes or in cars and assured us we would eventually see an occasional whale spouting and diving farther out in the Channel. Tremendous! In the vastness of the sky, sea, and sandy shore there was a regular watery zoo. Those dawns were surely some of the best times of day, whether there was a soft, misty fog or a bright sun coming over the hill to the east.

Finally, our house was officially declared finished, and we could migrate south. Filled with the various possibilities of life beside the sea, I sold our home/office property, while Dan retired from a teaching career that had spanned thirty-three years. There were no gold pens or watches, but there were several fine staff parties with laughter over many nostalgic memories. "Ah, do you remember when...?" Then, just like that, we moved and were "out to pasture."

Somewhat dazed, we asked each other, "Well, is this all there is? Are we supposed to now just sit back and smell the roses? I'm not sure we can or even want to sit back, but let's get on with this new chapter of our life, OK?" Most of the old furniture never lived to be "antique." Some of our nondescript, scratched, dented, cracked, bent, faded, or not-working belongings had disappeared to the first homes of the kids as they married—salvaged to "make do" until they had full-fledged careers. Several now came to take a bit more furniture and belongings and see the new home down south before we moved.

A married college couple then drove south with us for a long weekend to help us unpack all we could load. The two mowers, my rototiller, and all the shovels, hoes, and rakes traveled south to find a new home in a storage shed near the water well in back. The five big steamer trunks of books came along to the extra large garage to settle in. So did an increasing clutter of "things" over a few more trips. My biggest garage ever was soon filled up to the point that a single car could barely make it through the door, so the Ford pick-up had to stay outside. That first evening, our tired helpers and we ate at a small restaurant on Coast Village Road. The celebration consisted of me and Dan and his student, George, and his wife, Karen, who gave us a thumbs-up and grin while proclaiming toasts with their glasses of iced tea, "To your new life beside the sea!" Actually, in many ways we were making a full circle. My parents and I had come to these same local beaches through all the years I was growing up, and Dan and I had come to Santa Barbara after we started dating in the tenth grade and even bought a row boat with another couple and docked it at the Santa Barbara Marina. Then, when Dan and I married we stayed in a Forest Service lookout tower just fifteen minutes down the coastal highway.

Even before unpacking many boxes, I rototilled part of the yard and quickly planted a big vegetable garden on the front side of the house behind a wall newly planted with salmon-colored bougainvillea, a hedge that I desperately hoped would quickly hide my most unusual front garden from the road. In January, I would plant bare root trees (dead looking bare sticks and roots, with a few branches) and fill the back yard with peach, plum, and apple trees, plus one avocado tree a couple of months later. With more space in front of the house, we set out two rows of various kinds of citrus trees. These served as a reminder of the many orange orchards in Ojai, the nearby small town where we grew up. Between the citrus rows, I set out small, rooted, berry plants, and several artichoke roots.

What makes a house a home? In the past it had been easy—most of our nests had been cozy and ever so small, with the exception of the fairly large Oak Hills Ranch. Now there was so much floor space! Yet it had the potential to become a fine home. There were the wood-burning fireplaces for the driftwood we collected on the beach after storms, plus a stack of oak wood piled up against the back fence; two rooms were ready with floor-to-ceiling bookcases and area rugs. There would always be animals allowed inside and out, and many windows to bring in the scene of the vegetation, ocean, and sky. Already Truffles and Wendy were excited and somehow knew this was their new home.

Had I, deep down, somehow desired more than "bare bones" living all those years before? I had always set a goal to simplify life and have the minimum of furniture, yet just the reverse was beginning to happen with this likely last home. What happened to my core belief that most good things can be simple, cheap, or even free? I knew this move was the perfect time to make do with less, but discarding anything was still a bittersweet job. If I couldn't remember things at some future time, the old remaining junk might become my memory of the past. Hence, the simple beach house filled up not with just the new but with a ton of stuff that was old, and the garage was overflowing.

I'd soon find out if all the elaborate, up-to-date "labor-saving equipment" would complicate or simplify our lives. The architect's blueprints showed the location for a dishwasher; a huge side-by-side-refrigerator that spewed ice cubes and cold water from spigots on command; a new clothes dryer and washer; an electronic security system; and phones all over the place. It would be a new world with an oven that cleaned itself, a disposal that loudly grinded out the sounds, "I'm taking your garbage," and a fan in the hood above the stove that sucked out all the homey fragrances of cooking, cooking that I now did less and less with just the two of us.

Even the long kitchen counters, drawers, and a walk-in pantry amazed me; somehow their vacant and seemingly excessive space immediately sprouted crops. The house was equipped with an electric can opener, a mixer, a juicer, a coffeemaker, a slicing board that swung out, a fruit-ripening bowl, and another closed bowl than spun water off lettuce leaves. Some of the machinery became "infernal monsters" to me, with innards that quit working the second they felt me turn on their switches or grasp their handles. They didn't behave any better for Dan. Moreover, my need for all these things was now almost nil compared to earlier years, and I often muttered, "Why now?" However, since much of the countertop contraptions were thoughtful housewarming gifts from kids, friends, and the architect, I clapped my hands and beamed appropriately with joy when receiving them.

The living room and bedrooms became furnished with the hope of hospitality and less chaos when we purchased eclectic pieces of no particular style and no great value. Pictures of the sea and its creatures, along with several farm, horse, and dog pictures, soon hung haphazardly on the walls. Floors were mostly tiled, and only two rugs graced the living room and dining room.

As is so often the case, I guessed the matter of compromise would work: simplify where I could but accept some of the equipment for some home comfort, time saved, and easier work loads. At least late in life I acquired not only central heating but also fireplaces that burned real wood.

The new stuff was nice, but growing old would not be trouble-free, when not only I began to break down with unplanned obsolescence, but planned obsolescence now seemed to be built into some of the next things that I acquired. None of it would endure hard usage like the old furnishings: toasters, chairs, hair-dryers, and lamps enjoyed visits to repair shops or wore out quickly. Even paint was poorer due to government regulations of the ingredients, which began to avoid lead.

At the same time, a new kind of repair problem surfaced. Few craftsmen hung their shingles out to repair anything. Where were the earlier, all-around, handyman "Fix-It" shops? Contractors, architects, and decorators only wanted to come for big jobs. Big job, no problem. Replace two tiles on the roof? Forget it. Everyone wanted to be a specialist and arrive for a week of work. At least I wouldn't be owned by "things:" none of it would probably last long enough to become antiques to guard.

Progress was also going to the dogs. Bones that never started out in meat markets now came in plastic, rubber, raw-hide, or biscuits called "Milk Bones." Someone told me dogs shouldn't have real bones, but for a while Wendy got some real knuckle bones as well as the fake factory-made ones. She needed rewarding for the terrific patience she showed living inside that office-building-turned-home for so long.

In the end, this ocean-front land became a prize almost as wonderful as any ranch, except maybe a ranch adjacent to the ocean. The cast of critters was smaller, and the kids were gone most of the time, but, like Wendy and Truffles, Dan and I reveled in being out of the large office building. Usually, just as the sun came up, Wendy ran free on a nearby beach while Dan and I tramped along the shoreline with her. She could also run around the yard, which was enclosed on all sides by fence or wall, and once again work as a guard-dog and "keep track of things."

For the cat, moving had been more than unpredictable and an inconvenience—it had been most upsetting. But soon Truffles could be let outside each day, and she quickly explored the whole property, inside and out—it was her new hunting area and home. She became lively and happy, and rewarded us with a bird or two, carefully placed beside the front door. Fortunately, she was never much of a hunter and quit catching birds entirely after the first few months.

My philosophy had always been that "happiness is mostly in one's own back yard," or close to it. And much of our future would, hopefully, be right here; yet we had also gambled that someday there would be some years left to see the world. Now was the time, and we traveled to faraway places in other lands and in America.

Wendy and Truffles always caught on to our travel plans, even without seeing the travel folders. Any piles of clothes on a bed or maybe just our talk was a giveaway. When the luggage came out, they were sure. Truffles curled up inside the suitcases and climbed back in every time they were open. She also tried to hide the morning we planned to leave. After one bad time when we almost missed our flight while trying to find her to take to stay at her favorite kennel, we kept her inside and in one room on departure mornings. Wendy, and later other dogs, knew even before the cat. And when we put the bag of their special dog food in the car to take to the kennel, they knew the worst, for sure. Were the dogs thinking, "We know where you're taking us, but will you really come back? If you truly love us, why can't we go with you?" They made it hard to leave, and our trips never lasted longer than a month and usually only happened once a year.

Since this became a time to change my mind about a lot of things, it eventually included the way we traveled. Trailers and motor homes had held my scorn, with their box-like shape and aluminum, fiberglass, or plastic sides, with their air-conditioners and luggage racks up on top, and sometimes a car hooked up behind. In spite of buying a compact little trailer years before that had followed us on a bumper-hitch as we traveled all over the U.S. for six months, most new ones seemed like movable houses and would surely insulate us from feeling and observing nature, or even finding beautiful camping sites.

Many of the primitive areas, rivers, mountains, Redwoods, and lakes could not accommodate huge trailers and motor homes. Did those people park rigs just to watch TV, listen to loud music, or play a game of bridge, and then cook meals on a Hibachi, with some smelly lighter fluid igniting charcoal briquettes?

In spite of these thoughts, the adventure of going to the lakes, rivers, and mountains of the country became a trail that beckoned. We finally joined the stream of camper, trailer, and motor-home enthusiasts out on the highways and byways with a thirty-two-foot fifth-wheel trailer, along with a one-ton, crew-cab pick-up truck to pull it. A main advantage was that the dogs and cat could go with us. For years, the long fifth-wheeler wagged along behind the truck all around the western U.S. and Canada, and our four-legged family members always traveled with us.

You young lovers and campers of the wilderness, don't laugh. Life changes. As you sit around a wood campfire and then crawl into your leaking tents to feel hard earth, rocks, and sticks beneath your sleeping bag, you are growing older. A motor home may come to look better and better as the years go by.

Even without pulling the trailer, the truck was handy, taking loads to the dump for a number of years; some old furniture, books, and childhood collections to the kids' homes as their families grew; loads of fertilizer and one-and-a-half-inch rock for drainage ditches to our own house; and ladders and paint supplies to continue painting rentals back in San Luis Obispo.

Motoring around the U.S. and going to other countries was far better than we had bargained for, and it didn't detract from the beauty or the adventure to step out of a trailer-home to soak up the views, ride horses to the bottom of Bryce Canyon, sit on a bench to watch Old Faithful spout, or bus out to a glacier in Glacier National Park. Hearing rain on a non-leaking roof or feeling the strong wind buffet the cozy room, while I reached in an ever-cold refrigerator for foods to prepare on handy stove burners or an oven, made sense. When mosquitoes were few, food could still be cooked over a campfire if I wished, and always the fragrance of pine trees or soft night sounds reached us through the screened vents, windows, and doors.

I kept wishing that all those who preach gloom and see only deep malaise and despair would walk, bicycle, drive, or take a bus out to rural parks, campgrounds, or trailheads near cities in order to hike or stop and really see and listen to all that's on or above the land. Even urban parks and playgrounds give respite and a quiet freedom to think about life and dreams—stretch out and become one with yourself and the grass or trees. Learn to value nature and work to protect it—make things happen. Consciously think about this great country, about love and kindness for others. Get further education, do hard work, plan and set goals. Don't expect birth-to-grave help from the government for everything, including food, shelter, clothes, health, education, and even recreation.

Raccoons once tried to open our trailer door just outside Washington D.C., and on one morning of soft, misty rain, citified deer, rabbits, and quail came down to nibble the little lawn and plants in a friend's back yard near downtown Los Angeles. Pigeons, sparrows, and other creatures now often live where there is mostly asphalt or cement, in the big cities of the world. These birds and other creatures are all taking risks in building their nesting areas, finding their food, playing, and raising their young within a city or other difficult environment. They can usually succeed and people can too.

So much of life can be lost grousing, waiting, asking for handouts, or worrying about "entitlements" from governments. Take risks and say, "I think I can" or "I'll learn by doing," to use the motto of Cal Poly San Luis Obispo.

One other thing—besides becoming in tune with the land, growing vegetation and animals, and working hard, I have a premonition of a bleak future if all of us don't do more to save the earth. Here in Santa Barbara, the area is really desert, or semi-arid, yet man continues to rely on dams, wells dug deeper and deeper, water by pipelines from up north, and a desalination plant using ocean water. Large homes multiply on the hillsides, and thousands of non-native shrubs and trees surround them, making large wildfires far more likely.

In this manner, more and more people move in on the narrow strip of land squeezed between the sea and the mountains, to the detriment of the wildlife and native plant life. New population floods in, and then the local government and the builders both agree that we must grow, grow, and grow some more to give the newcomers housing, utilities, transportation, and other services. Social engineering people have a field day.

We can still, perhaps, save part of the planet if we help stem the tide of irrigating the desert, paving over the farm land, damming the rivers, and destroying the forests. Study and learn from the thick smog and lowering water expectations of places like Phoenix, where planners also decided, "People use less water than farmers, so we'll do away with farmers and give the water to the increasing population."

Here, growth is also in the name of tourism. A place long kept from dense development, is suddenly opening the gates to motels, restaurants, hotels, gas stations, "destination resorts," golf courses, and other attractions for the entertainment of crowds arriving in a stream of cars on additional lanes of highways to new and bigger parking lots. It will soon occur to the visitors that they have the same crowds, slow traffic, smog, cement, and asphalt at home, and there's little need to come.

Plant trees and vegetable gardens, walk more, bicycle more on safe bike lanes, and help your neighbors, kids, and animals. Make back yards and front yards places to entertain, talk, and be centers for family again. Help keep the beaches, mountains, and towns clean. Preserve nature and don't take the crab, starfish, rocks, and flowers home as souvenirs. Keep the trees favored by Monarch butterflies growing—a thousand things can be done that are easy on the environment.

I'll savor it in the meanwhile. In some ways, I feel I've come full circle back to this sea of no beginnings and no endings. In addition to the ocean, about twenty minutes south is the tall mountain where Dan, on bended knee and with Hereford steers crowding near, presented me with a ring. Here, ghost-like childhood memories also come back to me of an even earlier time, when my parents and I made this same beach and town a frequent destination. We drove over from the town of Ojai to avoid some of the hotter weather, either for the day or to stay several months during several summer vacations. Often we stayed on this beach, or others nearby, to watch the evening sun drop and slip below the edge of the sea.

Do their spirits come here still, like the endless and ancient tides, especially in the early light of dawn or early evening hours, when seabirds often come in to rest on the sand, and a couple of seals, who have so far evaded death by man, come when there's a low murmuring tide to sleep on the rocks or sand below the nearby cliffs? How deeply I wish they could have lived or somehow followed my life, known their grandchildren, one, two, three, and four, and now this move beside their long loved ocean.

Chapter 39
Truffles in Santa Barbara

Except for moving day and the car ride, Truffles made the transition to a beach life with few complaints. She loved the freedom of being outside during the days to study and explore within the safety of the fenced and hedged yard. Even here, I saw the mounds gophers had made and realized there were also rats and field mice. The number and different species of land birds were amazingly large, but, so far Truffles seldom wanted to hunt.

One night, after searching the neighborhood for a couple of hours, I went to bed without getting her in the house. She'd gone out like a happy lion that afternoon but arrived at the door the next morning, not saying a word and looking like a cold, dripping, wet rat about half the size of her usually fluffy self. She was disgusted, furious, and perhaps embarrassed to look almost naked, and came in the house shaking each of her four paws in turn and giving me a long, hopping mad stare. I toweled her somewhat dry and warmed her some cat food.

Finally, she sat on a dining room chair and spoke meows that clearly stated, "I've had it up to here! You can help me get drier than this. It's probably your fault, anyway." Cats have much dignity, and hers had been thoroughly shaken. I put a blow dryer on low, and she decided that the warm air was worth taking a chance with a new contraption.

Since she had lived her first years with a swimming pool in the back yard without falling in, and since there were no wet paw prints on the decking around this new pool, I wondered if she had tried going across the road to the beach. Maybe a wave caught her unprepared for flight. I would never know. I do know that I never found her anywhere near that well-traveled road or the beach for the rest of her life.

Friends remind me that cats are easier to have than dogs and tick off many reasons. One is that they don't have to be taken for walks. No, I didn't walk the cat on a leash, but we didn't let these last two cats, first Smoochie and now Truffles, stay out all night if we could help it, and it would have been easier to keep them leashed than to find them every night at bedtime. This area didn't have the isolated safety of open fields, big barns, and few cars, so Truffles could have no nights out on the town. For a while, puss stayed close to the house after her big fright, but eventually she went inland and explored the yards behind us.

Most nights, I could be heard calling, "Here kitty, kitty! Here kitty, kitty! Here Truffles!" Finding a cat who didn't want to be found on a warm, moonlit night was never fun, especially when I had to repeatedly call out the name Smoochie or Truffles for all the neighbors to hear.

Not anxious to be jailed for unlawful search and seizure while prowling around private neighboring yards, I changed tactics after a few weeks, making low, quieter calls of "Here kitty, kitty. Here Truffles, Truffles," before hissing, "Come here you awful cat, wherever you are!"

After wandering the whole circle of houses around us, shining my flashlight down the driveways and peering over backyard fences, I would finally go home, only to go through the same process an hour later unless Truffles had come home ahead of me and was casually meowing, "What's all the fuss about? Where's supper?" I soon decided to give no food to the cat after breakfast; she got dinner only when she came home for the night. I also made her stay in the house any time I could find her after two P.M. Still I went out searching for her too many nights and, if unsuccessful, waited up for her like I'd waited for the children years ago when one came home after curfew. So, just how wonderful is it to have an independent, self-reliant cat that doesn't have to be walked? These cats could have become totally "indoor cats," but we had never demanded that before, so it seemed inhumane (though I have since learned that it is often done easily and successfully).

Friends also liked to remind me that cats can stay alone in a house for days and not eat up their ten meals in the first ten minutes like a dog would. I knew that, and, with Smoochie it worked quite well. In fact, when we once had to leave him for six days, I set bowls of water all over the place, in case he spilled some, plus about a dozen servings of food. Much of it was dry cat food, but I decided to also try some well-wrapped packages of "moist" food. It might be entertainment—something for him to figure out. It was a good thought; I found the moist packages opened as neatly as I could have done. The wrappings were pulled back about halfway, and Smoochie's favorite flavored foods, like liver, fish, lamb, and chicken, had all been sampled. This self-reliant cat greeted us at the door, as though he would show us into his domain, happily running ahead of us into the rooms. "Look, guys, all is still here and in good order."

Truffles was another story. Our absence never made her heart grow fonder; when we opened the door after being away for a few days, she acted as if she didn't know us, or want to know us, and continued to sit on a window-sill to look out, pout, and not greet us at all. Another reaction was for her to run and hide under a bed or behind the sofa the moment the key was in the lock. Then I'd panic when not seeing her and begin to fear she had gotten out some way during our absence. Cats can be hard owners of their people—couldn't they be more predictable and cooperative, like a dog?

Dinner and breakfast times continued to be very different affairs for my dogs and cats. As with all our dogs, Wendy wolfed down everything in her dish and begged for more. She also found it sociable and polite to eat almost any food the family was eating, from oranges, strawberries, and apples to tacos, potatoes, and squash. The cats, however, wanted their own special chef to train and were apt to change their minds about the menu on a daily basis. Dogs would have tried to eat a completely frozen meal of most anything; while the cats required food the perfect temperature, a particular size of bites, consistency, taste, and a most agreeable scent. Even the eating location and type of dish were noted and judged. Go down the aisle of any supermarket or pet store, and the choice of specialized cat foods is endless; don't tell me cats don't bully their chefs shamelessly.

Still, I loved the graceful and complex cats as much as I did the dogs. Like children in a big family, cats come with endless personalities and characteristics. Most showed love and caring, sitting on my lap and softly purring all evening while I did some bookkeeping and then sleeping peacefully on the bed with us the rest of the night. They are happy, curious, and easily entertained, sometimes passing long tracts of time studying a fly or rain drops on a windowpane. They talk with voice and body language when the need arises, often rubbing around ankles and softly crying to insist, "It's dinnertime!" And, in spite of the spell of a moonlit night, they can learn their names and come when called—and when they feel like it.

Cat-lovers also mention that cats don't bark noisily like dogs, and they arrive as kittens nicely potty-trained by their momma cat. And cats groom themselves more carefully than dogs. Some dogs try to clean themselves with a bit of shaking or licking of their paws or fur, but cats fastidiously and thoroughly bathe themselves daily with tongue and paws.

Most cats tend to be spunky, like many dogs, and, if able, will try to play until the last day of their lives—perhaps crawling into a sack to peer out and pounce on the dog, or stalking a pen on the desk and suddenly grabbing it and rolling over with it between two paws. They can go from charming and appealing to tough, adventurous, and secretive. Maybe it's because of their long, relatively rough history that they are often so difficult to understand.

These wonderful animals, both dogs and cats, were often the teachers, and I the pupil. As in earlier years, I still sensed very strongly that they seemed to understand me better than I understood their thoughts and needs. Like humans, animals vary so much as to personalities and intelligence, with different levels of fear, joy, affection, stubbornness, curiosity, cooperation, desire to travel, spunk, and so on.

Cats are incredibly agile and love challenge, especially if it involves getting high off the ground, as in tall trees, rooftops, and telephone poles. For many years, when Truffles decided life was boring in our new home, she put on athletic shows on the seven-foot-high, heavy wooden valances that we used for the curtains and drapes in some rooms, valances that were level with the tops of the long bookcases and cabinets in those rooms. She would leap from a chair to the mantle of the fireplace and then to the top of a bookcase, after which she managed to circle the entire room by jumping across the doorways to the narrow valances and additional bookcase tops.

Truffles also learned to enjoy going in cars as much as any dog we owned, since both dogs and cats can get cabin or yard fever. The animals adapted to transportation with great ease and compliant spirits; they loved to take trips in the travel trailer, the motor home, and the car with us. These were years when we often took the animals north to visit the children. The Santa Rosa kids had built a tall, two-story house on some wooded, rural acreage that was itself surrounded by extensive park lands of hundreds of acres for hiking and horseback riding. Their family animals were as sociable and welcoming as the parents and children.

Their Bogie was a huge orange cat—probably twice as big and heavy as Truffles—but the big fellow always played carefully and gently with her, especially as both of them aged. They had long games of hide-and-seek, stalking and surprising each other and later settling down to nap on the same couch or bed.

Truffles and Bogie usually sniffed noses when Bogie discovered she'd just arrived with us. I always wondered if they didn't say more than just hello. Bogie had lived in an apartment complex with many other cats when the kids were new in town. Never did he show any sign of having fought with other cats, and the huge guy remained a delightful pacifist and gentleman toward all animal guests, including our dogs and cats. This was strange, because Bogie never wanted to be touched by any humans other than his immediate family. Bogie sometimes slept with us in the guest room, but I got bitten or scratched if I tried to pet him. Only in great old age did he finally come to sit on my lap once in a while.

I'm not sure Bogie saw Truffles fly out of the upstairs laundry chute while she was investigating. Bogie would have been impressed, since it was quite a distance to fall with the houses high ceilings and she crashed on top of the washing machine in the room below. We all heard her land and give an immediate howl. I'm not sure if it used up one of her nine lives, but she came out to us in the living room speaking short, irritated meows and walking rather stiffly. I also don't know if it's true that cats always land on their feet, but that day I think both her feet and her legs hurt.

Truffles continued to travel with us for many years. She made several long trips in our big crew-cab truck and thirty-two-foot trailer around the western half of the U.S., plus dozens of shorter trips. She never made the trip down the laundry chute again, but Santa Rosa continued to be her favorite destination. I even trusted her to the outdoors there, with its four and a half acres of ferns and forest of oaks, redwoods, and other trees, surrounded by the large Annadel State Park.

I believe few cats live to be as old as Truffles. Once she almost died when we boarded her in a kennel for over a month. I think they had just finished spraying for fleas, and she may have gotten her feet in a wet spot of the poison on the floor. A staff member rushed her to our vet, and he had her pretty healthy and well upon our return. Maybe she had used up another one of her nine lives.

Fine veterinarians and Dan get credit for a part of her good health and amazingly long life. Although he started out married life not liking cats, Dan had changed his mind with the arrival of our first stray cat, Sage, in Arizona, and he now spent a number of years preparing old Truffles special diets. At first, meals were ones that the vet suggested might be best for her, but in Truffles' last year or two, on a daily basis he fixed her anything that she might eat. Truffles' gourmet foods became almost all freshly cooked liver, fish, beef, lamb, egg, and a variety of foods we were eating, such as rice, a taste of spaghetti with meat, or even cottage cheese. Her teeth were almost all gone, so all foods were finely chopped. After all the food preparation, he then had to watch her eat just a bite or two and leave the rest.

Despite her uncommonly old age of twenty-three, Truffles managed to take several long trips with us the year before she died, and, almost up to the very end, this special cat played like a kitten and still stretched out on the desk beside me while I wrote or read. She was almost blind, but could still scatter my papers all over the room. She still loved to be lifted onto any bed I was making so as to feel the top sheet billow up as I shook it and then let it float down over her. She didn't seem to really hurt, even as she became skin and bones with some kind of age-related problems, and still padded around the house following me as I worked. Dan tried giving her water injections to hydrate her toward the end, but that didn't do much good, and we finally had to take her to the vet for a different kind of injection. Gentle, and seemingly fragile, Truffles turned out to be one spirited and hardy cat and lived a great and graceful life to the ancient age of almost twenty-four.

Chapter 40
Chip's Beach Social

There were eight playful puppies, all tumbling, wiggling, and shoving each other about on a slippery-clean kitchen floor. We stood there with the puppies' owners, our oldest son, and two grandchildren. For a second time, I warned the owners, "We've just come to look." Since we had almost always gotten our dogs from a friend or the Humane Society, this was an uncommon venture. The ad in the paper was compelling, though, and Dan Jr. had mentioned that same afternoon that his family was finally going to get a dog.

I'd insisted, "Come on, it's just a little outing while the roast and potatoes bake and before you kids eat and have to leave for home. You just might want a Lab when you start looking for a pet." Dan Sr. was also very reluctant to make this visit.

These were Chocolate Labrador retriever pups, all a beautiful, dark chocolate brown, with thick soft fur. The owners mentioned how these dogs have a double coat, and, for the most part, haven't been as cruelly in-bred as some other breeds. "Perhaps," he informed us "this is because they are still such a popular breed for hunters and are often put through field trials." They assured us that the dad and the mom were both sound and healthy labs with no hip problems. I had heard about an alarming number of hip problems, not only in Labs, but in many other breeds as well.

Sweet, square-faced guys and gals looked with inquisitive, shining, dark eyes for our shoe laces or a chance to bite, paw, or shove over a brother or sister, while I asked, "If we were to actually buy one, would we take this big, friendly, guy, or would we choose one of his smaller littermates?" We picked up each puppy and looked them in the face, all the while smelling their milky breaths and puppy fur. The females' faces seemed less square, but would also be lovely. From "just looking," to, "if we buy," to "how much," and, "let's buy" didn't take very long. Unanimously, we all chose the large, stocky, square-faced, and out-going male puppy with the huge paws. Since size of feet is an indication of future size, someday he would be a very big and heavy dog.

Since Dan hadn't been anxious to come and Danny drove us home, I handed Dan the fat puppy to hold on the way back. Bonding between them came then and there. Of course he knew my scheme and has laughed and talked about it ever since. Even at eight weeks, the puppy's whole body tried to wag, and with his needle-like baby teeth, he chewed on Dan's fingers and tried to lick his face. His fur was like soft velvet. I, too, was totally smitten with him by just watching him win Dan over there in the back seat.

This trusting and awkward baby whimpered and cried the first couple of nights, for he had only known his mom and romped and slept with his sisters and brothers. The pup also kept us running, keeping him warm, loved, and fed while trying to cope with his constant puddles and crying. At night, Dan and I took turns getting up to give him a bit of milk, pet him and put him back on a baby blanket I'd found in my old cedar chest. All of us considered names; it would be fun to register him, even though we didn't plan on letting him become a father. The bear-like cub received the name Chip, as in Mr. Chip's Chocolate Mouse Friend. With endless numbers of brown dogs, it was difficult to think up a name not already used.

A cardboard box full of blankets made him a happier pup after those first nights, and, within a few days, he clearly decided, "Life is a ball, an adventure. I'll love everyone and enjoy the simple, good things each day, like chewing on socks, shoes, curtains, and pant legs." He also chewed on Wendy, and Truffles.

This one puppy made me wonder how I had ever raised four kids and all the other animals. A puppy is for the young or for someone with little else to do—he rained puddles and more at one end and at the other end chewed up new boots, magazines, and the sack that held an economy-sized bag of unshelled peanuts intended for hand-feeding a couple of friendly blue jays next door. For several weeks, he continued eating and drinking several times a day and usually ended up getting a snack at midnight.

When Truffles whacked Chip in the face with her paws, he just went over to Wendy and chewed on Wendy's paw, or climbed and tumbled over her. Dogs know if they are truly liked or not. At first, he thought Wendy must have a milk supply handy and rooted around her underside. That irritated her somewhat, and she jumped to her feet to sit somewhere else.

Then, with a mother's wisdom, Wendy suddenly decided she would bond and become a surrogate mother to this puppy in perpetual motion. After all, she had raised her own boys until they were about three or four months old. She washed the little guy all over with her tongue and let him play with her tail, ears, and nose. I prayed for the day Chip would stop gnawing on everything in the house and yard, but he chewed anything chewable until he was at least two and a half. More and more I kept him in the kitchen or outside. I had heard that an outgoing and strong puppy is the one to choose. If so, we had chosen well.

However, Chip's social life didn't get off to a very promising start. A month later, we took the dogs and cat up to see the Santa Rosa kids and their dogs, and our dogs, along with their Kona Labrador, slept in the extra large garage. The next morning our precious puppy became a great embarrassment. He had been a demolition squad of one; a large sack of birdseed was spread out all over the floor, one rubber boot of a new pair would never be worn again, a good ranch jacket needed to be dry-cleaned, and all the dog blankets spread out on the floor now had dozens of little holes. Perhaps everything was like chewing gum for his teething period, or maybe it was just fodder for boredom and play. Of course, all puppies chew on things, but Chip continued to gnaw away at everything he could get his jaws around, including the legs of furniture, all the small throw rugs, drapes, shoes, magazines, books, bath mats—even part of the car's upholstery.

When I later complained to other Lab owners on our beach walks, I learned that most owners know about this breed's demolition timetable. With rueful laughs, several owners responded with comments like, "You got that dog without anyone telling you that these puppies attack and ruin everything they can get a hold of until they're about three years old? Yes sir, it's about three years of non-stop destruction." I got off easy; it wasn't quite three years—it just seemed like it.

As he grew and grew, Chip developed a strong macho look but remained just a sentimental, loving guy. Most dogs and pet people on the beach were dog-savvy and knew Labs were sweet, but, at first, a few grownups snatched their dogs up in their arm as he approached and asked me what breed he was. Some had only seen yellow and black Labs.

With his whole body wiggling with excitement and friendliness, his first and main targets were people, rather than their dogs, and he was ecstatic when they were people and dogs he'd met before. Before long, I tried to postpone our walks until it was late enough for others to be walking just so Chip could have his "party time." Chip had a slobbery, licking tongue, and a wagging tail greeting for about ninety-eight per cent of all those he met, human or animal. The few adults or dogs he avoided I always studied carefully, even if I usually couldn't decide why he left them alone. Still, I trusted his judgment.

Chip's whole body was big and strong, and his tail was like a stiff, hard rope; and to have it whip back and forth against even panted legs was punishment, though he only intended a joyful welcome. A beach walker remarked, "Your dog gets extra tail-power by wagging his whole body at the same time as that lethal tail swings back and forth." Several others tried to bend over to hold his tail, but then they got a big wet face-washing from the other end. We tried to keep him away from small children after he vigorously licked a few faces and bowled over a couple with his tail.

Most of the dogs brought to the beach were taken off their leashes, which instantly transformed them into more friendly dogs. At home, many of them probably rushed to their fences to bark, snarl, and show their teeth when strangers walked by. But when running free and with lots of sticks and balls to chase, almost all the beach dogs wished to be friendly and play, or at least be tolerant and keep a balance of power going. Like people, they, too, needed an emancipation proclamation—a change of pace and place without the stress of just some tiny yard or house with little or no company. Fortunately, these were years long before all dogs had to be on leashes, or at least years before the law was enforced.

There may be something to the "love me, love my dog" thinking. I gravitated toward those who liked animals, and they did the same. The pooches became a bridge to happy smiles and short conversations or hellos with the owners of the other dogs, and maybe that, too, communicated to the dogs and made them friendlier. Actually, I recognized the humans by greeting the dogs they owned, and for quite a while I seldom recognized the people by sight if I met them in a restaurant or on the street without their pets. Chip never picked a fight, but the hair on his back often rose as he and other dogs met for the first time. Of course, at the same time, his tail wagged and he smiled greetings.

Some of the little dogs had a way of yipping and yapping as they ran up to Chip, but he met them with a tolerant smile and politely walked away. I wondered if the tiny dogs really believed they were big wolves, or maybe that a strong attack would be their best defense. For whatever the purpose of their yippy barks, both Chip and our other dogs looked down at them and then seemed to decide they were just out of control puppies and should be ignored. However, he did play with several of the smaller dogs, especially a teen-aged boxer, and they always ran in endless circles, chasing each other in and out of the surf. This lively socializing left him no time to chase birds like Wendy loved to do. Since this was a daily beach festivity, Chip must have felt he might miss some pats on the head and some reciprocated licks and tail wagging with his beach buddies if he went off dashing after birds with Wendy.

Chip's party beach was redecorated daily by the incoming surf that tossed upon the sand driftwood, seaweed, stones, shells, parts of boats that had broken up in storms, and, occasionally, empty plastic bottles that Chip liked to carry in his mouth or tried to bury in the wet sand, for some obscure reason. With a hotel and dining room adjacent to the beach, often hosted guests and members dropped bits of food over the wall to the sand. Overweight Chip sniffed diligently, hunting for those appetizers. It was like a daily treasure hunt or an Easter party on the sand, and he ate some very gritty but elegant hors d'oeuvres. At first he also loved to pop any party balloons that littered the beach after they'd decorated the club the previous evening, but after several years balloons stopped being used, at least on the beach.

Only once did a dog attack Chip when he went up to the owner of a dog on a leash to say "Hi." Chip immediately rolled over on his back in the position of submission, but that doesn't always work, and the owner had to pull off his large, mixed breed dog. Fortunately, his dog was on a leash.

However, later Wendy had one potentially deadly near-miss. She didn't always bother to stop and size up other dogs, opting instead to just run up to greet them nose-to-nose. This time the other dog was a very large, muscular, pit bull terrier, held with a very heavy short chain and wearing a wide black leather collar with spikes sticking out all around it. Holding the dog was a squarely built man with heavily muscled and tattooed arms. Man and dog seemed similarly built and probably had the same outlook on life. Dogs, in addition to their ancestry, often take on the moods and personalities of their owners, whether for good or for bad. They want to please. This fierce dog lunged at Wendy, barely missing her throat. The tough-looking man yanked his dog up on his hind legs and held him there, and by then Dan was able to leash Wendy and get her and us away from them. Being female wouldn't have helped her a bit and neither would the short hair on her skinny, vulnerable neck. Few breeds seem to have that attack-and-kill gene as strong as some pit bulls.

In spite of Chip's sociability, there's something hereditary about how most dogs greeted each other—fixed social patterns that are followed each day. Dogs who met daily were friends that could usually skip some of the greeting protocol, and the routine behavior appeared as common as people doffing their caps or shaking hands. However, some other dogs seemed to be saying, "I'll sniff your nose and turn around and sniff your other parts, but I am not backing down or leaving quite yet." The other dog was doing and saying the same thing. Maybe it meant rank mattered; each didn't want to be attacked, yet wanted to remain the dominant dog, alpha dog, or whatever other name means "top dog." Some who didn't want to be submissive or feel inferior would proceed in a fashion that seemed to say that they were taking charge. Heads were held high and eyes were alert. Hair along their backs and shoulders sometimes rose, and they stood tall and walked stiff-legged. At some mysterious point in time, both dogs seem to have saved face, and they could then relax and play or catch up with their owners. Chip and most dogs knew there was no need for actual combat, especially dogs who weren't leashed. I suspect that, like horses that kick and bite, dogs, for the most part, only bite through fear or because they have been mistreated. Of course, a few are trained to attack and bred for such aggressive jobs as guarding or police work.

Several beach walkers reacted to Wendy more fearfully that they did Chip, since she was a Doberman, but Wendy only had a gentle, loving and kind heart and soul. All the regular beach walkers knew her sweetness. The dogs and I met many other Doberman pinschers throughout the years and never met one who wasn't friendly. Several walkers even looked carefully at Chip and asked if she was a Rottweiler, although Chip was all Lab and a rich, chocolate color.

Some other dogs just lived to play, and, completely forgetting any formal meetings, they came flying up to Chip at a full run, raced around him or pawed the air, while he stood still and wagged his tail. By mutual agreement these dogs and Chip could start playing or leaving each other in just a moment or two. Other dogs lived to chase balls or sticks. And some, like Wendy, preferred chasing birds. Still, other dogs crouched down low on the sand and only got up when Chip was quite close. I'm not sure why—maybe they were undecided about how to meet another dog. They needed to come to more beach parties. I still wondered if the owner's outlook on life was catching; happy people had happy dogs, and those with problems sometimes had neurotic dogs.

Labrador retrievers have a super fine sense of smell and usually, as their name suggests, make great retrievers. They normally love the water and can bring back birds over land as well as water. A hunter told me the breed learns willingly and with lots of enthusiasm. However, purebred Chip never really wanted to retrieve, hunt, or swim. He usu-ally swam only when we did, since it then became social. Our son's labs Kona and Mega lived to retrieve and could find sticks or balls thrown long distances into thick brush, down hillsides, or into water. Both dogs swam until they were exhausted, whether in our pool, the ocean, or a lake, pond, or creek near their home.

Many beach-walkers' pets, both big and small, also liked to swim and fetch sticks and balls from the surf. One such dog even dived to the bottom and brought thrown rocks up to the surface for his owner. Doug's Mega often swam far out—even through heavy winter surf—for over an hour to fetch sticks and tennis balls. She followed that workout by then swimming in a pool and, going in circles, trying to paw the bubbles she created. After that, all of us had to try to keep her tied up and away from water for the rest of the day.

Chip continued to demonstrate his non-sporting view of birds when a large, rather plump brown bird came to our patio for a spell for sev-eral years to eat small crumbs of dog food in the dog dishes and on the concrete. At first, the bird cocked his head to one side and then the oth-er to consider the danger of Chip lying there. Each day the bird came nearer, less concerned about any move the dog might make. Finally he was pecking crumbs within a few inches of Chip's nose. The dog just slept or idly watched the bird find food. The bird finally trusted this big beast, who was also colored the same nice brown.

Wendy, the Doberman, and Nicky, a German Shepherd soon to join our family, seldom wanted to play games or meet other dogs or people along the shore. Their passion was to chase birds up and down the edge of the surf. There were some different birds at different seasons, but com-mon ones were the various sea gulls, terns, godwits, stilts, a few Great Blue herons and Snowy egrets. The birds, mainly the smaller ones, devised a game to keep the dogs frantic. Instead of flying out to sea or to another part of the beach, the birds flew just a short distance ahead of us, land-ed on the sand, and then took off again as the dogs raced toward them.

Recently, more and more large crows have become "shore birds", scavenging people's picnic scraps and eating dead sea creatures such as fish, crabs, and lobsters, as well as small creatures in the wet sand.

In old age, Chip only briefly walked ahead or tried to play with another dog for very long. The rest of the time he walked along between us. If Dan walked with him at a club while I swam, Chip made one circle of the tennis courts and then pulled Dan to the car door to certainly say, "I'll just let that do me for today. Put me in the car, and you go on." As happens with older dogs, we began to take two walks—a short one with Chip and then a longer one without him. Even a short stroll gave him fresh memories for the day, and as he stretched out on a rug beside me, he snored, grunted, and twitched his body in good dreams.

It may not be too many years more before Dan and I will be kept at home ourselves, but what a lifetime of memories of companionship, love, and shared delight these precious animals will have given us.

Chapter 41
Nicky Comes to Stay

Nicky was one of our super-dogs whom we took in when she was quite old. She was a small German Shepherd, the kind that has creamy white or light tan on the undersides, the legs, and around the head, while her back and sides were a dark, grayish black. I never found out if the dog was purebred, but she was beautiful, especially her huge, expressive, dark eyes.

This shepherd was Nancy's dog, but as Nancy had to be away from home longer and longer hours as the only breadwinner for her daughter and herself, the dog became lonely and, perhaps out of desperation to do a job and gain recognition, she became overly protective of Nancy and their house and snapped at one or two people. Nancy then tried taking her to school and leaving her in the car while she taught college English classes; however, Nicky soon jumped out of the open windows and tried to protect the car from students walking by. When left at home, she would jump the backyard fence or dig her way out under it and disappear. Nancy's daughter had left for college, and with the little girl whom Nicky had helped raise no longer around, the dog became ever more desperate.

On a trip north to San Luis Obispo, Dan and I discovered Nicky chained in the back yard, completely tangled up in a large shrub and unable to move. She had turned over her large watering pan and was hot, thirsty, and frantic. Since we had Wendy and Chip at home, Nancy said she hadn't wanted to ask us to take in a third large dog. We quickly insisted that we'd love to have her. The bright dog quivered with anticipation and relief and seemed to know exactly where we were going to take her. Content in the back seat, with her leash, water, food bowls, a favorite bath towel, and a few tennis balls, she quickly went to sleep.

Where in the world could we keep all these animals at night? When left outside, our two barked at every real or imagined danger, so we usually kept them inside at night. Dogs and cats had never used any of the fine beds I had furnished them for sleeping, whether they were soft pillows, large baskets, private doghouses, or cute futons. I didn't want three big dogs in the house at night, and conventional doghouses wouldn't be used or look good on our patio. Of course, the critters' first choice of sleeping quarters would be on our bed; second choice would be as close to our bed as possible; and third choice would be where something exciting or involving food might show up: a refrigerator door opening, an open door to escape to the great outdoors, or someone nearby to hug and talk to them.

Quickly I thought of an answer. "You dogs and we will all sleep soundly," I assured them. Very soon after, a cabinetmaker built them a deluxe "duplex" plus a single room. Both the double and the single were made to look like fancy serving tables on all sides except for the entrances. The top of the duplex was roofed with patterned tile that matched the tile around the pool, and I placed a clay flowerpot in the center. The other sides were solid wood siding, painted off-white like the house. The doors of the dog-quarters faced the sliding glass doors to our bedroom; they would be fewer than two yards from us at night and would know we were near. The carpenter made the single dog house the same, and we placed it near the other one against the patio wall. No one on the patio or coming up to our sliding door would be apt to notice that these were dog shelters. We could remove the single one after elderly Wendy was no longer living. It worked! All three dogs felt close enough to us to enjoy their spacious bedrooms. These three dogs were the only ones I ever had who liked doghouses.

Nicky and Wendy tied each other in their great intelligence and devotion to the family. Nicky understood that Wendy was the old, top dog, and decided that sociable Chip could be middle-dog if he wished. Being least dog didn't bother Nicky at all—she just loved all of us— and never again did she bite anyone or any dog. This German Shepherd seemed to sense so much about life and could easily understand and accept us wholeheartedly.

When Nancy came to visit, Nicky loved to see her, but would never go anywhere near her car. There was one time when, for some reason, we took two cars, and Nancy tried to get Nicky to go with her in her car. The dog quickly wheeled about, dashed back into the house, and hid in a closet.

As the years went by, Nicky willingly continued to play and wrestle with Chip around the yard, but on the beach she became an accomplice with Wendy to endlessly chase sea birds. Even with two dogs running, they never caught a single bird, and Nicky agreed with Wendy that they should leave any sick or injured seagulls alone when those birds were unable to fly away. Fat and slower Chip, in the meantime, continued greeting all of his regular beach friends and any strangers, hoping to be petted, perhaps called by name, and occasionally given a small doggy-biscuit from someone's pocket.

Nicky and Wendy couldn't have loved us any more sincerely than they did and were rather gregarious by nature, but they had no desire to be like Chip and greet every dog and human like a long-lost friend. Those two also did a great job of sensing insincere people, somehow figuring out who was for real and who was just putting on a show. When there were no birds to chase, they greeted most people with polite enthusiasm, but didn't gloss over any bad impressions they had of dogs or people and just walked away to avoid those they questioned.

Then one day, Wendy and Nicky truly showed their independent yet loyal and protective nature. They had a chance to use their German-Shepherd and Doberman instincts regarding people and their family's safety when a large, extra rough and tough looking man climbed over our backyard high gate. The man had probably first tried our front door, which was fortunately locked, and had then started walking down our driveway toward the street in front when the dogs saw him beside the house. There was no need to sic the dogs on him; they knew their job and knew what sort of man he was.

Both began roaring with voices I had never heard before, and I ran to a front sliding door to look out. This man was trying to shoo the dogs away with an old book he was clutching and was shouting back at them with foul language in a guttural, nasty voice. I had a sudden strong suspicion that he had recently been in prison and the "book" might even hold a gun. I opened the front gate from inside the house, while Wendy and Nicky circled and circled him; not biting, but showing their teeth and barking. When he was once on the road and definitely leaving, the dogs turned around as a team and trotted back up to the house, somehow knowing they shouldn't go on to their beloved beach on the far side of the road and hedge.

My dear friend, Babe Selby, phoned from Sweet, Idaho, some time after that incident and amazingly told me about the two Dobermans she felt had saved her. "My dogs have always greeted everyone at home and at our business building with great friendliness, and they also let the grandkids sit and crawl all over them and do as they please, but the other night I couldn't believe these were my same house-dogs! Two men in black suits and ties came up to me in a car while I was home alone and on my hands and knees planting bulbs near the house. They got out of their car, and they started to say a few crazy things that didn't fit in with anything concerning our business, the house, or anything legitimate. Almost immediately, our Dobies arrived, right there between the men and me, showing their teeth and growling like mad. Both dogs kept trying to back into me, to push me further away from the men. You can't believe how quickly those guys said they must have the wrong address and left. No wonder you love those dogs of yours." Since we only talk for an hour or two a few times a year and exchange long letters with about the same frequency, she hadn't known before that I also had dogs who, like hers, could do great guard work when needed.

She and I agreed that dogs seem to have, or develop, an extra sensory perception for our feelings and the intentions of others. The proof comes again and again to those who live with animals. I don't know how animals read their owners' minds and those of both friends and strangers, but they do.

Incidentally, way back in 1938, Babe and I vowed, while still in high school, to meet in the year 2000 for a horseback ride together. Since we could both still get on a horse, we met in Santa Barbara soon after the year began and took a trail ride along a beautiful canyon creek and then up to a high ridge near the Reagan ranch.

There are books out now saying how much you can tell about people from their "body language"—the way one stands, moves, holds one's head, and things like that. If this is so, the dogs have it down pat. I sometimes wondered what they read in it when I crossed my arms, crossed by legs, or tapped my foot. Maybe instead animals detect some kind of vibes or subtle odor, a scent humans give off on their skin or their breath in times of anger, fear, excitement, hatred, or even acceptance and love.

Our bright new family member, Nicky, only lost her wits once, and it was on Nicky's first Fourth of July with us. Since I had decided she was unflappable and noise would never faze her, I left her outside that day and evening. Our other dogs hadn't feared the noise and lighting displays and had always just gone to sleep when we did. It happened to be an extra big year for fireworks on the beach, and there was, as always, the big display of fireworks up the coast near the harbor. Even aboard several boats at sea people were setting them off. At bedtime, Nicky was nowhere to be found.

Dan and I drove the neighborhood for ages, and finally found several people who had seen Nicky go through a condominium complex down the road. They thought she had been heading for the beach, beyond most of the fireworks. That was where we finally found her—wet, muddy, sandy, and almost beyond recognition. She was completely exhausted and still terrified, probably thinking it was the end of the world. Needless to say, she spent the rest of the night in the house after a warm, soapy bath, a drying off with towels and my hair dryer, plus countless apologies and hugs from Dan and me. After that we stayed home on the Fourth of July, and Nicky always had access to our bed or closet, usually way back behind the shoes. When Wendy and Chip eventually decided her fear of any bang, crackle, or hiss of fireworks in the sky just might be justified, all three dogs wanted to be in the house. From then on, we celebrated not only the weekend of the Fourth of July, but also New Year's Eve at home with the dogs huddling in our closet or bedroom. They were also left in the house any other evenings when we went out.

One other event colored our animal family's life during those years. One summer, we kept the whole family of Nicky, Wendy, Chip, and Truffles with us in a big, long, fifth-wheel trailer in Buellton for four months. A realtor friend had a client who thought he would like to rent our entire house for four months and offered an enormous sum of money. We'd had a small financial setback, and this seemed too good to pass up. I scrubbed and painted for weeks and moved all our personal belongings into several large closets.

For the first five weeks of our renter's stay, all the animals went to a good local kennel, while Dan and I toured Australia and New Zealand. When we came home to hook up the trailer behind our one-ton crew-cab truck, we saw no one around the house and no cars, so we picked up all the pets from the kennels and brought them home for long, soapy baths on the lawn, with the exception of Truffles, who got bathed later in the trailer's kitchen sink. I had put cheap covers over the new carpeting in the 5th-wheeler and sheets over the couch and matching chair to escape wear and tear from so many critters and two people living in such close quarters for the remaining three months.

The fine mobile-home manager in Buellton was willing to take all the pets and us. There was a large green field adjacent to the park to walk the dogs, and a good-sized pool for Dan and me to swim laps. The park had large, nicely tiled showers in the bathrooms and laundry rooms, although we had a shower and full hookups for gas, water, electricity, sewer, and our own telephone and TV in the trailer.

A neighboring man there, as soon as he decided the three dogs wouldn't be barking, made the comment, "I guess you folks know you've really gone to the dogs!"

The dogs immediately understood the ropes, somehow, that they had to remain in the back, living room end of the trailer and could later spread out on the dining and kitchen floor after we went to bed in the roomy front end. They never fought or disputed each other's choice of sleeping spots, and only the cat came now and then to sleep at the foot of our bed. All the animals had finely-tuned inner clocks and knew they had to lie quietly, if not asleep, until our daily "appointment" at 7:00 A.M. to walk out to the large open alfalfa field south of the park.

The trailer was parked under shade trees, and most days we left elderly Truffles in the trailer with the air-conditioner on low and took the three dogs back to Santa Barbara with us. We played tennis and swam at the club, walked the dogs on the beaches, and found shady spots for the truck while we ate our dinners at noon. Some days we ate where there was outside seating and the dogs could be with us on some far end of a patio or porch. We dressed up and attended every Channel City Club luncheon meeting that summer. Four special animals in a trailer with us? A piece of cake!

And for the first time, we actually turned on the TV set for the news and several programs. News flashes in the past had seldom reached us. Now a common question that news journalists asked people when they run out of current news was: "Where were you when Japan attacked Pearl Harbor?" or, "Where were you or what were you doing when the President died?" I hadn't a clue for any correct answers. Of course even the dates of birth of my kids escaped my memory, and I was actually present at those. If asked a kid's age, I sometimes had to fudge and said things like, "Old enough to know better," or, "Somewhere between twenty and fifty."

Soon we were back home and all was well. Our renter had actually only used our home about a month of the four he had rented. I always felt that both Wendy and Nicky, maybe more than Chip, understood much of what we felt or said. They both matched our moods and right to the end of their lives wanted to be part of the action. We often sneaked out just one dog, without the others seeing, to take with us in the car while we ran short errands, yet I soon noticed that Nicky never sat up in the car to look out the windows as she always had before.

One morning not long after, I noticed Nicky was not feeling well, but we were almost late for doctor appointments, so I gave her a hug and told her we'd take her to the vet in about an hour. When we got back, we found that she had died beside the house. Our vet did an autopsy and found she had a number of advanced internal cancers. It never got one bit easier to lose a pet, and she was one of the very best. Like almost all of our animals, she had just needed daily closeness to family to love and appreciate her. Both Chip and Wendy knew she had died and needed a great deal of petting and hugging for a surprisingly long time. Slowly, the relationship between Chip and Wendy, who had mothered him as he grew up, became even stronger.

Chapter 42
Bear and the Watermelon

Who says old dogs can't learn new tricks? Bear came to us at age six. We were his third or fourth home, and, as far as I knew, he had always lived a dumbing-life in small back yards, with only quick walks around a block for exercise.

I had no wish for another dog. Wendy was getting old, and she and Chip were both lots of company. They, too, would have voted to keep the family as it was.

However, Don, Director of the local Humane Society, phoned me to report he had an extra nice Chocolate Lab, purebred like our Chip, who desperately needed a home. This older dog was owned by a friend of his. He had found homes for the friend's two other dogs, but not Bear. "It would be nice for Chip to have a pal, and you folks would then have two great Chocolate Labs."

After talking it over, we decided against more dogs. "No," I told Don, "we'd love to take him, but we're here on somewhat limited space now, and I still miss losing Nicky. We still have both Wendy and Chip, you know."

Don phoned two more times to say he still hadn't found a home for the dog, each time saying, "I don't want to twist your arm now, or be a nuisance, but Bear is still waiting for a good home."

Dan and I began to waiver. Dan suggested, "Perhaps we should relent and take him. The yard is big, and what's one more dog to feed?"

The fourth call came while Dan and our son Jeff were both in the garage. Jeff became my witness to what his dad suddenly promised. As I
reported, "Don's on the phone again, and that Lab still needs placing.
What-da-you-think? Shall I tell him a definite, final 'No'?"

Dan went into one of his typical great sales pitches. "Honey, let's
take him. I'll feed him, bathe him, and take care of him. It's just as easy
to walk three dogs on the beach as two. It would save a dog and give
him a great life. Don't you think it would be fun to have two Chocolate
Labs?" I couldn't refuse, and told Don that we'd take the dog.

The owner, Mr. Johnson, drove his dog to us, and with tears stream-
ing down his face, he handed the leash and the dog's pedigree papers to
us down at the gate. We had not seen the dog until then, and it came as
quite a shock. Bear must have weighed a hundred and fifty pounds or
more. He would have been a hefty guy, even with normal weight, but
he was nowhere near a normal weight. He was almost square and just
stood there in one spot, his eyes bulging. Still he was a beautiful dark
brown, with a statuesque, purebred Lab's head, and looked at us in a
sweet uncomplaining manner.

Tears continued to spill out of Mr. Johnson's eyes, and he wanted to
leave, but I finally convinced him to come with Bear up to the house.

"You really should see where your dog is going to live. Come on,
sit on the patio and watch us introduce Bear to our Wendy and Chip.
Since the dogs will immediately like him, that will give you comfort
and a good memory to hold." I knew our dogs were used to the kids'
and several friends' bringing dogs to visit, so Chip and Wendy wouldn't
be concerned. Family dogs sometimes visited us for a week or so, and
ours knew that visiting dogs were just making a social call and would
leave when their owners returned. They even walked out with us to
say good-bye when guests or family members and their dogs drove off.
Hopefully, it would be a number of days before the dogs realized Bear
would be with them permanently. Perhaps Bear, too, thought that he
was just visiting, for he was polite but not outgoing as he sat and panted
in the shade of a chair.

Mr. Johnson continued to wipe his eyes. He was an elderly man
and was suddenly losing so much: a fine large home, his wife, and three

beloved dogs! I imagined he might have spent the last few months sitting outside with his pets and feeding them fatty treats all day long. It must have been something like that made Bear so huge. Mr. Johnson left us with the pedigree papers, medical records, and an overweight dog who could barely walk. The American Kennel Club had the Lab registered with a name along the lines of, "Johnson's Cocoa Bear."

After the owner left, we decided to take the three dogs for a walk on the beach, but we quickly discovered this obese fellow could only waddle along the sand about ten feet before collapsing and panting, so we left him lying on the sand while we took short walks back and forth in front of him to keep him in sight. Bear must have gained this weight rather recently or he would have died. For several months we made two beach walks. One very short one with Bear, and another long one with Wendy and Chip.

This genial but rather indifferent fellow seemed to have little personality. He didn't welcome hugs or petting, but maybe it was because he feared Wendy and Chip's jealousy and felt very insecure: "Am I here for a visit, or have I lost another home?" Right from the start Chip tolerated him, but also made sure that Bear recognized him as higher in the pack hierarchy. Wendy was probably still alpha dog without even knowing or wanting it.

With a strict diet, slow but slightly longer walks each day, and lots of one-way conversation with me, Bear began to look and feel somewhat better, but he still tried to avoid hugs and attention, and oh how he could snore! With our crew-cab truck, Dan, the three dogs, and I went up to visit our Santa Rosa family now and then. And at home, if I could get him into the car while out of sight of the other dogs, I took him along while I ran errands in town, hoping that an enriched social life would change this pooch from being so lackadaisical, but I couldn't figure him out. Wendy continued to like him all right and sometimes licked his face, but she didn't find him very interesting, since he didn't try to play or run.

In time and in spite of Wendy and Chip, Bear changed in small ways. I often put a spread over the bed and let each dog have five or ten minutes of "quality" time alone with us as we read or watched the evening news. The dogs were brought in one by one. Bear could now jump up on the bed with very little help. On the beach, he occasionally began to wander out into the surf to just stand or swim for a few seconds if a wave suddenly made the water deep. If we were throwing tennis balls or sticks for the dogs to fetch in the water, Bear sometimes got a stick in his mouth if it floated his way, only to have it yanked away by Chip out there in the shallow breakers. The best news was that after a number of months the monstrous dog was reduced in size enough to join us in making the three-mile round-trip walk down the beach and back.

Another change came when, like Chip and Wendy, Bear began to try different human foods. Chip especially loved to eat all, or almost all, human foods. If the other dogs were out of sight and wouldn't try to steal his food, Bear now also began to eat adventurously. Little bites from our plates—bananas, spaghetti, tacos, oranges, apples, carrots, cooked chard, and especially avocados. The dogs had also discovered that I grew apple, peach, and avocado fruit in the back yard, and, along with the other dogs, Bear learned to stand on his hind legs, with his front paws on the tree trunks, to pick fruit, even when it was still green. He was becoming one of the gang.

I knew I really had a dog with a new lease on life when Bear then did a truly hilarious and amazing thing. One day, I was sitting in the hot spa beside the pool, when, suddenly, Chip started running up to me while looking back toward the vegetable garden, which was out of sight behind a row of orange trees. Chip continued to run toward the garden, then rush back to me while turning his head toward the garden. He kept up an excited, whining gibberish, and was clearly telling me something very unusual was going on in the garden or front yard and that I should get out of the water and investigate.

At that moment, Bear came walking slowly, ever so slowly, up to the patio with a watermelon in his mouth that must have weighed about ten pounds. Of course, it didn't fit entirely in his mouth; he somehow had opened his powerful jaws wide and taken a deep bite of it. He placed each foot carefully to keep his balance and progressed past me toward the front patio entrance to the house. His head was held high, and he held the melon against his chest. Bear's tail, which seldom wagged, was up high and slowly going back and forth. No Labrador retriever had ever been more proud and successful looking than he at that moment. Chip couldn't believe this was happening and was still frantic. He was coming up to me and then running around and around Bear.

I wanted to dash in and get Dan to see this funny sight, but I got to thinking, "Is there any way Bear can now set that melon down and get his teeth out of it without breaking some?" I took hold of the melon and asked him to release it. Then I got Dan.

I wasn't sure this was a ripe melon. As an experiment, I had planted watermelon seeds for the first time that year, because I had decided that the weather would never remain warm enough for melons to become sweet and ripe, and they take up a lot of garden space.

However, now I suggested, "If this melon is ripe, we've got to share it with Bear." It was a red and juicy-ripe watermelon! Dan cut it into five large pieces, giving the parts where Bear's teeth had been to the dogs. Dan and I ate our fill of the other two pieces while standing and watching the dogs eat theirs on the patio. We were still laughing when Dan finally hosed the watermelon remnants off the cement. Bear remained one happy dog, pleased as punch that he had not only discovered a delicious treat, but also managed to bring it back to his family.

All these dogs, even Bear, had so much going for them. They were ever so intelligent, clever, and had lots of dignity, a dignity that could easily be bruised by their also being sensitive—actually, in most ways similar to human beings.

Bear was with us when Wendy died on one of our trips to visit the Santa Rosa kids and their pets. Their home was always a big happy place, with four foresty acres, two children, their Kona dog, and the huge orange cat who liked Truffles. Their yellow Lab, Kona, had taught all three dogs not only the joy of eating blackberries alongside the state park road down the hill from the house, but also the fun of swimming in the small, cold creek up the road a ways. There, under big Redwood trees, there were always a couple of large, deep pools, perfect for dogs to dive in and swim a short distance or retrieve sticks or tennis balls.

Wendy had been ailing for some time and become very skinny; the vet said he had done all he could for her. Wendy lay down much of the time in her very old age, but there were few signs of discouragement or quitting. She wanted to be part of the action until the day she died.

On this day, all the dogs joined us on a trip to Bodega Bay. Wendy tried a step or two to walk along the surf, while their Kona and our Chip avoided gigantic waves to chase tennis balls near shore. It was too hard for her, so she stayed behind and kept Bear company guarding our picnic baskets and towels. Bear hated big waves.

By picnic time, Wendy was trying to dig herself a hole in the sand to lie in and wouldn't even try a bite of barbequed chicken or drink some water. She lay down all the way home and had to be lifted out of the car. She couldn't stand up or walk, and Dan said she weighed almost nothing. We took her to be put down by a local vet that evening, while I hugged her and told her over and over how much all of us loved her.

Like Treve, Boomerang, and Nicky, Wendy was one of the great family members in our lives, and it was terribly hard for us to say good-bye. I miss them all to this day. Like friends I enjoy most, Wendy was always whimsical rather than whiny and never made even a sound of complaint on her last day.

However, a very strange thing happened the next morning. Chip attacked Bear and they had a terrible fight. Chip was still a strong dog, while Bear was getting quite old and white about the face, but he fought mightily. Chip continued to attack Bear all day, and we finally separated the two dogs by keeping Bear in the house.

Somehow, Chip knew that Wendy had died and would be gone forever. Whatever he knew about death, he certainly didn't know how to grieve or handle his feelings. Obviously, he was terribly lonely. Wendy had constantly been both his buddy and "mom" from the time he came to us as a puppy, and since Wendy had had puppies of her own, she had always seemed to know how to relate to Chip. Chip would be top dog now, but poor Bear didn't care about that and didn't need to be beat up constantly. It didn't make Bear a very happy dog, to say the least, and I tried to give extra love to each of them when the other one wasn't around.

I could only wonder about the inner conflicts, the despair and grieving, that triggered Chip's fighting. Maybe it also included fear and anger.

Though senior, Wendy had never seemed to use her position and had always nurtured Chip as her baby. Even when he grew big and strong, she had been his tutor—if Wendy barked at the mailman, so did Chip. Without Wendy as a mother figure and as top dog, he may have felt lost, and Bear was the only one handy to blame. It didn't help that he'd never liked Bear very much and, on very rare occasions, had shown an aggressive side. It wasn't territorial—we were all far from home, and the dogs found lots to do and see while visiting.

Like people, animals differ in their reaction to stress; some responses are learned, and others just bubble out. Once again, I felt there had to be some sort of psychic, chemical, or other kind of communication, both between animals and between animals and humans, but why had it seemed to break down? Dogs often show compassion, yet where was Chip's for Bear?

It didn't get any better, the fights continued, and Dan and I were forced to buy Chip a leather muzzle to wear when the two dogs had to be together. Several months went by before Chip got over most of his terrible wrath and grieving. In the meanwhile, it was hard to explain to all his human beach buddies why this amiable, friendly fellow had to wear a muzzle on walks.

Eventually, Chip seemed to bond somewhat to Bear, and even licked his face and became solicitous toward the aging dog. Bear, too, continued to change and, finally, late in life, not only became an affectionate dog, but enjoyed life more and more. It was almost as if something had just clicked into another gear in his head. He even tried getting in the swimming pool for the first time in his life when Doug and Robbie encouraged him one hot summer day. Bear swam around and around in small circles near the steps and then got out, with some help, only to turn around on his own, totter back down the steps, and swim some more circles. It helped that everyone clapped their hands and cried out things like, "Right on, Bear! Go for it!" That made Chip jealous, and he had to swim some. Usually Chip only swam in the ocean, and we had never encouraged him or any of our other dogs to go in the pool.

Chip and Bear were no high-jumpers. One place the dogs had to stay out of was my vegetable garden, which was now confined and hidden in an area between two rows of citrus trees. Being heavy, furry guys of about 85 pounds each, they could sink their oversize feet deep in my seedbeds and nothing would sprout. As a barrier, I placed two long ladders, one above the other, on the sides along the pathway to the garden and front lawn. The dogs never tried to jump over the ladder fence, which was only about two or three feet high. Talk about old and laid-back fellows!

As I have mentioned before, all animals, children, and adults, too, respond to varied, fun, and stimulating environments—ones that also had lots of love and caring. Bear and one of our cats had taken a long time to awaken to family life and all that was going on, but it happened, and in the process, these animals seemed to become more intelligent, responsive, and sprightly.

In retirement, our animal farm had several other guest-performers who came to visit. Nancy's Sasha was a black toy poodle, with dark, ever so bright, observing eyes. She had an interesting background. Sasha's mom had had a "husband" in Paris, France, and had then traveled, while pregnant, to the United States and on to California. Sasha was the only puppy born, according to the owner, and Nancy had bought the little girl, Sasha, when she was about four months old.

She and the poodle visited often. However, this time Nancy boarded the dog with us for several weeks. While Nancy was seeing exotic animals in Africa, we had what seemed to be an exotic animal to baby-sit, and one as beloved by her mistress as an only child would be. I felt an awesome responsibility to keep the pooch safe and healthy.

Poodles are one of the most intelligent, playful, curious, and loving breeds. Poodles are also good about not shedding, and that helped Nancy, who has a slight allergy to dog hair. These dogs can also be high-strung and perpetual motion machines, and, moments later, calm and thoughtful.

Eager and courageous, Sasha, as well as Nancy's next poodle, Tony, loved to swim out to fetch tennis balls and sticks through waves, which was a great challenge for their small bodies to overcome. Both dogs were polite house guests, but they knew sand and sea were nearby and begged for walks by bringing their leash or ball to us countless times each day.

Some people seem to discount this breed and hold it against them that many owners have their dogs clipped with silly and outlandish circus or chorus-line hair styles, or rather like gardeners sometimes trim shrubs and trees—in the shape of horses, elephants or a number of balloons. No one should hold haircuts against the hapless dogs. I told a friend Nancy had a poodle, and she raised her eyebrows and said with a definite sneer, "Oh, really?"

Sasha seemed to understand all our conversations and behavior to an uncanny degree. She also constantly tested the boundaries of living with us, such as jumping up to sit on a chair to eat at the table with us, or making the cat play a cat-run-dog chase game. Sasha had a talent for playing many roles, most of them designed to get lots of treats as we ate, as well as love, walks, car rides, and games with a ball.

The poodle constantly badgered Chip during this long visit, and he must have tried to slow her down one day by putting a big paw on her back while they were down on the lawn. She immediately howled theatrically and refused to walk. I picked her up and rushed her to the vet, fearing Chip had broken her back. The vet took x-rays, checked her carefully, and finally decided she was "just putting on a show. She's a con artist."

At bedtime, Sasha still refused to walk and gave out a number of yowls, whimpers, and soulful, reproachful looks with her dark, intense eyes. She played the part well, because Dan decided he should sleep in a sleeping bag on the rug, while Sasha snuggled beside him and gave out a series of final pitiful whines.

It still seemed too early to fall asleep, so I got up to heat a glass of milk and make a sandwich. Dan agreed to join me and turned on TV, while I cut slices of a beef roast and tucked them between slices of bread.

The minute I set the food on the table and called Dan to eat, Sasha immediately completely forgot the role she was playing. Without even a limp or whimper, she came running over for some of the beef, pantomiming her wishes by standing on her hind legs and patting my wrist that held my sandwich with a front paw, her shiny eyes looking first at me and then at the food. Before I could hand her a bite, she jumped into an empty chair, to dine at the table, as she was often allowed to do at home.

In spite of the veterinarian's reassurances, I had continued to worry. Now, with Sasha's virtuoso performance of no pain, she and we could sleep soundly and long.

Doug's family has had two yellow Labs besides their current chocolate Lab, Keela; all three were scripted by their genes to be great retrievers and swimmers. On a local beach, Kona, Mega, and Keela liked to swim through rough waves—no matter the season—to fetch sticks or tennis balls, and, even when exhausted, come back to the house and immediately jump in the pool. It sometimes took the long chain that I had saved from the years when we had goats to keep the dogs dry for a spell.

Mega was an even more accomplished retriever than Kona had been, especially on land. In Santa Rosa, we ate some meals on the upstairs outside deck, which has stairs to the yard. Mega never came up the stairs to beg for food, but brought sticks and tennis balls for anyone willing to throw them as far as possible down into thick brush, big trees, and a very steep embankment. If no one took the stick or ball immediately she dumped them on our laps, so we always threw them and then watched as the dog systematically tracked back and forth over that large area until the ball was found and she raced up the open stairs to do it all over again.

Mega has another challenge now that she shares with the whole family; there's a new cat named Rusty who has the whole family, and many a friend and relative, bamboozled. At first, the small kitten attacked our pant legs and any part of the dog she could bite, and it seemed cute. Mega often put a good portion of the cat's head or body in her mouth to slow her down or rolled over on her back to play with the cat on her chest. The fearless cat loved it and didn't mind being slowed down a bit by the dog's rough response.

However, their old cat, Bogie, had a terrible time, because the kitty refused to quit her leaps, scratches and bites, even when Bogie tried to fight back. A house rule was adopted to put Bogie outside the house an hour before Rusty each morning, so that the old cat could find a secret hiding place or do some exploring before meeting up with the youngster. At night, Bogie slept in a separate part of the house, away from Rusty and with the door closed.

Rusty is the only cat I ever met who scrambled to the top of a number of gigantic trees and never cried to get help coming down. The puss is old now, but remains undeterred and still goes up and down a number of trees without help.

The family believes that Rusty really thinks she's a dog. She sleeps beside Mega and still attacks the dog, wrestles and rolls around the floor with the dog, and bites the dog's legs, neck, and ears. Mega is often forced to jump up to try to stop the play and seems to say, with surprise, "That really hurt, Rusty. What do you think you're doing?" And in her later years, Rusty still tackles pants with short or long legs.

Chapter 43
Sunday Gal Lost in Santa Barbara

One day, I suddenly realized that I had company. A large panting and smiling dog was following me up and back along the edge of the club pool, plainly saying I should get out. "Come on, lady, I need to talk to you." He was almost a look-a-like of our dear Wendy, with long, thin legs and bony elbows on a thin body, a skinny tail curving up, and the same floppy ears framing a thin, dark face. Instead of Wendy's black body, his was a coat of black, brown and tan, all mixed together, like tweed. There were also the same wonderful dark brown eyes and smiling lips that continued to plead, "Come on, get out; I'm lost and you've got to help me."

I stood up in the pool and decided the pooch looked very tired, shivery, and was limping a little. No collar. Cupping my hands full of water, I asked if he wanted a drink. He politely drank a bit but wasn't really thirsty. There was, of course, a small, still flowing creek nearby.

As Dan and I continued swimming, I watched the dog try to leave through the gate with anyone going to their cars. "Hey guys, I'm lost and you could take me home. You know where I live, but I have no idea where I am or where home is."

No one stopped to help. He kept trembling all over and continued to come back to talk with his eyes, tail waving, and an occasional soft whimper, as he followed me up and down the pool.

Hoping he would stay to dine, as I went in to dress I stopped at the snack bar and ordered him a "plain hamburger—no bun, no pickle, and no mustard. Sure, give him a few potato chips." The amiable, weary guy not only stayed, but sat facing the pick-up-window and waited for the meat smoking on the grill. It was about then I realized he was a she. The lost pooch ate daintily and only ate the potato chips when I encouraged her. Was she not hungry, too tired, or too nervous to eat? Maybe she had once been scolded for getting into a bowl of chips.

The lost dog followed me into the lounge area, and the staff behind the front desk and I pondered options for her. If only all animals wore ID tags, not only dogs and cats, but other pets like parrots and rabbits! ID's are also very much needed in times of floods, fires, earthquakes, or broken fences. Keeping food, leashes and pet carriers handy will also save many animals whenever time is short to take action.

The pound would be closed on Sunday, but, from experience with previous lost dogs we'd turned in, I knew I could get a list of numbers to call on the answering machine if I called the Humane Society. The recording finally gave a number for "lost or found animals." A helpful man at that number took the dog's description and current location, as well as our name, address, and phone number. He suggested that I could put her in a lockable pen that had food and water in it, out in Goleta at Animal Control. She would be checked in by the staff on Monday.

I had never been to that County Animal Control location, although it was near the fine Santa Barbara Humane Society buildings. We had taken home a number of lost and roaming dogs over the years, but mostly they had collars with tags listing phone numbers of the owner or of a pet clinic. I would reach the owners, and they would come and retrieve their wandering pets from us, or we would deliver the pets to the veterinarian hospital listed on the dog's tag. Sometimes we would just report the location of a lost animal that we couldn't catch.

Oh, what to do? As she stayed near us in the clubhouse, she continued trying to leave with tennis players, and some said she had been out on the courts and had tried to get petted or chase their balls. One lady said, "Oh look, she's trying to catch her tail. How cute." Actually, I thought she was trying to reach fleas near her tail; I parted her hair and found a nest of flea activity there.

Finally, I asked Dan, "How can we take this distraught, shivering Sunday Gal out to a 'closed-hours-receiving-cage' and leave her there all day and night? She's already scared and suffering. The cage would have food and water, but dark clouds are drifting in, and it looks like rain by evening." Our hearts were melting. "What a special dog! Anyway, she has to have a flea-bath," I concluded.

The gal came home with us, possibly trying to memorize the route on the way by looking out of both backseat windows to keep track of the scenery, but she was so tired that now and then she collapsed in a heap to close her eyes for a minute or two. She lay in awkward and unnatural positions, with a hind leg twisted under the other leg, her whole body so tense and weary she didn't even try to get comfortable. Had she been running frantically up and down the streets and hills all night and morning trying to find her way home? Maybe more than one night?

"Dan, how do you think we should introduce her to Chip?" Chip was becoming a senior citizen and might be a problem. He was becoming more and more jealous whenever we so much as petted other animals.

"I know, I'll tell Chip we're going for a walk and that she is Nancy's dog. No harm in a little transitional lie; he must understand he's our only dog and must be gracious to visiting dogs and cats."

Chip obviously responded, "A walk, a walk? Great! Hello, Nancy's-dog, want to go for a walk?" It was perfect. Chip loved her at first sight, and Sunday Gal clearly knew Chip was top-dog and, what's more, liked it that way. Did this Sunday Gal remind him of our Wendy or did he like her just because she was a she? Was it because they shared a happy beach walk together, walking side by side, bodies bumping, just like long ago when there had been other dogs Chip shared walks with? Maybe Chip actually needed this pal in his life.

For the sake of cementing this friendship, Sunday Gal had to summon energy for this walk, but she clearly decided, "I may be half sick and bone-tired, but this is a wonderful, sandy beach, even if they keep me on a leash. Walking along the edge of the waves makes my sore feet feel good. They'll take me home later."

She met other dogs and was friendly, but one small black dog crouched down low some distance down the beach, and Sunday Gal suddenly froze in place, as if ready to go after that dog. Was she "pointing" at what she thought was a wild animal? Was she part retriever? Would she have hurt the dog? I don't think so. However, she knew seagulls were for chasing, and she strained against the leash like Wendy used to do when several gulls landed ahead of us on the sand. When Chip met some of his friends, Sunday Gal appeared to enjoy meeting people and dogs, but she was too weary to be exuberant.

Dan took Sunday Gal down to the front lawn upon our return for a long, flea-killing shampoo, and then, because of her ongoing shaking, brought her, still wet, into the house to warm up and be toweled dry some more. Oh well. In fact, because we let her sleep beside the bed and stay in all evening and night, we got to know her. To know her was to love her, but I knew we had better not give her a real name…a loving owner might claim her at the pound the next day. Sunday Gal loved all the pats and hugs, and she and Chip licked each other's faces. She tried to start a game with Chip by dancing around him, touching him with her paws, or rolling over on her back and looking at him upside down. Then she came to put her face in my lap and smile. No wonder Chip and we adored her: she was a carbon copy of Wendy.

Sad and wondering moments came to her, she stopped to gaze out the glass door, and, when let out, stared through the patio gate. "This has been a lovely way to spend a Sunday afternoon, but when are you taking me home?" At bedtime, she still wanted no food or water but curled up on the blanket at the foot of our bed and promptly went to sleep.

All night she softly whimpered her troubled and frightening dreams, twitching and trembling, but the gal stayed in the exact same place on the blanket until we got up. She must have either had strict training, or was trying to be a perfect guest and not get up until her hosts did.

Chip came in the following morning, still not jealous, and she caught his enthusiasm when I suggested, "Another walk?" It was a beautiful day to be with the this special dog: The clouds and showers were gone, and the sky and ocean were ever so blue. The water was like a glassy lake, with very small low-tide waves along the shore. Somehow it seemed like an omen that we might get to keep the dog.

This time, two people on the beach tried to tell us her breed and also tell us her age by looking at her teeth. No way would she open her mouth for them, but one lady decided the gal was about four. Both thought she might be a Doberman-Ridgeback mix. Dan thought she might be five or six. In spite of her enthusiasm and quick leaps inviting Chip to play, I saw white on her chin and remembered Wendy had loved life to the hilt until the day she died, so I guessed eight or nine. Both Dan and I believed she was mostly of Doberman ancestry because, except for her coat, she was so like Wendy.

A regular meal finally seemed a good idea to Sunday Gal, but the tremors continued. She came to sit up against my legs, while I talked and talked to her and stroked her, but still her shivering came and went. Maybe she was catching a cold.

"We love you, and we'll help you find your owners. But if they turned you out from a car without a collar or any dog tags and don't get you this week, you will love it here, I promise." Shake, shake. "You're beautiful, especially your eyes and your smile."

It's so scary and devastating for an innocent, domesticated pet to become a stray. She made me think of all lost and suffering animals. They become petrified and just can't figure out how to avoid being hit by cars, where to get food and water, and, most of all, how to get home to give and get love.

I decided to call the Humane Society first, before calling Animal Control, because I wondered if there was any way we could keep her home, and they could give our name to anyone phoning about her. Waiting until 10:00 A.M. seemed an eternity. We would want to own her legally. Could we claim ownership and put her in the Boarding Kennel to be claimed?

Cheryl, a Humane Society friend of ours, said, "No, guys, you have to take her to Animal Control, but since you brought her in, they will let you be first in line for adoption if she isn't claimed by her owners. If the Humane Society took her, it would be like taking stolen property. Because you don't own her, we can't take her."

Another staff friend of ours there then came on the phone and jokingly said, "If I become lost will you take me in and give me a home?"

Animal Control sounded very reassuring. Sunday Gal would be put up for adoption Friday morning if not claimed, and if we brought her in on Monday. She would get all her shots on Tuesday and be thoroughly checked over by a vet. "Don't worry, she will have good care. Owners usually claim their pets soon after the animals are brought in, so if she has an owner, you might know more quickly if you bring her in today."

Best to go right away, like getting a tooth pulled. No way to explain to Sunday Gal why she would be put in a pen, maybe for days. The dog was anxious to go in the car, and she again watched the road and scenery very carefully. Finally, still tense and tired, she went to sleep and left the driving to us.

The office staff were great at Animal Control. I explained that she was now free of fleas and asked if this bony, trembling dog could have in her cage the piece of carpet that I'd brought. They said yes. Several staff members gathered around her and, with no trouble, opened her mouth to check her teeth for her age. The staff pronounced her "an older dog—maybe eight or nine." I assured them we would take her on Friday, no matter what her age, if she were not claimed. I was thinking, however, that nursing dogs through their final ailments of old age is always such a heart-breaking time, and Dan and I had spent much time debating the breed, size, and age of our next, and maybe, last dog. The staff couldn't seem to decide on her breed, but finally wrote down, "Doberman-mix."

We rushed out to try and catch up on errands and work, but couldn't free ourselves of worry about our new friend, caged and frightened among the barking dogs. We told ourselves that at least she had had a good sleep, a big breakfast, and probably knew we would not take her to a bad place. Most strays probably came to the pound in the scary, dark compartments of a Animal Control truck. Chip looked all around for her when we returned home. Two dogs are often good companions for each other, but it was strange how clearly he missed this and looked around for her for many days.

The phone never rang on Monday. I decided we just might acquire this polite, bright, and joyful girl who had joined Chip and ecstatically danced around us upon hearing the word, "Walk?" Tuesday the call came that her owner had claimed her.

How could Sunday Gal be a part of our family for only one day and night and become such a deeply loved animal? With increasing devotion and comprehension, Chip shared our home alone with us, but I somehow believe that he, as well as we, still remembered Sunday Gal.

Chapter 44
Rooms with a View

Afeeling of astonishment comes over me daily. How did Dan and I end up here, free and mostly untethered to kids and endless daily jobs, in a habitat at land's end with the wide and vast ocean stretching to the horizon outside our window? Today it is in the seventies, though it's only March, and a slight breeze and the sun spill into the new upstairs bedroom and writing area, calling my attention away from my computer and the mounds of papers and books on the glass table. We have a wall of floor to ceiling windows and sliding glass doors face the front garden and the sea beyond. For one who never wanted to look back on my life, I am suddenly doing a lot of it—finally heading down our very long past in memory walks and writing. Yet, I still like to focus on the present, or impulsively make plans for something in the very near future.

No day is ho-hum; each one is a sort of celebration, like frosting on a party cake, but much more substantive. No more broken fences, over-flowing sewer lines, lack of water to flush toilets, or going hungry. Instead of cleaning barns, doing daily loads of wash, and performing taxi service for children almost around the clock, we have a dog to lead us down a sandy shoreline; there are plenty of activities, with swimming, tennis, kids and grandkids coming to visit, and even time to read books! Best of all, I can live it with my trail-partner of sixty-seven years. Fate may, now and then, actually become what one plans.

With the hypnotizing sound and view of the waves and the far-reaching sea, I find myself constantly scanning for dolphins, seals, and sea lions. However, the dolphins are the most common. Our bit of land is far more populated than I'd imagined, with more shore birds and land birds than in any of our past locations. There are dozens of varieties, some in permanent residence and others arriving and leaving during different seasons of the year. I only know the names of a few of the birds. With tails acting as a brace, woodpeckers hammer holes in the tall palm trees next door, probably putting away a supply of food or making nests. Hummingbirds come, flashing and dipping here and there, seeking nectar from our flowers and nesting in the hedges or the olive tree. Doves are here, as they were on the ranch, and sometimes they perch on the railing outside my upstairs window and coo. Bold, large crows seem to multiply and now and then manage to steal oranges and other fruit to eat. As the years go by, they seem to also become shorebirds—finding food from leftover picnics and dead sea life on the sand or pecking and watching for creatures in the wet sand at the water's edge. For some years, blue jays ate peanuts from the hand of a gardener next door, and sometimes there are the sweet songs of mockingbirds. Clever little house sparrows or wrens abound, with their chirps and messy nest making under the eaves and red tile roof. One year there was even a pair of Great Blue Herons nesting in the top branches of an extra tall pine tree that we see on one of our walks in the neighborhood. Like the white egrets, seals, and other creatures here, herons have become rare sights along our walks at dawn.

Even here, not very far from downtown, many wild critters, in addition to the birds, managed to survive. Unfortunately, as I feared, there are also many gophers, moles, mice, and rats. However, even raccoons, possums, and the other small creatures are finally becoming a rare sight for us as additional homes continue to be built in the area.

Some years ago there were two green parrots, perhaps AWOL from the zoo, which is only about one and a half miles west as the crow (or parrot) flies. The pair hung out in the neighbor's tall palm trees for most of a year, and then there was only one parrot. I worried about the lonely one as well as the fate of his or her mate. Eventually, there were no parrots. Maybe both just winged it back to the zoo for regular meals and safety. They were a mixed blessing, for as lovely as they were to watch, their voices were ever so loud and strident.

Three or four years ago, we watched an extremely rare sight close to shore when five whales swam by and stopped to lazily drift through some kelp beds before going on their way far to the north for the summer. These gigantic and intelligent sea mammals played and moseyed a little bit like the dolphins.

Many clear days I can see several of the Channel Islands, and I contemplate trips (still not taken) to visit them. Today, some seagulls are giving their high-pitched cry as they follow a number of pelicans diving for fish.

At least this vast unconquered sea can seldom be put to its "highest and best use" and it's a Pacific Ocean wilderness that stretches for several thousands of miles west to the Orient. I had envisioned these years would be a time of withdrawal and less. Instead our world has expanded both north and east to the mountains; south and west to the islands, other horizons of open sea, and, finally, the city and harbor coastline to the west.

Soon after our move south, several of the grown children spoke as though they, too, saw us doing less, and I tried to explain, "Wait a minute. You talk as though this stage of life is an ending, a winding down for us, and I sort of thought that it might be too. Then Dad and I discovered something very fine: we're gung-ho over a big bunch of new beginnings, so many beginnings, we can barely keep up with them, and every year we keep repeating that the preceding year was the best. The secret is that we create them with continuous happiness; there are my fall and spring gardens, new friends, adopting the latest dogs, Sammi and Tucker, and just going up the coast to see you kids. There's lots of laughter, even without my earlier pratfalls, and with luck, I don't even have to feel completely grown up or feel old, unless I look in a mirror.

"Yet, old habits die hard. Dad and I startled some new friends who were poring over wine lists at dinner last week when we said we would just order Cokes. But you kids noticed we gave in to age last night when we graduated from the middle rows of the theater to sitting near the stage in order to hear. However, that, too, is OK, since Dan and I've decided it's where the most youthful sit."

After a lifetime of expected and normal routines, the travels we have taken each year have included the unexpected and untried fun of meeting new people to talk to, new ideas to consider, and new parts of the world to see. Yet right here I can also explore both the present and the past with new eyes and thoughts. In the hours of writing Book One and now Book Two, time and place become lost. Everything around me is forgotten. A whole morning can pass, and Dan eventually comes to ask if I'm not getting hungry. Other times I begin in the stillness of night, around 3:00 A.M. and write until 6:00 or 7:00 A.M. The books are my new occupation these last years, but I'll do it as I have in the past—one faltering step at a time.

The views from the upstairs addition still mesmerize me, even after living here twenty-seven years: the palms and eucalyptus trees nearby, the beautiful, crumbling cliffs next to the water's edge for several blocks up the nearby hill. Stearn's Wharf and the breakwater are visible beyond and become strands of lights on the sea after night comes. Far off, behind the breakwater, the land extends out toward the ocean, crescent-like and higher. However, from our south facing home and land we can only watch the sun sink into the sea at sunset during the months of December and January.

Windows on the back side upstairs give clear views of the high peaks of the Santa Ynez mountain range with their constantly changing moods, such as the many shades of darkness, or reflecting bright sunshine, and their tops, sometimes frosted with clouds and, once in a very long time, a bit of snow. Chumash Indians once roamed and lived in this area and had a community living in nearby Hammond Meadow. They hunted throughout these foothills, mountains, and meadows, and fished these coastal waters.

Surfers in wetsuits are also early risers, perhaps so they can still rush off to school or jobs after surfing. They sit on their boards out in the water just to the east to wait for the right waves to propel them to shore. On the road in front, some of these surfers pass by on bicycles, or even on skate boards and roller blades, carrying their boards and gear under an arm. Others arrive with their boards strapped to the top of their cars. They now and then come in droves when the "surf's up," but even on small-wave days a few may go out to sit on their boards to hope and wait. Experienced surfers know exactly the best surfing locations up and down the California coast.

Back on our lot, a silvery, gray-green leafed olive tree was our first tree planted and has slowly grown up to frame the corner of our house at the edge of the patio. It hasn't given me golden oil or black or green olives yet, because I've neglected to learn how to cure olives, make any oil, or even pick the fruit. The evergreen tree has gradually grown a gnarly trunk and a rather crooked shape after it lost some large branches to recent storms and trimming. Still it proves its long growing history, noted for survivability and strength, by enduring on a small steep slope and clinging to ever-eroding soil at the end of the concrete. I take courage by looking at it each day: we're both survivors.

If the kids feel our lives might be simplified to just basic needs—food, shelter, clothing—they surely know we also consider laughter high on the list of essentials, yet I'm still confused about what's "essential." I've noticed many elderly friends deeply savor the physical trappings of their lifetime, like silverware, fine dishes, special pieces of furniture, and walls of treasured paintings, and I wonder about our house. While it's more elaborate and complicated with labor-saving devices than I had planned or ever wanted, with these creature comforts coming late in life, beyond the treasure of husband, kids, and animals, I too, feel deeply possessive, not about the house or belongings, but about place—this location, being here. It fills my inner senses and thoughts. I treasure the land itself, the sea in all its countless moods, the seasons, and the many wild birds, animals, and sea creatures. I treasure the time to finally think, to reflect about all that has been and is yet to be.

It's a halcyon time to goof-off, but it's not exactly bliss; I still feel vestiges of the earlier years—the thought of working at anything less than full speed ahead remains scary, while the days and months seems to fly by faster and faster. Time is weird and still confuses me. My inner clock continues to warn, "If you don't get started by 5:00 A.M. you won't make progress." But if I'm constantly busy, time flies, so I need to do more and more, and then time flies even faster.

I still feel the need to plant vegetable gardens both spring and fall on my "south forty," although there are now wonderful, well stocked, fair-like farmers' markets minutes away with produce from the surrounding areas: fresh fruits, vegetables, eggs, flowers, nuts, and honey. The growers often display many of my favorite foods, such as figs, the older Globe variety of artichokes, asparagus, Hass avocados, and brown eggs that are advertised, "From hens that range free on the land and are vegetarian in their diet."

Small farmers or their family members arrive early to set up tables and umbrellas in rows, for these farmers' markets are almost always daytime affairs. Frequently, musicians play a guitar, harmonica, banjo, or even a violin. Happy crowds greet friends and soon have their arms, bags and carts overflowing as they carry the flowers and other produce to their cars.

Even if forever is not forever, just for a knockout I plant beds of color with flowers in addition to the vegetables, and I always take time to fill vases on tables, even when company isn't about to arrive. The first flowers I planted so many years ago were sweet peas and the occasional geranium, but they have now been supplanted by others. Roses of a variety of colors grow beside the house and, with gladioli facing them from the other side, line the driveway down to the road. A row of a dozen bougainvillea climb the front wall, and several hibiscus shrubs are drowning again this year with the arrival of heavier than normal storms. Impatiens fight for space with ferns, camellias and gardenias beside the walkway to the door, and bright orange and yellow beds of nasturtiums beyond the driveway crowd around and climb a struggling-to-live fig and two avocado trees. Narcissus, daffodil, and other bulb plants try to survive each year on a narrow band of poor soil between a tall wall and the far side of the driveway.

My inability to sleep soundly continues. Often at 3:00 A.M. I turn on the light to read or write. Each day is different with sun, rain, fog, a ruffled or calm sea. Today was a rare occurrence: the sun came up in a blaze of reds, pinks and yellows to the east at the same time a full moon was going down in the west near the still shiny lights near the harbor. Perhaps because of some warmer than usual ocean currents, dolphins are in this area much of the time, and this morning they're circling around a small kelp bed to find breakfast. A lone, shiny black cormorant, with his long thin neck and small head, like a sub's conning tower, ignores the seagulls, pelicans, and dolphins, and powers along searching for a fish to eat,

Sometimes a lone seal stretches his head up as high as he can to see our dogs, perhaps curious about the strange brown animal with four legs who can walk and run on land. A beach-walking friend watched a seal actually swim up into knee-deep water to sniff her dog Libby's nose.

It's good to be on the beach with only the dog and Dan, but so many people would benefit if they, too, would come here at early dawn—to hear, see, and feel all that's here on this walk up the shoreline, whether a bright sun rises behind us, or a soft misty fog lingers.

Some one hundred thousand people live in this town, with many more in suburban areas, yet I can easily count the number who are here right now walking or throwing balls and sticks into the surf for their dogs. It's now known that people who have animals for companions live longer, and I wonder if these excursions might also extend the lives of not just people but their dogs. There is a push on to enforce leash laws after eight or nine in the mornings, but we will always try to walk much earlier, if need be, along this shoreline.

The onslaught of pollution caused by the growth of cities and the great increase in the number of people is having a great impact upon the sea as well as the land. How long will these and other great and small creatures of the sea last against the onslaught of human population growth, their pollution and destruction? Otters are no longer often seen around here, and seals are sometimes killed to achieve a "proper seal population." It's an almost certain outcome: when supposedly good people do nothing, suffering occurs and species become extinct. I and everyone should do more to help save both the animals and the environment on land and sea. The gulls, flying up from a night on the sand as we approach, will probably take longer to become extinct or endangered, because they have adopted so well to civilization, even feeding in flocks at the city dump.

To get back to the beach, I continue to feel a special delight when the waves during the night have washed all footprints away, and we make the very first ones in the hard, wet, and smooth sand. It's also the best time to search for a new crop of seashells that may have washed up during the night. As the sun rises, waves often show lime-green and gold as they rise to curl over and break toward the shore. Sunset, of course, is also a special time, and we try to take another walk, this one on the surrounding streets.

Then one day Chip left us. He had woken up that morning and couldn't walk. We phoned our veterinarian and he reminded us that the cancers he had found were not curable, so he came out and put her to sleep at the old age of fifteen.

In spite of our advancing age, Dan and I soon decided we should give a home to a new dog, perhaps a middle-aged one so we might outlive the dog, and a chocolate Lab, if possible. The Humane Society said they would keep us in mind. However, a worker overheard our request and said he lived next door to a young couple who couldn't keep a yellow lab—a dog so lonely he had gotten out of a cyclone wire fence and had been hit by a car and whose owners planned to take him out to the Humane Society that very day. We gave Tucker his new home, but the tale doesn't end there…

No matter how much love and attention we gave him, he grieved day and night for his former home. Months passed and it got no better. Would a second dog help? We visited all the pounds and Humane Societies up and down the coast. Finally we heard about a female chocolate Lab in Ojai that had never been to a vet, may have had puppies, and needed all sorts of help. We brought her home to our vet, who was appalled at her condition and took over. Sammi was her name and she came home after her shots, some ear infection medicine, and a flea treatment.

Tucker didn't seem to like her when they first met, but these unfortunate dogs were now ours for good. We added several cyclone wire fences around our home and one across the yard, along with several gates. The large lawns back and front would be good areas to throw balls. As the years passed, Tucker and we grew to love each other deeply, though Sammi remained less affectionate.

Days in this area are not always tranquil, carefree ones, and, surprisingly, people talk a lot about the weather. Some newcomers lament that there are no seasons. Of course, we have seasons, and they are a lot more than shorter days and longer nights. "Snow bunny" tourists, who come to avoid their cold winter months back home, and transplanted people who rent or buy homes here and sink roots seem to think our storms will be just a few gentle rains. They often get quite a surprise—now and then a big winter storm can be a whopper and catch even old-timers unprepared. Creeks overflow on their way to the sea, streets flood, and one winter the water was high enough that teenagers even dived off a retaining wall into creek water almost as deep as the stoplight at an intersection—that caught the eyes of the nation and showed up on national TV. Houses spring leaks, umbrellas can't be found, and cars get caught midstream in some intersections and other creek-flooded areas. Fortunately, most homes here don't have basements to fill with water.

I love days when sheets of rain hit the windows, strong winds create whitecaps on the ocean, and powerful waves break and boom against the rocks or walls, sometimes throwing spray over into the street. Soon all the mud drains down from the mountains and the city turns the sea a frothy brown, the color of a cup of chocolate.

As an almost lifetime farmer, it becomes some consolation to me that I no longer have to lead livestock to safety from fire or floods, plant garden crops in order to have enough food, or hunt for raincoats in the back corners of closets. Tucker and Sammi have their nice tile-roofed doghouse duplex but spend their days inside. I didn't mind feeding horses and other animals in the rain in earlier years, but to stay warm inside and watch rain storms through the upstairs windows is ever so nice, especially when I'm tiring sooner and gradually getting retreads—new lenses in my eyes, hearing aids in my ears, crowns over my teeth, and even special walking shoes and a cane.

Having always been quite indifferent to the appearance of our cars, houses, furniture, and clothes, now, in the only home we ever built new, I have a home that's beginning to grow on me. It's almost an embarrassment to turn somewhat materialistic late in life. Maybe it's special because I have time to look at my surroundings, contemplate them, and love them. I vow to stay here the rest of my days—it's my castle and base to come home to. When several of the children just asked what I really wanted for Christmas, I replied, "Just give Dan and me more years here."

This morning the beach was a wide ribbon between the sea and the wall of countless rocks, logs, branches, seaweed, and other debris brought in on the waves after some heavy rains and wind. There were new little creeks, as well as the regular, larger ones, cutting into the sand with the water's rush from the hills and mountains to the sea. Some were too deep to jump over, so we returned to the shoreline road to finish our walk. In the soft morning light, it began to rain again, but it was finally a gentle rain, so we walked several miles before coming home dripping wet.

Laughing, I reminded Dan, "Down here we decided not to just rest and take it easy, but we may rust out doing this." A seven- or eight-year dry spell was still fresh in our minds, so we actually treasured the rain, knowing that reservoirs of the area were filling and all the trees and chaparral on the mountains would get needed water.

The winter season brings on vividly colorful red, yellow, and rose sunsets and, as luck would have it, offers us the two months when we can actually see the sun set into the sea from the house. On those days days, while a low winter sun glistens dazzling bright and silvery off the ocean, it's easy to feel almost a part of the sea. Then the sun gradually takes a higher arc to slide down behind the harbor and the hills up the coast from here. Rains turn all hills, fields, and roadsides green, and soon it is spring and time to plant my vegetable garden. Fogs, soft and gray, roll in from the sea at night, especially in late spring, and help keep the ground moist.

Summer brings tawny, golden hills and fields. Crops ripen, a large Fiesta Parade streams down State Street and along Cabrillo Boulevard, and it's hard to not get too much sun on our skin.

There are many warm Indian summer fall days in October and November, and the apples ripen on the trees. In town, sweet gum trees blossom with flowers of yellow, red and even purple, and the farmers' markets fill with apples, pumpkins, squash, pears, and yams. In the fall, the area is very dry, and we wait for those needed rains of winter again. Of course we have seasons!

This seemingly benign, placid county also gets an amazing number of special events from nature. Recent years have witnessed not only large rain storms, but also flooding, wildfires—one in 1990 that burned hundreds of homes—winds that toppled small and huge trees, and long years of serious drought. More rarely, we feel one of the California earthquakes, during which our dining room chandelier swings back and forth and the water in the pool sloshes back and forth, and I quickly turn on TV to learn where the earthquake is "centered."

The word has been out for quite a while that a truly giant earthquake is "in-the-making," "due" for some unlucky area in California. I imagine that most people living here probably just mentally cross their fingers and hope it will only occur in some faraway, desolate, and uninhabited area of the state, and no time soon.

The only thing wrong with these seasons is that they should come for a longer visit and quit seeming to whirl by faster and faster. It is hardly worth putting Christmas decorations back in boxes and climbing a ladder in the garage to store them up above the cabinets when the holidays arrive again so quickly. I need to stretch out these precious years, even to snag more time to find lost items each day! What undone things should I do before I become too old and addled? There are walks to be walked, places to see, waves to hear, and children to visit. There are things to be said, thoughts to be sifted through, and maybe even books to be written.

No longer is there a messy house of six, all going in different directions, with days of complicated school schedules, dates, jobs, clubs, assignments, play rehearsals, tennis practices and matches, and water polo games. Too many activities, even though they were necessary or worthy.

There's still my wish for simplicity in both routines and surroundings. I've eliminated some of the ought-to-dos and the should-dos, but I'm still impulsive as ever and hate to plan ahead. I phone friends at eleven and ask if they'd like to meet us for lunch at twelve—that can make for a restricted friendship. Maybe I overdid those should-dos in earlier years, even though they were fun most of the time. So what if thirty years of photos were still in boxes instead of albums? And I don't "have to" cook, keep the lawn short and super green, or maintain a spotless house. However, the worst words I've heard when referring to older people's lives are those calling these our "declining and reclining years." I plan to stay upright as long as possible, and perhaps "declining" can jolly well stay in the mind of the beholder and not in my thoughts.

I think about some friends we've met. "Dan, why do the Browns always feel they should have no leisure in retirement and must look for work to 'fill' every moment of their days? They still seem bored, even as they're puttering so much—making pies, polishing their car, playing bridge three times a week, and keeping every hair in place—you name it."

We promise ourselves to make more time to see family, but "eight-day-weeks" still happen. Most of the kids' accumulations stayed with us through their college years. Now, only photo collections remain to be sorted and mailed later this fall. All children are in different lines of work. Most have both cats and dogs, and one, Doug, has a horse—the six of us are becoming more and more diverse in some ways and still more similar in other ways, with new and old likes and dislikes, habits, internal clocks, plans, and dreams. There are more of us, with the children's partners and our grandchildren. No one stayed "down on the farm" to sink rural roots, and no one has a career in the field of agriculture, but there's a lifetime of love for each other in all of us, and we stay close.

Some accumulations are gone, but as a pack rat through and through, I still save. I turn off lights, shut doors to lock in the heat, and then open them a half-hour later to cool things off. Empty boxes are stored within larger boxes, and kids are well aware of our shoe sizes and desired brand of dog bones because of the many gifts that go their way in these secondhand containers. Ribbon, string, and used wrapping paper fill more boxes, stored where I can never find them at the right moment... instead, I open paper bags to use as wrapping paper and go through endless rolls of adhesive tape. We built a guaranteed-to-break-the-back mezzanine in the garage, and it's only now starting to show some empty spaces.

One of the things we joke about is that I no longer tell the children to "straighten up those shoulders and tuck in that tummy." These grownups, whose diapers I once changed, are telling me to straighten up, or I'm telling myself…and losing the battle. Today I caught sight of myself in a three-way mirror—I'm going to sleep on the floor tonight before my back is like a camel's.

More and more we've become daily pill-poppers. A shoe box in a drawer is full of vitamins, herbs, and other pills of various sizes, colors, and shapes for real or imagined ailments, or for preventing the advance of an army of health problems waiting in the wings. A few battles are being lost—turtleneck sweaters and buttoned-up collars no longer hide my aging skin. Wrinkles are continuous from my neck up to my receding and thinning hairline, but I've made one firm decision: real old age is best considered to begin fifteen years after the date of my last birthday. I used to worry about the children's report cards, but now I worry about my grades. Am I dying if the doctors and labs only check me as "Satisfactory"? Not one "A" or "Excellent"?

More and more years pass and the generations are repeating themselves. Family visits are wonderful, but the children have begun to steal my lines of long ago, and there's reverse applause. Instead of my telling one of them, "How pretty this bouquet of mustard is! Did you find it in the meadow?" They now come in the house to say, "What a beautiful bouquet, grandma. Are the flowers all from your garden?"

When they arrive two hours early and find dirty dishes still in the sink, I'm sunk and apparently not doing my housework. Their next question then becomes, "Well, what did you do today?"

Even one of the grandchildren observed my lack of a cleaning lady a few years back. "Grandma, you're full of cobwebs, they're right up there in the corner, and there are more in my bedroom." Later, the same child wondered, "Mom says you lose your purse all the time. Why do you do that? I bet there's a dollar in it? Will you pay me to find it?"

"Don't worry, sugar, " I responded to this cute remark. "It's in the house somewhere, and losing it turns my purse into a piggy-bank—I can't spend money while it's lost."

All the kids correct me on another point. These adult children, who forever thought I was too strict, now complain, "Why don't you train the dogs and be more strict with them? They don't have to be in the house this much. All the dogs should at least sit and stay down when you tell them to." Actually, these current dogs seem part-and-parcel of long-ago other fantastic ones who knew that life is about enjoying it, not sitting on command.

"Aw, come on, you know I've never been able to train a dog, or even wanted to. There's no way to overhaul me at my age. But do notice: we've washed all the windows and mopped the floors in honor of your visit." I shouldn't have been on the defensive, for as soon as these children left home for college, their beds were often unmade and the rooms messy until they married and had kids.

Still, I notice we're getting some unneeded care. More and more the children try to "help" or "ease" our work, and, in the process, they do things their way. Another cycle within cycles is occurring. "Let's set up a modem, so if you get stuck on the computer we can fix it and talk to you from home," or, "How about going out tonight? We'd like to treat you," or, "We'll wash Tucker and Sammi before we leave." I try not to always acquiesce.

On a most unwelcome note, these four children and some of the grandchildren seem to have suddenly gotten total recall of their long ago childhoods, miserable ancient history that's probably become largely fiction. Now they feel free to blithely dump these stories in my lap, to graphically and in great detail, tell "the real stories." At a time I should be telling them old mom's tales, I hear for the first time about escapades and tricks they played. Danny had accidentally put a hole through the ceiling of the living room the day after he was given a gun. He ran out for a bit of mud to fill the hole, found the matching can of paint, and, with his finger, smeared some over the hole. Dad and I never knew about it. Nancy adds, "He asked me to go get the ladder, but I told him, 'I don't like your gun any more than Mom and Dad do. Get the ladder yourself.'"

Then the younger two perpetrators of reckless adventures plunk down in living room chairs and more tales leak out. The younger boys had a long car race—one driving the family station wagon, the other his own car—up by Santa Margarita Lake years ago.

Another one remembered a hair-raising time when he dove into Laguna Lake among the willows, tules, and rushes at a very young age, only to become entangled under the surface of the dark water in the thick growth. He was barely able to break loose before his breath ran out.

All these escapades would have put me over the edge at the time, and were flooring me even at this late date. They'd get no "Thanks for the memories" from me for spilling the beans. Where were my perfect kids and their flawless mom as they grew up? Then they roast and toast me with things I could never possibly have said or done. Too late for nit-picking; I decide I might as well try to laugh and protest, "I don't know what you're talking about; you're rewriting the script." Instead of inno-cent little children, there had been an innocent dream-world mother. Innocent or not, it took a lot of doing to keep that show going, though I admit they all did their own thing much of the time, and I had had only a limited awareness of their escapades.

"Wake up mom," one of the boys continued, "Aren't you going to say, 'It was small potatoes'? Every time something big and terrible hap-pened to us, like being called a name at school, you said, 'That's just small potatoes.' Wherever did you learn that saying?"

"Pshaw!" I responded, " I was merely thinking that probably your tales' bowling me over at this late date are better than having us old folks rambling and re-telling your stories a dozen times; and the splendid thing is, we all visit one another, laugh together, and love one another."

Last week, one of these middle-aged children whom we were visiting asked me if I was satisfied with the way I'd lived. "Mom, would you do all that ranch work and raise four kids if you could choose to live your life over again? I'm glad you had four, because that means I'm here, but did you actually plan on four?"

I got up to peel spuds and cut up some salad makings. The ques-tion caught me by surprise, but the answer was surprisingly easy, "What might have been if I could have seen the future? Yeah, I would probably have made the same decisions and had the same dreams. It just seemed a good idea, and the right number of kids at the time—big families were still the norm back then. Also, I'd been an only child and often I found it lonely.

"There are a few battle scars—your mom was a plodding workhorse, with marathons of daily labor, but it was by choice: I willingly enslaved myself, not only by having you four kids, but taking on 100-hour work weeks. Maybe I did better at growing crops than providing insights to life. It just needed a long program, and it seemed such a natural, right thing to do at the time—as though I'd been programmed for that country life. My hands and feet run cold these days, but my heart beats with wonderful, warm memories—Thanks for the memories! You're all in so many of them. It wasn't mountain climbing, hang gliding, skydiving, whitewater rafting, and other thrills like that, but it was still a lot of testing of myself and of your dad. I should have kept a journal instead of a lifetime of constant mumblings.

"I'm not sure wisdom comes with age, but Dad and I believed then and we believe now that each of us makes most of our own destiny; Dan and I decided life was doing everything with both endless perseverance and often desperation. Opportunity is all around every one of us, and we can decide to be happy or sad about anything. As each of you left home, each of you became in charge of and responsible for yourselves and your families; it becomes your call. Remember, too, that one person can change himself, or herself, and even the world, in countless small ways. As you go along in your life, keep your eyes on some objectives, some dreams, or you can flub it. In fact, some things are bound to go wrong, but just change paths, detour, and keep on truckin'—never, never give up!

"You were born after our Arizona years, when even the state of Arizona was still very young. We started out in almost a pioneering fashion on a frontier-type farm consisting of a house with two tiny rooms, set on two dry acres of weeds; but even the hardships of those years have faded, and only good memories remain. The trails we took weren't paved, but gads!, it was great to start having you children in our lives. And the countless animals who continue to give us a large extended family were also wonderful.

"It included more action and challenge than you might think to take hold of the land on that totally mortgaged first place and on a series of other small acreages, turning them into farms and homes as you were growing up. Dan and I not only had land, home, children, and all those animals, but many expectations that created happiness. Now, that had meaning for me. Even with no high living and with us constantly working our tails off, believe it or not, it was fun.

"And you and the other kids have been the biggest treasures—you know that. I don't know how you all ever turned out so well, when I could seldom teach even a dog one thing; I once, long ago, felt great success for just getting each of you to swallow your Pablum and eventually getting you toilet-trained. There was nothing humdrum about raising you. I don't know how to describe it all—there was so much wonder about you kids—a treasure and uniqueness, plus a connectedness with love and lots of hugging and laughter. I often jokingly told your dad that any postnatal depression would have to wait until all of you finished college.

"Unlike you and your brothers who ski, fly solo, or boat in the Pacific Ocean in winter, at least I couldn't easily drown or fall very far. But, as the saying goes, we all march to different drummers, and you'll all continue on different paths. There's a world full of different paths, and I have no monopoly on ideas on which trails are right for any of you. I just hope you and the grandkids always remain hardworking and optimistic, because I think we get what we expect and earn, and I know that being decisive and not wimpy helps.

"Even though you're all unique, you all have spirit, gentle feelings toward other human beings and animals alike, and are quick to laugh. Since you're all sound thinkers and believers in yourselves, perhaps I did a few things right, or I lucked out. I'm pleased as punch that every one of us, including dad and me, got both our bachelor and masters' degrees plus a couple of doctoral degrees. Plus all three of you boys are Eagle Scouts, and Nancy is a Torchbearer."

Maybe Doug was searching for something deeper, but my thoughts had never had the leisure to see the big picture, to go deeper than the surface, beyond the present, or what had to be done the next hour, day, or week—such as getting a washer repaired, or new tires for an old car. In earlier years I had rarely looked back, but now I find there are few walls to memories.

As Dan and I got in the car to leave, orders were still evident. "Be sure and call us as soon as you get home. We'll still be up."

One frustration here, that I've mentioned before, is that I spend more time than ever looking for things. Even when we lived in just two rooms, I could lose almost anything, from keys to a sack of potatoes. My carpetbag-sized purse has about twenty compartments with snaps, zippers and dividers, but size and organization does little good when I can still lose the whole purse in the house, car, garage, or on the back steps. Before it's found, I shift into total panic, wondering if I left it at any of the half-dozen stops in town that morning.

The new inside staircase is the first in my life. It should have shown up during my fit and strong years, not at the end. I stack so much stuff at the top to take down and so much on the first few steps to take up, that by the time I've toted a load one way or the other, I've forgotten why the stuff was moved.

Right now, I can't find an important letter. I've looked for hours in every likely spot at least a couple of times. Tucker and Sammi are bored, so they've been following me around for a while. They are supposed to be retrievers, but they only look at me with big brown puzzled eyes and try to guess my mood and thoughts. "Why are you so agitated? We'd fetch it if we knew what you're promising." I continue to look in the same places, or very unlikely places, whenever I have time. Time that I don't have because I've already wasted it looking. I'm glad it's not old age: I was born this way.

At least the new second-floor addition is good exercise. There's an elevator "for when we're really old and in wheelchairs." No one uses it now.

On this summer-like day, I have all the doors open, both downstairs and upstairs, and the dazzling sun on the water is also spilling deep within the house. It's one of many extraordinarily beautiful days.

As I reassured a son, I have a few regrets. I would like to have owned and known pigs; intelligent, clean pigs, who like clean mud to cool off, not filth. I could have given a good home to one, but the problem would have been that the animal would grow too big and it would have been impossible to me to have it butchered. It was a similar problem when we tried to save injured wild critters, such as coyotes, raccoons, and a doe to raise when it lost its mother. Wild animals can only be happy running free, and they need to be returned to the wild when made well. I'd enjoyed meeting and being pulled by a dolphin and riding an elephant, both very intelligent. I also wished I had somehow found the time to read more books and had ridden Pepper more often. And time to have laughed more and done more for others.

I was always indifferent to the field of genealogy that keeps many of my friends in their later years enthusiastically researching their past. I had always repeated without much thought, "It's who you are and what you do that counts. I can choose my friends but not my ancestors." Or I said, "Why worry about roots when I'm setting out these new roots to grow? I don't have time to dig into the past."

Now, in these last years, I've changed my mind, and as I read several U.S. history books, I wonder, "Are any of these people my tribe?" I don't wonder enough to do anything about it, but I understand now why many enjoy working on the history of their relatives. What happened to all my dad's relatives in England? And on my mother's side, were there any of my kin who took part in the Civil War or the Boston Tea Party? Were there relatives who came to feel the magnet of the West? Did some take part in the fencing, the growth of towns, and the explorations of the country? Am I a survivor or offspring of any of these people? Probably so.

My whole life has been rich with so many great dogs. The still vivid memories of all their love, zest for life, and sharing the fun or hard times with me come to mind—Sister, Jerry, Treve, Boomerang, Wendy, Nicky, Chip, Bear, Sammi, and Tucker. It hasn't helped that most of the dogs were beyond middle-aged when we gave them a home; the last two were about fourteen or fifteen years old when they passed away last fall. There were also the equally wonderful cats, horses, cows, goats, sheep, and other family critters. Now there may be only one more dog in our lives.

It's good to have a stock of memories, but I want to hang on to a bunch of dreams to pursue. Trips become a bit harder, especially to drive long distances; still, I find myself smiling this bright day and remembering that we found lifelong happiness in trying mightily and taking action every step of the way. Life is not over until it's over, and, fortunately, growing old takes a lot of time. Dreams should always have room for small side-trips and diversions, and action is more fun than procrastination.

To my pal and lifelong conspirator, I suggest, "Dan, let's not get put on hold to become old fuddy-duddies or sticks in the mud. We've still got mobility. Let's drive north and see all the children; stop in San Luis Obispo, Orinda, Los Gatos, and Santa Rosa. For one thing, I've got to see the horse of the Santa Rosa kids. Maybe I'll even force them to let me ride. It will, as always, be special to bring our suitcases into the their house, with big logs burning in the fireplace, a bubbly brood of kids, and their dog Mega meeting us. With nothing important on the calendar, let's leave by the weekend. The trip home can have equally fun visits with the rest of the gang—loving and keeping in touch is what it's all about."

"No kidding? You're my kind of impulsive gal; I was just thinking we should go up north. There's still no planning ahead or sitting still for long, is there? You'd better phone and see what the kids are up to this weekend. Maybe they've also developed wanderlust and won't be home."

"OK. First, though, I've got to plant some of the spring garden, even if it's early. The need for self-sufficiency and seeing crops grow must reside deep within me. Déjà vu: where's the shovel and pick?" Still an indifferent housekeeper inside, outside I needed orderly, neat gardens and loved to pull weeds—so much so that it was always a temptation to pull weeds along other people's front yards or beside the town's parking lots. This time, the soil was damp and easy to prepare; I would shovel over the whole plot, weeds and all, this time.

Dan shook his head, "Mark my words and take it from an old teacher: even without any freezing here, those seeds need to go in the ground a lot later than this. You know that."

"Well, if it's not spring, it's exactly like it. I'll just buy the seeds this morning and plant when we get home. This trip is just a short intermission, and there's somewhere inside me, a cycle, a clock of nature running, or something, that says there's no time like the present—it's time to go out to shovel." As always, words "new and improved" on the seed packets enticed me with visions of ever more perfect, delicious, and easy-to-grow vegetables and flowers. Happiness can come unexpectedly and seemingly out of the blue. It's usually somewhere near, and, as in the past, involved the land that was always there waiting. Lying stretched out near us in one of the furrows, knew we were taking a trip and that he would go with us. His tail flapped occasionally as I talked to him now and then.

My well-worn shovel turned over beautiful rich dirt—dark chocolate and friable. Dan came out and found himself leveling the rows and making the furrows for both the seed and the six-packs of small plants.

Don't push your luck? Fiddlesticks! The best is yet to be if I push boundaries and think it's possible. And many wonderful moments may be small, simple, quiet ones near home. On this bright and warm day, in spite of the dire warning, I went ahead and planted all the seeds and plants, and watered them thoroughly. If heavy rains come, the seeds can be replanted. I stood on the nearby graveled path at the end of the day, feeling tired but restored while I admired the dark, straight rows, scented with the newly turned and wet topsoil. Such land was a treasure, a warming of the heart. It was love.

Chapter 45
For the Life of Molly

Interacting with animals has been a large part of book two, *Laughing with the Animals*, and it seems only fair that the book should end with the story of our last wonderful family member, a young, spirited, and very intelligent dog named Molly. She will be three years old in November 2007, as this book goes to press.

As with most of our dogs, her constant and greatest wish seems to be keeping her family safe at all times. This means staying alert for any sounds inside and outside the house. She alerts us of everyone who drives by or walks up to our door. Are they friend or foe? We open the door slowly, and she waits just long enough for us to give our greeting. Once she sees that they are not enemies, she can begin to say "hi" to our visitors, vigorously wagging her tail and wiggling her whole body. When we take her on walks, she loves to meet friends' pets. Only once in two years has another animal tried to attack Molly while we were walking around the neighborhood.

Molly arrived in our lives a day or two after our trip to see all our children and their animals. Don Cole from the Humane Society had phoned to tell us that, while he knew that we were looking for a chocolate lab for our last pooch, he had a marvelous dog turned in that we should strongly consider. She was a golden colored American Lab that was only eleven months old, but extremely steady and well behaved for that age. He could keep her for training for seven days.

It was an easy sale to us, but we hated to leave this youngster out in their kennels and frightened of all the dogs and others, so we brought her home and paid the trainer to come to our house to train her a number of times.

This was one extremely wild and excitable dog, it turned out. She was strong, jumped high constantly, raced around the yard and the house, and was as large as common black, brown, or yellow labs, but with a more slender build and thinner face.

At our ages of about 86 and 87, she was not the dog we should have chosen, but she had had a rough, unsettled first eleven months—we kept her hoping to give her a better life. It means, too, that we will try our very best to be here for her as long as she lives, which may mean that we have to reach the old age of one hundred. With her unconditional love, empathy, trust, and loyalty, it will be far more likely that we can reach that goal.

From day one Molly slept on a special bed upstairs with us, and kept up a habit of waking us up between 5:00 and 5:30 a.m. to go out to the lawn. Luckily, we're on her schedule of early to bed, early to rise, and with a large lawn we can often placate her.

Molly's diet not only has her two meals of dog food, but she has decided to eat much like we do and enjoy carrots, broccoli, tomatoes, tortilla chips, mangoes, etc. We try to buy her lots of the strongest toys, and she chews them all up.

She is a splendid dog, and we are so happy to have her with us. What a wonderful final destination for us to reach, after so many years of hard work, and loving and laughing with animals.

If you enjoyed this book, please consider browsing our current selection of classic and contemporary books! Available for purchase online, from your local bookstore, or directly from the publisher at www.bramblewoodpress.com

www.ingramcontent.com/pod-product-compliance
Lightning Source LLC
Chambersburg PA
CBHW060243100426
42742CB00011B/1620